NOVA SCOTIA *at* WAR

1914–1919

BRIAN DOUGLAS TENNYSON

NIMBUS PUBLISHING
NIMBUS.CA

Nimbus Publishing Limited
3731 Mackintosh St, Halifax, NS B3K 5A5
(902) 455-4286 nimbus.ca

Cover Image: A detachment of troops from the 1st Regiment (Halifax), Canadian Garrison Artillery, arrives at Fort Charlotte on George's Island in August 1914 to help defend Halifax Harbour.

Printed and bound in Canada
NB1201
Cover design: Heather Bryan
Interior design: John van der Woude, JVDW Designs

MIX
Paper from responsible sources
FSC www.fsc.org FSC® C013916

Library and Archives Canada Cataloguing in Publication
Tennyson, B. D., author
Nova Scotia at war, 1914-1919 / Brian Tennyson.
Issued in print and electronic formats.
ISBN 978-1-77108-523-6 (softcover).
—ISBN 978-1-77108-524-3 (HTML)

1. Nova Scotia—History—1867-1918. 2. Nova Scotia—Social conditions—1867-1918. 3. World War, 1914-1918—Nova Scotia. 4. World War, 1914-1918—Social aspects—Nova Scotia. 5. Canada—History—1914-1918. I. Title.

FC2324.T46 2017 971.6'03 C2017-904127-4
C2017-904128-2

Canada
Canada Council for the Arts | Conseil des arts du Canada
NOVA SCOTIA

Nimbus Publishing acknowledges the financial support for its publishing activities from the Government of Canada, the Canada Council for the Arts, and from the Province of Nova Scotia. We are pleased to work in partnership with the Province of Nova Scotia to develop and promote our creative industries for the benefit of all Nova Scotians.

To Massimo, Zoe, and Breeanna
with love from Grandpa

CONTENTS

CONTENTS

PREFACE

Many books have been written about Canada's involvement in the First World War. As someone recently asked me, "What more is there to say? We know how it ended." That is undeniably true, but it has always seemed to me that the journey is as important as the destination. When the war ended more than four years after it began, Canadians had gone through the most traumatic collective experience in their history. And in a very real sense, the war didn't end in 1918, even if the killing stopped. Its impact on those who went overseas, those who waited at home and prayed for them, and everyone else was profound and haunts us still.

As a Nova Scotian, even if only an adoptive one, I have long been struck by the fact that we don't know very much about our province's role in the war. Only one book was written on the subject and that was M. Stuart Hunt's 1920 compilation entitled *Nova Scotia's Part in the Great War*, and it remains a useful source almost a century later. Joseph Hayes published a history of the 85th Battalion, also in 1920, and Ralph Lewis and Francis MacGregor wrote brief memoirs of their experiences in the 25th Battalion. In 1983 F. B. MacDonald and John J. Gardiner published the 25th's war diary and brief interviews with a few of its surviving veterans in *The Twenty-Fifth Battalion Canadian Expeditionary Force: Nova Scotia's*

Famous Regiment in World War One, but it was not until 2013 that Robert Clements's history of the 25th, in which he served with distinction, was published.

The best—and best-known—Canadian memoirist, of course, was Will R. Bird, a Nova Scotian who wrote two books, many magazine articles, and an account of revisiting the trenches many years later. But Bird wrote about the experience of Canadian soldiers generally, based on his personal experience in the 42nd Battalion.[1] In recent years three collections of soldiers' letters have been published as well.[2]

These are all valuable books, but none, with the partial exception of Hunt, tried to tell the story of Nova Scotia: its soldiers and sailors, those who served at home as well as those who went overseas, and the civilians who worked in the fishery, on the farms and in the forests, or in the coal mines and steel mills to keep the country going and able to support the war effort. Nor has anyone written about the sharp political divisions that arose during the war, as much in Nova Scotia as in Quebec and other parts of the country. And finally, no one has written—at least for the general public—about how the war affected Nova Scotia, shattering its dreams of becoming the Atlantic gateway and the industrial heartland of Canada.

This book attempts to address this need to some extent. It makes no claim to be the definitive work on the subject because I did not undertake any archival research in the papers of relevant prominent Nova Scotians like Robert Borden, W. S. Fielding, George Murray, Edgar Rhodes, and others. It is based on extensive research in several newspapers and any publications that I could find that touched on the subject. My goal has been to present what I hope will be an interesting and informative introduction to an important but neglected subject. I also hope that this book will inspire other scholars to pursue the subject further.

Many people have assisted me in writing this book. The staff of the Nova Scotia Archives, where I spent a lot of time in the past year, were as always very patient, helpful, and supportive. Similarly, the lovely staff of South Shore Public Libraries obtained a steady flow of books for me through the provincial interlibrary loan system. Local historical societies and museums are invaluable for this kind of project, and it is a pleasure to acknowledge the assistance of Barbara Thompson and Linda Bedford of the DesBrisay Museum in Bridgewater; Linda Rafuse and Kathleen Stitt of the Queens County Museum; Lisette Gaudet of the Yarmouth County Museum and Archives; Lyne Allain of the Mahone Bay Museum; Richard Sanderson of the Naval Museum of Halifax; and Dr. Keith Mercer, Cultural Resource Manager of Parks Canada in Halifax. Pat Townsend and Wendy Robicheau of the Acadia University Archives were very helpful, as was Kathleen MacKenzie of the St. Francis Xavier University Archives. John Brehaut of the Department of Veterans Affairs helped me to sort information from the Virtual War Memorial database. Tim Coulter of Delray Beach, Florida, shared his vast knowledge of the history of North American shipbuilding to clarify a point on the Nova Scotia Steel Company's shipbuilding program. Brigadier General Greg Young of the 15th Battalion CEF Memorial Project and William H. E. Day of Port Maitland kindly gave me permission to use photographs in their possession, as did Bruce MacDonald of Antigonish. Sara Beanlands allowed me to use material from her fine report on the Jewish Legion in Windsor. Dr. Philip Smith of McGill University provided interesting information on John Gallishaw and F. B. McCurdy. John Orr and Spud Roscoe also kindly shared information with me. Matthew K. Barrett, who among other things writes fascinating articles online about the Canadian Corps's battalion commanders, helped me to discover that the papers of Sir Robert Borden are now available online for consultation. Finally, I want to express my great appreciation to Whitney Moran, managing editor at Nimbus, for her enthusiasm and support even when this project grew much larger than she had anticipated, my copy editor, Paula

Sarson, who was not only thorough but proved to be exceptionally tolerant of a sometimes cranky author, and Elaine McCluskey, non-fiction editor, who very efficiently assisted with the final layout, cover design, and images. They were a delight to work with.

Lindsay Tennyson, Michele and Gemma Coley, Peter and Heather Nowlan, and Jennifer Faulkner and Peter Robichaud all contributed significantly to this project by providing accommodations during my extensive research trips to Halifax and Yarmouth. John Boileau and Bryan Elson were good enough to read draft chapters and make very helpful comments. I, of course, am solely responsible for any factual or interpretive errors that remain. Finally, as always, I want to thank my long-suffering wife, Sandra Atwell-Tennyson, who has shared yet another exploration of the Great War, assisting with research, copy-editing, and general encouragement.

Brian Douglas Tennyson
Oak Tree Cottage, Bridgewater
July 6, 2017

Chapter 1

THE SUMMER OF 1914

Serene and still are the waters of the harbor; silent are the streets after sunset, peaceful and beautiful are the parks and the Arm. Nothing occurs to disturb the slumber of the residents of dear old Halifax![1]

AT FIRST GLANCE, NOVA SCOTIA IN THE SUMMER OF 1914 appeared to be much the same as it is in the summer of 2017. It was a small place, the second smallest province in Canada, comprising about 34,351 square kilometres. It was small in population as well, with about 500,000 people, slightly more than half its current population. But it was growing dramatically—by 7.1% between 1901 and 1911 and another 6.4% by 1921, even though many young people left every year seeking better opportunities in New England or the Canadian west.

Halifax was the largest city, but with only about 50,000 residents it did not dominate the province then as it does today. Most people lived in small towns or villages and worked in the fishery, agriculture, or forestry, although an industrial economy had been developing since the 1880s and was attracting people from rural areas and immigrants into the towns, especially in Cape Breton, Cumberland and Pictou Counties.

Although small, Halifax was important because it was the provincial capital. More importantly, it was the Royal Navy's major base in the Northwestern Atlantic. It was also the closest North American port to Britain and Europe and aspired to be Canada's major east coast port. Those who had supported Confederation had hoped that a railway connecting Halifax to Montreal and Toronto would bring this about. That had not happened because Central Canada continued to import and export primarily through Montreal, except in the winter months when the St. Lawrence River was frozen. Adding insult to injury, Central Canada didn't even use Halifax in the winter months, preferring to trade through Portland, Maine, because it was closer, even if situated in a foreign country.

And so Halifax had not prospered as the Atlantic gateway to Canada. Beckles Willson, a well-known journalist and writer, described it in 1912 as "a comfortable, tranquil, pleasant city," but "dingy and shabby."[2] Thomas Raddall, who arrived from England that same year with his parents, also later recalled pre-war Halifax as "a small and depressing community" that "had a look of stagnation."[3] The *Halifax Herald*, writing in May 1910, did not disagree: "Serene and still are the waters of the harbor," it said, "silent are the streets after sunset, peaceful and beautiful are the parks and the Arm. Nothing occurs to disturb the slumber of the residents of dear old Halifax!"[4]

What they didn't know was that the new federal government headed by Halifax lawyer Robert Borden was planning to invest

$36 million—a huge sum at the time—to make the port of Halifax more competitive. In 1913 it made the remarkable decision, with the enthusiastic support of the provincial government and the Halifax business community, to replace the Deep Water Terminal with the new Ocean Terminal, closer to the open ocean. This required cutting a new railway line through the city's genteel South End, but would, promoters confidently believed, greatly increase the importance of Halifax as a major Atlantic port.

Although Nova Scotia had been part of Canada for forty-seven years, its identity was still decidedly British. Halifax was perhaps the most British community in the province because of its British Army garrison and the regular visits of the Royal Navy. This was reflected in the reaction to the Canadian government's decision in 1905 to assume control of the fortress and to man it with Canadian soldiers. Instead of welcoming the change as an important step in the long march to autonomy—to use the word "independence" would have been considered tactless if not revolutionary—Haligonians, at least those who were part of "society," were deeply disappointed.

When Beckles Willson suggested in 1912 that "the regulation uniforms denoting the British officer [were] as much in evidence as ever...the supercilious rejoinder of one fair damsel, lying back in a canoe on the shores of Bedford Basin" was, "Oh, those! They don't count. They're Canadians." Although nobody complained of how the Canadian officers performed their duties, Willson "heard many complaints as to how [they] had received their appointments at Ottawa."[5] Apparently patronage dispensed in Ottawa was inherently inferior to patronage dispensed in London.

When the government followed up in 1910 by establishing a Canadian navy, the response was the same if not worse. "One had only to mention the *Niobe* and the *Rainbow* [the navy's first two ships] to excite a smile. The officers may turn out to be good fellows, but they will need all their tact, good looks, and gallantry to overcome the prejudice the fair Haligonians feel towards them as delegates from Ottawa instead of from the British Admiralty."[6]

Hugh MacLennan—himself a Nova Scotian—later said that Haligonians

> *lived...in an anomalous permanency, still tied to England, suffering when she did but rarely partaking of her prosperities, unreconciled to be Americans or even Canadians, content for the moment to let their status drift with events, convinced that in being Nova Scotians they possessed a peculiar cause of satisfaction, an excellence which no one had ever troubled to define because no one outside the province believed it existed, and everyone on the inside took it for granted.*[7]

In other words, many Nova Scotians were still reluctant Canadians, which was hardly surprising in view of the fact that most of them had voted against Confederation in 1867, or at least against the terms of the agreement, and as late as the 1880s were electing provincial governments that vainly advocated separation.

Most people, if asked, would have said that Nova Scotia's economy was based on the sea that virtually surrounded it. Bluenose men either fished or built ships or sailed them all over the world, and the more prosperous of them did all three.[8] In fact, while fishing, shipbuilding, and shipping were all important to the foundation of the province's sense of identity, agriculture employed far more people. Forestry was a major component of the economy too. Although it didn't employ large numbers of men, there were logging operations and mills, large and small, scattered throughout the province, and it exported more than 214 million board feet of lumber and wood products annually from a number of ports. Agriculture, forestry, and fishing were intimately intertwined because many men worked in more than one of them, according to the season.

But Nova Scotia's economy had been changing in recent years, and many people in 1914 would have been surprised to be told a century later that their business leaders had failed to make the transition from wood and wind to steam, steel, and railways. It was precisely because men like Charles Tupper and A. G. Archibald had recognized the significance of the industrial revolution sweeping the western world that they had advocated joining Confederation. They understood that coal and steel were the future and that Nova Scotia possessed massive amounts of not only coal, but also iron and other minerals as well. If a new nation was going to be created in British North America, it seemed obvious that Nova Scotia, because of its resources and location on the Atlantic seaboard, would emerge as its industrial heartland.[9]

When the federal government built the Intercolonial Railway that linked Nova Scotia with Central Canada, it encouraged industrial development in the province by establishing a preferential freight-rate schedule that subsidized goods moving west but not goods moving east. This was deliberately intended to offset the disadvantage of distance for Nova Scotian businesses trying to market their goods in the largest Canadian market, i.e., Central Canada. And it worked to a significant degree. Businessmen, including at least some shipowners, invested in industrial development, and by the turn of the century almost every town in the province had factories producing a variety of products ranging from shoes to pianos, including textile mills and iron foundries that produced machinery and other products.[10]

To cite just one example of how the economy was changing, let us look at Yarmouth, a town typically regarded as a diehard fishing and mercantile community. In 1911 it was the home of the Milton Iron Foundry (founded in 1841), the Burrell-Johnson Iron Company (1856), the Yarmouth Woolen Mill (1881) and the Cosmos Cotton Company (1883), the Nova Scotia Steamship Company (1887) and the Yarmouth Steamship Company (1887), the Yarmouth Street Railway (1888)—reportedly the first street railway in Nova Scotia and only the third in Canada—the W. H. Redding and A. A. Durkee shoe factories, the Minard's Liniment Factory, three carriage factories, a cigar factory and two candy factories, among others. As the town rightly proclaimed in 1911, manufacturing "has become an integral part of Yarmouth's activities."[11]

By 1912 the province's manufacturing sector was employing almost 34,000 people producing goods worth more than $70 million.[12] To a significant degree, this reflected the astonishing growth of the coal and steel industries in the last years of the nineteenth century. Coal had been mined on a large scale since the 1850s, and Londonderry was the foremost iron mining district in Canada.[13] By the 1890s the Nova Scotia Steel Company, based in Pictou County, was Canada's leading producer of iron and steel products. Then it acquired the rich iron ore resources at Wabana, Newfoundland, and the General Mining Association's coal mines at Sydney Mines, and it built an integrated iron and steel complex there that was described as "the most efficient and technically advanced in Canada."[14] At the same time, American entrepreneur Henry Melville Whitney formed a syndicate that acquired the other Cape Breton collieries and built a steel mill in Sydney. The result was that Nova Scotia was responsible for almost half of Canada's annual coal production and more than a third of its iron and steel.[15]

This did not mean that there weren't problems. There were, although they weren't very obvious in 1914. Essentially, Nova Scotia's economy was being forced to adapt to external factors over which it had little control. In the fishery, the number of vessels working the Grand Banks and the annual catch had been declining since the 1880s because the market for salt fish was declining as demand grew for fresh fish.[16] To compete, fishermen would have to shift from sailing vessels to steamships with refrigeration, which were too expensive for most of them. W. C. Smith and Company, the forerunner of National Sea Products, made the transition but it was an exception. On a more positive note, the demand for lobster had grown dramatically in recent years, and there were 220 lobster-canning factories scattered around the coastline.[17]

In agriculture, the number of farms and the amount of cleared acreage had been declining since 1891 as the demand for high-bulk, low-value perishable products intended for local markets was increasingly replaced by low-bulk, high-value, non-perishable products destined for more distant markets. This meant that large farms concentrated in the best agricultural areas like the Annapolis Valley thrived, but smaller, less efficient, farms were in trouble.

Fig. 1.1: Fish drying, Lunenburg, c.1900. Many Nova Scotians made their living from the sea before the war.

It was the same story in both manufacturing and forestry. Larger companies in Central Canada or the United States were absorbing smaller rivals in order to dominate the market and better control prices, but this meant that control over the industrial economy was beginning to move out of the province. Dominion Steel was controlled by outside interests from the outset; the large Rhodes Curry manufacturing operations in Amherst were bought out, as was the Davison Lumber Company in Bridgewater. Nova Scotia Steel held out longer, but the local investors eventually lost control there as well.

In short, Nova Scotia in the summer of 1914 was not just a traditional community of small towns and villages and rural communities engaged in fishing, farming, forestry, and shipbuilding. It was actually a place in transition, and therefore not as tranquil and untouched by modernity as it might appear in retrospect.

Its population was growing rapidly, but mainly in the northeastern area where the most industrial development was taking place. And it was becoming more urbanized, but again mostly in the northeast. While Halifax's population grew by 14% between 1901

Fig. 1.2: This photo of an ox team in front of the Bridgewater railway station, c.1900, dramatically illustrates how society was changing.

and 1911, for example, Sydney's grew by 70%.[18] The population was also changing. The young men and women who continued to leave the province for New England or the Canadian west were being replaced by immigrants from Europe, Newfoundland, and even the United States. This meant that the composition of the population, especially in the industrial and mining districts, now included many French, Belgian, German, and East European immigrants, who brought their languages, cultures, and religions with them.

The growth of industrial towns, which was welcomed by local politicians and businessmen who equated growth with progress, had unforeseen consequences. Industrial towns, as opposed to semi-rural villages, required affordable housing, water, and sewage systems, electrification, and other services, while industry required some level of regulation regarding working conditions. Neither towns nor employers were quick to respond to these needs, so growing numbers of people were working in unsafe and unhealthy environments and living in wretched slums. The *Sydney Daily Post*, not a progressive newspaper, once suggested that the area's poor neighbourhoods would be "a positive disgrace to the most filthy parts of Constantinople."[19]

The emergence of factories, mills, and mines changed not only working and living conditions but also social attitudes. The concept of a "working class" was emerging as workers began to realize that they must join together and bargain collectively if they were to avoid excessive exploitation. Not surprisingly, industrialists resisted this development, which in fact was illegal until 1872. Coal miners—the most exploited industrial workers in the province—led the way when they formed the Provincial Workmen's Association, a moderate union founded in Springhill in 1879 by Robert Drummond, who has been described as "one of the most significant figures of 19th-century Canadian labour history."[20]

Between 1901 and 1914 almost two million workdays were lost to strikes in the Maritime provinces, mostly in Nova Scotia.[21] The two most serious ones occurred in Cape Breton in 1909–10 and in Springhill in 1910–11, when the US-based United Mine Workers (UMW) fought for recognition as the bargaining agent for the miners. Both companies fought back ruthlessly, evicting the miners from their company-owned houses, employing strikebreakers, and bringing in troops to "protect" their property. Both strikes eventually collapsed, keeping the UMW out of the province for a few more years but leaving a disturbing legacy of bitterness in the mining communities.

The election of a new federal government in 1911 had changed the political landscape in Nova Scotia. The province had been electing Liberals provincially since 1882 (and continued to do so until 1925), and didn't embrace the Conservatives in 1911, even though they were now led by Robert Borden, a native son. Perhaps their mixed feelings about the change were justified, because the country sank into a recession in 1912 that lasted until the war stimulated the economy.

The recession had its greatest impact on the industrial sector of the province's economy. The steel plants at Sydney, Sydney Mines, and Stellarton struggled with depressed markets, forcing Nova Scotia Steel to actually shut down its Sydney Mines mill, while Dominion Steel kept its plant open but laid off many workers. The reduction in steel production naturally reduced the sale of coal, so there were layoffs in the mining industry as well.

IN THE SUMMER OF 1914 THOSE WHO HAD THEM WERE AT THEIR cottages—"camps" as many called them—enjoying the heat and chilly waters of Nova Scotia's always too-brief summer. Others had to make do with urban attractions. Youngsters swam in the quiet parts of Halifax Harbour, at Evangeline Beach at Grand Pré, all along the LaHave River, even right in Bridgewater, at Mira Gut and elsewhere throughout the province. People enjoyed picnics, boating, band concerts in the parks, or perhaps just strolling on a summer's evening and enjoying ice cream from the local creamery. There were the usual summer fetes, such as the unique garden parties in Lunenburg County, and the annual celebration in Yarmouth of the town's founding on June 8, although J. M. Lawson, the *Yarmouth Herald's* editor, complained that there should be some organized activity instead of people just fleeing the town for a day in the country.[22]

He was pointing to the growing tendency of people to leave town on weekends and holidays to visit relatives in the country or just to enjoy beaches, especially with the growing popularity of automobiles. There were almost 1,800 cars and motorcycles registered in the province by this time, although there were not that many actually on the roads, "quite a number having gone out of commission since registering."[23] If the early cars were unreliable, the province's highways didn't help; they were unpaved and rough, and there was a growing demand that something should be done about them. One non-event in many communities in Nova Scotia was the celebration of Dominion Day, a reflection of the resentment still felt by many Nova Scotians at having been dragged into Confederation against their will.

Communal picnics organized by churches, companies, and fraternal societies were popular. In Bridgewater they usually involved cruising on the *Trusty* down the LaHave River to a beach for the day. In other communities, special trains carried crowds to picnic parks or beaches for their outings. The Yarmouth hospital picnic was typical of these annual events throughout the province. It took place across the harbour at Bay View Park, so people were ferried across on the *Hippolyta*, which was "decorated with bunting" and "kept busily occupied until 10 o'clock at night." Baseball and other games were played during the day, while the Yarmouth Concert Band "enlivened the occasion with their rendition of favorite melodies" and "the ladies" served "an excellent fish chowder, ice cream and other refreshments."[24]

The major event every summer in communities throughout the province was the arrival of the Mighty Haag Shows, a travelling circus from the southern United States that toured Nova Scotia every year. It came by train and announced its presence with a colourful parade, which generated much excitement. When it took place in Bridgewater during the last week of June, the *Bulletin* enthused that "too much" could not be said of it because it was "free for everybody, and is one mile in length," and included "features never attempted by any other show." The *Bulletin*'s editor was especially enthralled by the calliope, "one of the finest calliopes in the world" of course, which was operated by "Signor Lamont, who is considered the premier of calliope players."[25] After entertaining the citizens of Bridgewater, Haag's circus went on to Liverpool and Yarmouth. When it left the province, Nova Scotians could not know that this was its last visit, just as 1914 was the last year of peace.

Fig. 1.3: Garden Party, Yarmouth, 1914. Garden parties were popular social events in the pre-war years. People dressed in their finest, sipped tea or lemonade, and sometimes enjoyed games.

Nova Scotians were not isolated from the larger world. In fact, because so many of them made their living on the world's oceans, they were probably less isolated than most Canadians. They could certainly relate to the greatest marine disaster in Canadian history, which occurred on May 28, when the Canadian Pacific liner *Empress of Ireland* collided with the *Storstad*, a Dominion Coal Company collier, in heavy fog in the Gulf of St. Lawrence. The *Empress of Ireland* was the pride of the CPR's fleet and was carrying 1,477 people from Quebec City to Liverpool. It sank within minutes, causing the deaths of 1,012 people, more than the number who had died in the better remembered *Titanic* disaster two years earlier. Among them was Dr. Murdoch Lindsay of Pictou, a young Halifax physician who was on his way to England to get married.

The international scene generally was relatively tranquil. The emergence of Germany as a major power in recent years had led to a naval armaments race, but most people saw no real cause for concern. Indeed, the Canadian and American governments were making plans to celebrate the centennial of peace between Britain and the United States since 1814. National committees had been set up in both countries to plan the celebrations, and Ernest Scammell, the secretary of the Canadian Peace Centenary Committee, toured Nova Scotia in May 1914 to encourage the formation of local committees.

His message was that the century of peace between Canada and the United States constituted "an object lesson to the whole world" because it demonstrated "that two peoples could live side by side and settle matters in dispute between them, not by resort to arms, but by the application of good will and common sense."[26] The clear implication was that other countries should follow their example, and one wonders if anyone remembered his comments three months later when Canada went to war.

Veterans were very much in the news that summer because the Borden government had agreed to award a bounty of one hundred dollars—a significant sum in 1914—to men who had served in the militia during the 1866 defence crisis, when the Fenian Brotherhood, an Irish Catholic nationalist organization dedicated to winning Ireland's independence from Britain, launched attacks on Nova Scotia, New Brunswick, and Ontario. The provincial militias had been called out—this was just before Confederation—and had been paid the usual service allowance, but there had been agitation for years that the men should be recognized. In 1899 the Laurier government did issue the General Service Medal to men who served but agitation continued, seeking compensation for the time taken away from their jobs. In 1912 the Borden government agreed to pay the bounty to 6,000 men in Ontario, Quebec, and New Brunswick, and 11,160 Nova Scotians. The high Nova Scotian number reflected the fact that turning out when summoned was compulsory there, but only voluntary in the other provinces.

The payments were not actually made until the summer of 1914. To collect, a man had only to satisfy a board that he had drilled with a militia unit for two weeks in 1866. That meant that every Nova Scotian man still alive who had been of age in 1866 was eligible for the bounty unless he had not responded to the mobilization. Because militia records were far from complete, however, a man had only to swear that he had served and have his claim corroborated by a neighbour. He, in turn, could vouch that his neighbour had served as well. No doubt there were abuses. James Cameron claims, for example, that only about 1,000 men in Pictou County had actually served in 1866 but 1,470 men received the bounty.[27] Liberals noted that the payments were distributed by Conservative politicians at a time, perhaps not coincidentally, when a federal election was expected to be called within months.[28]

It was a rather comic opera affair, to be sure, but it took place in the context of a society that, on the whole, did not take military matters seriously. Canada had no enemies and in any event enjoyed the protection—most people thought—of the Royal Navy. As for the Canadian Army, or permanent force as it was then called, it had been carved out of the militia in 1885 and consisted of only 3,110 men. In the event of a crisis, it would form the professional core that would train and lead the militiamen called out for active duty. Most people, however, regarded the pre-war militia not so much as a defence force as an outlet for patronage appointments important primarily for the social status they conferred on its officers.

This was not quite fair. Frederick Borden, the Nova Scotian minister of militia, had increased the defence budget from $1.1 million in 1896 to $8.1 million in 1911, and Sam Hughes, who succeeded him in 1911, had further boosted it to $14 million by 1914. Over the years, Borden had also introduced major reforms in the militia and expanded the permanent force, including the acquisition of modern equipment. He had also been the chief proponent in the government for taking over the Halifax garrison and building a Canadian Navy, which he thought was essential to effective coastal defence but would also transform Halifax into a dynamic regional shipbuilding centre.

Fig. 1.4: The Royal Canadian Regiment at Wellington Barracks, 1906. The RCR was the infantry component of the permanent force and replaced the British garrison at Halifax in 1906.

Borden had also beefed up militia training and established an annual national training camp at Petawawa, north of Ottawa. The 1914 national camp, which took place in July and was presided over by the governor general, the Duke of Connaught, involved the rapid mobilization of 13,000 troops and was the first time that all components of the army trained together on a large scale. The event included a three-day mock battle in which 10,000 militiamen divided into two opposing forces engaged in manoeuvres that the Ottawa newspapers thought constituted "the nearest approach to real battle ever staged for men in training."[29] We know from hindsight, of course, that it did not represent the nature of the coming war, but people at the time didn't know it, either in Canada or elsewhere.

The remarkable growth in defence spending when most Canadians assumed they had no enemies aroused much controversy. Conservative newspapers defended the increased spending, while Liberal newspapers denounced it as patronage that was all the worse because it encouraged militarism and tawdry flag-waving. When Hughes was criticized for his extravagance, he retorted that what he really needed was $17 million.[30] The *Liverpool Advance* expressed mock astonishment in April 1914 that even though Parliament had been in session for three months, the government had "not even hinted at a German menace."[31]

Meanwhile, if great progress had been made in developing the permanent force and militia, the government's naval policy had proven to be a total failure. The Conservatives had rejected Laurier's plan to build an independent navy, but the Liberal-dominated Senate had blocked the government's attempt to contribute financially to the construction of naval ships for the Royal Navy. The government eventually accepted that it had no practical alternative to developing a navy, but by the summer of 1914 it had only the *Niobe* and the *Rainbow*, both acquired from the Royal Navy, and the *Canada*, a ship built for the Canadian Fisheries Protection

Service but also intended as a training ship for naval personnel. The government's enthusiasm for the navy was distinctly muted, and Liberal newspapers complained that the main role of the *Niobe* appeared to be to visit communities "for picnics and other celebrations...at the request of various Conservative members or defeated candidates."[32]

Throughout this mostly pleasant summer, while fishermen fished, farmers worked their fields, and miners and steelworkers worried about their jobs, few paid any attention to brief newspaper reports of an assassination in an obscure city somewhere in Eastern Europe. Perhaps it was this unawareness of what was going on in Europe that lends the summer of 1914 in Nova Scotia its bittersweet sense of innocence. More typical of the news in local papers was the announcement of the first garden party of the summer season in Bridgewater, which was to take place on the evening of July 6. "A special effort," the *Bulletin* assured its readers, had been made "to make this even more attractive than usual." One no doubt popular attraction was Madame Babette, who would "give a forecast of the future."[33] One wonders how accurate she was.

Chapter 2

THE OUTBREAK OF WAR

On every hand the hope is ardent that the great catastrophe may be minimized or averted, but if duty calls, Canada's answer is ready.[1]

THE EVENT THAT TRIGGERED THE OUTBREAK OF WAR WAS the assassination of Archduke Franz Ferdinand, the heir to the throne of the Austro-Hungarian Empire, on June 28, 1914. Because the assassin was a Bosnian Serb and Serbia had been destabilizing the multi-ethnic Austro-Hungarian Empire for years by stirring up South Slav nationalism, this incident appeared to present the opportunity to deal with the Serbian problem once and for all. After obtaining an assurance of support from Germany, Austria-Hungary therefore declared war on Serbia. Russia, which had its own ambitions in the area, supported Serbia, with the result that France and Britain were dragged in, and Europe—somewhat to its own surprise—found itself at war. This process took more than a month to unfold, culminating in Britain's declaration of war on August 4.

The Balkans were a long way from Nova Scotia, and there was little interest in the assassination of an obscure archduke in an obscure corner of Southeastern Europe. It is somewhat surprising, therefore, that the incident was reported in a front-page story in the *Halifax Morning Chronicle* on June 29 with a banner headline, supplemented by extensive coverage of its possible implications on page two. The *Amherst Daily News*—one of the more cosmopolitan newspapers in the province—also reported the event on its front page. More typical were the *Bridgewater Bulletin* and the *Antigonish Casket*, both of which published only a brief report on page five on the thirtieth. Other newspapers ignored the event.

There had not been a major war since the defeat of Napoleon in 1815, and the idea of permanent peace was in the air, despite the sabre-rattling of the European powers in recent years. May 6 had been celebrated as "Peace Sunday" in Canada's Protestant churches, and the *Wesleyan*, the newspaper of the Methodist church in the Maritimes, marked it with an editorial declaring that British involvement in any future war "would be an indelible dishonor to our nation, [and] a blighting scandal on Christianity."[2] The *Morning Chronicle* had written as recently as July 9 that "thoughtful people" were convinced "not only that war is abhorrent in itself, but that it is a ruinous game, win or lose."[3]

Less than three weeks later, Austria-Hungary declared war on Serbia, triggering the chain reaction that engulfed Europe in war. The Reverend Clarence Mackinnon, then principal of Pine Hill Divinity Hall in Halifax, no doubt spoke for many people when he expressed his astonishment that a crisis in a little known corner of Europe could provoke a general war. His impression was that the Austrian ultimatum to Serbia aroused "very little" concern among most Nova Scotians, whose "main anxiety was whether the ice in the ice-house would hold through the present heat."[4]

The *Truro Daily News* couldn't believe that the major powers would allow themselves to be drawn into a war because of "the little snarlings of these Balkan races." The *Morning Chronicle* agreed that Germany would not turn a regional conflict into a general war because it had "far more to lose than she can ever hope to gain," while the *Acadian Recorder* rightly pointed out that Austria "has acted the bully all through the piece" because it had long "desired to wipe out" Serbia "and the murder of the Archduke Ferdinand has supplied the excuse, atrociously unjust as it is." The *Amherst Daily News* could not resist pointing out "on what a thin shell after all is our boasted civilization built!"[5]

All agreed, however, that if Britain found it necessary to go to war, it would, as the *Truro Daily News* said, have "the full force and support, to the limit of their resources, of the Canadian people."[6] The Conservative *Sydney Daily Post* took the opportunity, however, to point out that Sam Hughes had been "sharply criticized" as recently as that spring for once again increasing the defence budget. "Was the coincidence accidental?" it asked. "Those who know the Minister of Defence best say that it was not."[7]

By August 3, the European powers were at war, with the exception of Britain, which was expected to join imminently. That evening, crowds swarmed downtown Halifax, gathering in front of the *Morning Chronicle* building at the corner of Prince and Hollis Streets. A screen had been mounted on the wall facing the square to flash the latest bulletins as they came in from the wire services, but the crowd was so large that bulletins had to be posted in the Prince Street windows as well for those unable to see the screen.

"Heated by patriotic fervor," the crowd "surged back and forth up and down the hill, cheering, singing, waving flags and handkerchiefs and good naturedly jostling each other, yet intense with the excitement of the moment." A gramophone placed in the doorway of the building played "national and patriotic airs," the crowd sang "Rule Britannia" and "La Marseillaise"—several times—and "every announcement from the British House of Commons was received with cheers."[8]

In Sydney, "hundreds" similarly crowded about the *Daily Post*'s bulletin board early on the afternoon of the third and stayed there through the evening as the newspaper issued the latest news "hot from the wires." A special afternoon edition quickly sold out and an extra edition brought out that evening sold another 3,000 copies. War fever was "sweeping over Sydney," the newspaper declared, and the announcement (actually false) that German forces had been repulsed by the French on that first day of war "was received with bursts of cheers. Greater still was the enthusiasm when it became known that Britain would undoubtedly declare war within twenty-four hours."[9]

It so happened that the *Ste. Jehanne*, a French hospital ship that served the thousands of French seamen who fished off St. Pierre and Miquelon, was in port loading coal that day. Coincidentally, the British Dominions Royal Commission, created in 1912 to investigate the natural resources of the Dominions and imperial trade relations, was in town as well. That evening the members of the commission enjoyed a cruise on Sydney Harbour, and when their vessel approached the *Ste. Jehanne*, "the engines stopped and the band struck up the stirring strains of the Marseillaise. Cheer upon cheer rose from the hundreds on the deck of the big hospital ship followed with cries of 'Vive la France' and 'Vive le Canada.' The visiting party replied with three hearty British cheers."[10] When the *Ste. Jehanne* left Sydney a week later to return to France, its decks were "crowded with officers, sailors and patients singing in loud chorus La Marsaillese [*sic*]." As it "slowly drew down the bay, all flags flying in the glory of the setting sun," a large crowd on the wharf cheered its departure while the city band played the British and French national anthems.[11]

The announcement that Britain had declared war reached Nova Scotia at eleven o'clock on the evening of the fourth. In Halifax, where "thousands of eager, anxious citizens" had stood for hours outside the *Morning Chronicle* building waiting for the latest bulletins, there was "for a brief moment…a silence, and then with one great voice the multitude broke into thrilling British cheers. These were followed by 'God Save the King' sung amid the waving of hats and handkerchiefs." This was followed by "Rule Britannia," which "resounded along the thoroughfares with a significance that has never been realized before in this generation." The crowd remained until after midnight, "cheering singing and awaiting every bulletin from the front." When a newspaper staffer opened a window and told the crowd (incorrectly) that the German Navy had attacked the Royal Navy even before the declaration of war, the news "was received with hisses and groans."[12]

The city was reportedly "restless" all night, and "there was little sleep in any quarter" as people "congregated on every corner and along the streets discussing the news." As the *Morning Chronicle* euphorically reported,

> *"God Save the King" was sung time after time, stanza after stanza, the crowd seeming unable to sufficiently express their feelings. Then followed the magic of "Rule Britannia," which fanned popular enthusiasm into a great outburst of song. Order would then be called and some one harangue [sic] the crowd calling for cheers. Cheers for the King, Canada, the Empire, "The good old Irishmen" and for every conceivable man or thing that sounded British, were demanded and given as only British throats can give them.*[13]

The same public excitement was displayed in Sydney, where a crowd again gathered outside the *Daily Post* building to read the latest bulletins. When the British declaration of war was announced, "there was an enthusiastic outburst of cheering and a number of people sang the Canadian anthem and 'O Canada' with enthusiasm."[14]

To their credit, the newspapers endeavoured to temper the exhilaration with a dose of reality. The *Morning Chronicle* reminded its readers that "we are faced with the prospect of appalling war and its inevitable carnage and waste."[15] The *Lunenburg Progress Enterprise* went further, suggesting that Canadians thank God that they lived on this side of the Atlantic and that they think of the many Europeans, including women and children, who would be killed "by shot, shell, starvation and disaster" in this war.[16] The *Casket*, voice of the Catholic Diocese of Antigonish, agreed, observing that "the Atlantic is not such a bad neighbor after all."[17] The *Bridgewater Bulletin* similarly reminded its readers that war meant "the wholesale murder of men to satisfy the war-like ambitions of kings and their counselors."[18]

But the *Amherst Daily News* had no doubt that Nova Scotians would stand behind Britain "for the maintenance of the Empire's integrity, and for the preservation in the world of Britain's ideals of democratic government and life."[19] Nor did the *Eastern Chronicle*, which reminded its readers that "the God of our fathers will not forsake His people, if they be not downcast, help one another and trust Him."[20] On a more practical level, the *Lunenburg Progress Enterprise* proclaimed that Nova Scotians and Canadians generally must unite in the common cause because "party differences fade into insignificance in the presence of the great crisis."[21]

The propaganda that would become so extreme and pervasive over time began immediately, without direction from London or Ottawa. As early as August 6, for example, Sydney's *Daily Post* denounced "the duplicity, the frenzied militarism and the unrestrained arrogance" of Germany, whose "true inwardness" was "the spirit of the Frank and the Goth of the Dark Ages with an imperfect veneer of modern civilization."[22] The *Progress Enterprise* more temperately argued that, because Britain and France represented "the loftiest ideals and noblest practice in present-day civilization," their defeat "would mean a set-back to what is best in civilization, [their] victory the widening of the bounds of liberty and progress."[23]

The outbreak of war actually posed a very serious dilemma for those who had hoped, if not entirely believed, that the world had entered a new era in which international disputes could—and should—be settled through goodwill and negotiation, not war. The Methodist and Presbyterian churches, which had been active in the peace movement before the war, now struggled to reconcile their beliefs with their patriotism. As late as August 3, the congregation of St. Andrew's Presbyterian Church in Halifax was told that war would be "insanely futile" and sang the hymn "O God of Love, O King of Peace."[24] The *Presbyterian Witness*, the newspaper of the Presbyterian Church in the Maritimes, shifted sharply from reminding its readers on August 15 that Germany "was a Christian nation" to arguing on September 12 that Britain was "fighting for honour, justice, and liberty" in a "Holy War."[25] The Methodist *Wesleyan* was much slower to fall into line, advising its readers in November to temper their patriotism with calmness and to suppress the temptation to "anger, wrath, malice, revenge."[26]

The Anglican Church accused Germany of violating not only international law but also God's law and argued that Britain had behaved in a Christian manner by honouring its pledge to Belgium and seeking to protect the weak.[27] The *Casket*, however, reminded Catholics that "a large percentage of national and racial prejudices...are due to lies first told in time of war" and expressed regret "that a start has been made to renew that outrageous custom at the expense of Germany." It was true that "we are at war with Germany," it said, and "we shall beat her; but neither patriotism nor military nor naval necessity requires us to lie about her."[28]

Dalhousie University found itself at the centre of an unwelcome controversy when Frank Graham, a law student, published a letter in the Dalhousie *Gazette*, the student newspaper, denouncing Canada's participation in the war. The *Halifax Herald* demanded that the "anti-British" article be "immediately repudiated and denounced by the Faculty, the Governors, and the Loyalist Students." The *Acadian Recorder* more reasonably thought the letter "unworthy of attention" because it was "disjointed, illogical, impertinent and written in a style of school-boy sententiousness." To his credit, A. S. MacKenzie, the university's president, took the sensible position that the *Gazette* was a student newspaper over which the university had no control. The editor of the Dalhousie *Gazette* also responded, saying that he thought the *Herald*'s reaction was excessive, although he distanced himself from Graham's views.[29] The Graham affair turned out to be a tempest in a teacup, not least because few students at Dalhousie or the other universities shared Graham's views.[30]

FOR MOST CANADIANS THE WAR WOULD BE FOUGHT IN EUROPE, which seemed a long way away. It was not so distant for Nova Scotians, however, for whom the sea had always been regarded as a highway rather than a barrier. They knew that the war might very well come much closer because they lived on a peninsula jutting into the Atlantic Ocean, exposed to enemy naval action as it had been throughout its history. The Militia Department agreed, and its first priority was to mobilize the defence of Halifax and Sydney Harbours and other strategically important coastal sites.

Halifax was the country's most important east coast port, partly because it was the Royal Navy's North Atlantic home base, which was defended by the Halifax fortress, but also because it was a busy commercial port. Sydney was also an important port because of its two steel mills and several coal mines, which were vital to the Canadian economy and fuelled most of the naval and commercial steamships operating in the Western Atlantic. As well, North Sydney was the Canadian terminal for the Newfoundland ferry service.

Perhaps equally important was the fact that Britain's rapid communication links with North America flowed through Nova Scotia. The undersea telegraphic cable stations were at North Sydney and Hazel Hill, near Canso, and the Marconi Company had wireless radio stations at Glace Bay and Louisbourg. It also operated a wireless radio station at Camperdown, on the outer edge of Halifax Harbour, the first of a network being built to aid marine traffic in the area. And of course there were many smaller coastal communities whose livelihood was based in different ways on the sea.

The country had been divided some years earlier into military divisions (later redesignated districts), and Halifax was the headquarters of Military District 6, which encompassed the three Maritime provinces. MD 6 was commanded in 1914 by Lieutenant Colonel, later Brigadier General, R. W. Rutherford. His appointment was an inspired one, not only because he was an artilleryman with a decade of experience in senior positions at Militia Headquarters in Ottawa, but also because he was a Nova Scotian. He had grown up in Halifax and Pictou because his father was inspector of mines, then manager, of the General Mining Association's operations in Pictou County.[31]

Because of its historic importance to the Royal Navy, Halifax had long been a defended port, but the Royal Navy had turned the fortress and naval dockyard over to the Canadian government in 1906 because it now believed that its primary role in any future war would be to protect shipping at sea, not to defend coastal ports. Even so, it required Canada to maintain the Halifax fortress and to garrison it if the navy was going to continue to use it as a base of operations. Thus, the Halifax fortress had been manned since 1906 by troops from the Royal Canadian Regiment and units of the Royal Canadian Garrison Artillery, both of which were part of Canada's permanent force, aided by detachments from local militia regiments.[32] Canada was very willing to do this because coastal defence continued to be very important to it, especially in view of the fact that it did not have a navy in 1906 and could only by a generous interpretation of the term be considered to have one in 1914.

The idea of coastal bombardment by battleships may seem fantastic a century later, but in fact it was not unrealistic. The question was whether naval bombardment of significant coastal targets was likely. Perhaps not, although during the war German warships shelled English towns of no military significance along the North Sea coast. The larger threats were actually the traditional ones: that enemy warships might attack shipping in coastal waters or even stage small local raids on coastal communities such as Nova Scotians had experienced in past wars. It would be the task of the Royal Canadian Navy to assist the Royal Navy by patrolling coastal waters, but, with the exception of Halifax, there were no coastal defences in the province in 1914.

Halifax fortress, the elaborate network of fortifications that protected the city's naval port and harbour, was fairly impressive. The British Army had spent a lot of money upgrading it in the two decades before it withdrew, so Canada inherited an up-to-date and well-equipped operation. The Militia Department had undertaken some work on the fortress between 1911 and 1914 as well.

Nine batteries of the latest concrete and heavy earth-bank construction mounted twenty-six modern breech-loading guns, and the garrison, although a third smaller than what the British had maintained, was sufficient to man the most important of them. The Militia Department also assigned additional units to reinforce the Halifax garrison in the event of war and improved training programs in fortress duties for them. In all, a total of 2,600 men provided the infantry detachments in and around the city and manned six of the nine batteries. The war plan developed in 1912 provided for the mobilization of more than 5,000 militiamen from across the Maritimes for service at Halifax.

Sydney, on the other hand, was virtually defenceless even though an Admiralty report had recently recommended that it be developed as a second defended port because of its importance for the fast refuelling of naval ships. Sydney already supplied fuel for the naval dockyard in Halifax and was the refuelling depot for steamships—both naval and commercial—of various nations operating in the North Atlantic. It was also strategically placed to guard the Grand Banks fishery and the Gulf of St. Lawrence if necessary.

The government had balked at the cost, however. Rear Admiral C. E. Kingsmill, the director of the Canadian Naval Service, inexplicxably dismissed Sydney Harbour as "not a place from which a great deal of trade goes, that is, valuable trade." More surprising, in view of the fact that Cape Breton was an island not yet connected to the mainland, was his suggestion that "the coal they ship could be carried by rail another way."[33] Clearly, the Militia Department shared his lack of concern and contented itself with designating Sydney's 17th Field Battery to protect the cable landing at North Sydney and Cape Breton's 94th Regiment to provide detachments to guard both the cable and wireless stations when necessary. They would be reinforced by troops from the Halifax garrison.[34]

When the crisis came in the first few days of August, the Royal Canadian Regiment was mobilized, all leaves were cancelled, and those training at Camp Aldershot were ordered back to Halifax. The *Morning Chronicle* seemed to take pleasure in reporting that "every soldier in the Garrison, including clerks...have [*sic*] received their equipment and Saturday teams with rifles for the pen pushers were to be seen delivering consignments, at the various offices."[35] Next day, a company of RCR men left London, Ontario, to reinforce the Halifax garrison.[36]

The port of Halifax was placed under naval control on August 3, with Commander Charles White in charge. Henceforth, ships could only enter the port after being cleared at the examination anchorage below Meagher's Beach. They would then be inspected and would have to provide a complete list of the names and addresses of their passengers.[37] Similarly, all vessels sailing from Halifax had to obtain clearance from the dockyard, which involved getting clearance papers from the Custom House and being searched before they sailed.[38]

Stuart Jenks, the province's deputy attorney general, quickly discovered that these regulations should be taken seriously. He was sailing from Herring Cove to the inner harbour with a group of friends on August 17, when one of the forts fired a warning shot "because he [had] neglected to report to a patrol boat as he should have done when entering the harbor." When Jenks ignored it, perhaps not grasping its meaning, another shot "was sent whizzing past his boat about twenty-five yards [twenty-three metres] ahead of his bow." This time he got the message, promptly stopped, and reported to the patrol vessel *Sea Bird.* The incident was apparently "the talk" of the Waegwoltic Club, where Jenks moored his boat.[39]

It wasn't the only incident of its kind. In March 1915 the battery at Ives Point fired two 12-pounder warning shells at the *Brandt,* a federal government steamship that attempted to enter the harbour without proper authorization. One of the shells skipped off the water and flew into the South End of Halifax, crashing into the roof of a house on Lucknow Street. Fortunately, no one was hurt, but the incident made clear that better coordination was needed between the naval port authorities and the coast artillery.[40]

The Royal Canadian Navy's cruiser *Canada,* one of the ships transferred from the Fisheries Protection Service, was stationed off the harbour to direct ships to the examination anchorage. It had been used before the war to train crew for the fisheries service and civilian sailors for the new naval service before the Royal Naval College of Canada was established in 1911.

The college occupied the old naval hospital building at the dockyard, near Pier 4, until that building was severely damaged in the 1917 explosion, after which it was moved to Esquimalt, British Columbia. Because of the growth in naval activity during the war, the Acadia Sugar Refinery's property, which was adjacent to the naval dockyard, was expropriated in 1917, adding about 275 metres of wharfage with a large storage shed that could be converted into barracks.

The Eastern Passage was closed to shipping, and just to make sure that no one tried to use it, the schooner *Advent* was deliberately sunk there on the third by using it as a target for machine-gun firing practice for the militia. Captains were warned that ships attempting to enter the harbour by that channel were "liable to be fired upon without warning." The usual signals made by arriving vessels—"flags, guns, bomb rockets, lights, etc."—were now forbidden. Finally, captains were alerted that it might become necessary, if an attack on the port seemed imminent, to remove buoys or extinguish lights without notice.[41]

The public was warned not to approach government vessels, the naval dockyard, or the dry dock without good cause, because they might be fired upon if their movements appeared in any way suspicious. The operators of small boats and fishing vessels were also told that they should not be "in the area outside a line drawn across the harbor between Reid Rock and Ives Knoll or outside N.W.A. [the North West Arm] beyond the line of Purcell's Cove Ferry between Sunset and Sunrise" or they were "liable to be fired upon by the batteries."[42]

Halifax Harbour's primary defence was provided by a minefield laid in the channel between McNab's Island and Point Edward and an antisubmarine net placed across the harbour from either side of George's Island. Because of the danger that German submarines might lay mines in the approaches to the harbour, a flotilla of ten minesweeping vessels was moored in the North West Arm, just above Chain Rock. Every morning they ensured that the channel into and out of the harbour was clear.

These defences were supported by the network of batteries. Two new batteries were under construction when the war broke out. Sandwich Point Battery was nearing completion at Herring Cove, but construction of the long-planned Connaught Battery had just begun.[43] Until they became operational, Rutherford reactivated two of the five inner works that had been mothballed before the war.

Initially, there were four searchlights at Ives Point and two at York Redoubt, but the lights at York Redoubt were later moved to Sandwich Point, where Rutherford thought they would be more effective, and two new searchlights were installed at Fort McNab to prevent submarines from attempting to run over the antisubmarine nets at high speed.[44] Three searchlights were also built at the Connaught Battery and a fifth searchlight was later added to Ives Point.

The Royal Canadian Garrison Artillery manned the outer forts, while the 1st Halifax Canadian Garrison Artillery (CGA), a militia unit commanded in 1914 by Major A. W. Duffus, manned the inner

Fig. 2.1: Troops from the 1st (Halifax) Canadian Garrison Artillery arrive on George's Island in Halifax Harbour, August 7, 1914.

batteries and several of the smaller forts. It already had a company training at the Sandwich Point Battery, its war station, when war was declared, and a contingent of thirty-five officers and men from the 1st CGA, which soon rose to fifty officers and men, arrived on August 7 to man Fort Charlotte on George's Island, "the keystone of the defence of the inner harbour."[45]

To accommodate the troops manning the harbour forts, the existing buildings on George's Island were renovated and large wooden barracks were built along the north and east sides of the parade square, with another smaller barrack and cookhouse on the south side. The Royal Canadian Engineers, part of the permanent force, maintained the forts, barracks and other installations, provided electrical services, and operated the searchlight system.[46] There was, for example, a detachment of twenty engineers on McNab's Island to watch over the antisubmarine nets and operate the searchlights there.

Meanwhile, Halifax's two infantry militia regiments—the 63rd (Halifax Rifles) and 66th (Princess Louise Fusiliers)—were mobilized on the third, making them, the *Morning Chronicle* thought, "the first Canadian volunteers ordered on duty."[47] On the evening of the fifth, "upwards of three thousand loyal and enthusiastic citizens" gathered at the armoury to witness their formal mobilization. The galleries and main floor of the building were so packed that "the police had the greatest difficulty in securing enough room for the men when the bugle sounded 'fall in.' It certainly was an enthusiastic crowd, the cheering hardly ceasing as the Halifax soldiers went through the necessary formalities for mobilization, and was strongly reminiscent of the scenes that took place here when the troops sailed for South Africa." In addition to their existing members, the two regiments enrolled 200 new recruits that evening, who "were rapidly served out with uniforms and equipment."[48] They were reinforced as well by detachments of the 62nd Regiment from Saint John and the 14th King's Hussars from Kings County.

The task of these troops was to protect not just the port but also to establish a defensive perimeter around the city itself, just in case an enemy ship landed raiding parties to lay siege to the fortress from St. Margaret's Bay in the west or from Lawrencetown Beach on the Dartmouth side of the harbour.[49] This perimeter consisted of a series of camps and fieldworks sited on or near major roads leading into the city. The smaller, outer ones were intended essentially to sound the alarm and perhaps slow down an attack, while the larger and stronger inner ones were intended to actually repel an attack. According to Bryan Elson, however, "for the most part they were not close enough to each other to be mutually supporting, and direct lateral road communication between them was usually lacking."[50]

With the exception of Camperdown, the positions on the Halifax side were manned by the 66th Regiment. Four companies plus a machine-gun unit were posted near the junction of the Bedford and Kearney Lake roads to protect Chain Lake and Long Lake, which were then the source of Halifax's water supply. There was another camp at Spryfield, covering the critical junctions where the Prospect, Sambro, and Herring Cove-Ketch Harbour roads diverge as they leave the city. Two blockhouses were built there as well as huts for the men, although the troops at the other locations were housed in tents. The positions on the outer ring were at Portuguese Cove, Ragged Lake, Hatchet Lake, Governor's Lake, Kearney Lake Road, and Hammonds Plains.

The 63rd Regiment was responsible for the Dartmouth side of the harbour and the Camperdown radio station at the entrance to the harbour. Already important in 1914, the Camperdown radio station became even more so in 1917, when the first radio direction finding (RDF) station in Canada was built there. Three more RDF stations were soon added, at Cape Sable, Chebucto Head, and Canso, as well as one at Cape Race in Newfoundland. RDF stations assisted ships in fog or in making landfall by enabling them to verify their calculated position, but these stations were potentially invaluable in wartime because they could also fix the position of enemy warships based on their radio transmissions.[51]

The 63rd positioned two companies along Woodlawn Road, mainly to safeguard the city's water supply at Topsail Lake and Lake Lamont, and forward positions were established at Yorck's farm on Main Street and at Kuhn's farm in Woodside, on the shore road to Eastern Passage. "Working day and night, the men started digging trenches, placing barbed wire and constructing blockhouses and dugouts to block a potential enemy landing force."[52]

Lest anyone think that these military positions need not be taken seriously, a notice was published in the Halifax newspapers on August 14 warning civilians that if they were challenged by sentries "they must immediately halt and reply to the challenge," especially at night. "Failure to comply," it was declared, "may result IN PERSONAL INJURY."[53]

Within a very short period, the number of troops on duty in and around Halifax reached 2,600 officers and men. Almost nobody, including Sir Willoughby Gwatkin, chief of the general staff in the Militia Department, seriously believed that Halifax required this level of protection, but the Militia Department's 1912 war plan had, improbably, assumed an attack by the United States, in which case coastal defence would be a serious concern. But no one had seriously thought war with the United States was likely, including Borden and Hughes, who had been warning since 1910 that war with Germany was imminent. Tying up this many troops to guard Halifax against a highly unlikely German attack was both expensive and inefficient; though not an immediate problem, it would become one when the number of men volunteering for overseas service began to decline.

Gwatkin tried to persuade Rutherford to reduce the number of troops deployed in and around Halifax but Rutherford was being pressured by senior Royal Navy officers for whom defence of the fortress was "all-important,"[54] not to mention local politicians and businessmen who were benefiting from the presence of such a large military establishment in the little city. Rutherford did cancel the order for the 3rd New Brunswick (Artillery) Regiment to go to Halifax in August 1914, but wanted more RCR troops for the garrison. When Hughes scotched that idea, Rutherford more realistically recommended the creation of a composite militia regiment formed from single companies drawn from eight of the Maritime militia regiments not yet called out. Gwatkin and Hughes agreed to this, and by September 10 the composite battalion was part of the garrison, freeing up men from the 66th Regiment.

It maintained guard posts throughout the war at the Gun Wharf, the King's Wharf, the Engineers Lumber Yard, the naval hospital, dry dock, and Richmond pier, as well as at Forts Clarence and Ogilvie and the Point Pleasant Battery. It also provided guards for German prisoners and enemy aliens confined in the Citadel and on Melville Island. By September 1915 the Halifax garrison had risen to 3,500 men.[55] Most of them were actually unfit for overseas service but this did not, as Thomas Raddall recalled, discourage small boys from taunting them with the rhyme, "Comp-o-zite, they won't fight."[56]

No doubt the Halifax militiamen found it exciting, at least initially, to be called upon to defend Halifax in a major war, but many if not most of them soon became frustrated because they wanted to go overseas. And the glamour associated with defending a port that, at least until the summer of 1917 seemed increasingly unlikely to be attacked, soon wore off. It was, in fact, as Stuart Hunt observed, "uninteresting work" and "altogether a thankless task."[57]

Those who could transferred into overseas battalions as they were being recruited. George Sylvester, for example, who was principal of Tower Road School but also a lieutenant in the 63rd Regiment, was posted with his detachment to McNab's Island with instructions to "challenge every boat coming in." At first this seemed important because he thought Halifax was "rather an exposed harbor" and it seemed "quite possible that we shall be attacked."[58] By the spring of 1915, he had had enough and enlisted in the 40th Battalion, which went overseas that autumn.[59] Sydney Creighton, a civil engineer from Dartmouth, stuck it out longer, serving with the Halifax fortress engineers until September 1918, when he joined the Royal Canadian Engineers. It's not clear if he actually made it overseas, but it seems unlikely.

Meanwhile, as planned, Rutherford had sent a company from the Royal Canadian Regiment to Sydney by train as early as July 30 to guard the North Sydney cable station and the nearby coal mines against a surprise attack until the formal declaration of war, at which point the 94th Regiment and the 17th Field Battery mobilized and assumed responsibility.[60] Between 2,000 and 3,000 people thronged the Intercolonial Railway Station in Sydney to welcome the first detachment and "as the big engine pulled into the station the uniforms and accouterments of the soldiers caught the eyes of the immense throng, and cheers commenced and continued for some little time." The crowd was disappointed when only ten men detrained but Captain E. B. Costin, who was in command of the detachment, explained that most of the company had got off at North Sydney. Those who had just arrived in Sydney were on their way to Glace Bay by special train to guard the Marconi towers.[61]

Another company left Halifax for Canso on a government steamer the next day to protect the cable station at Hazel Hill, and thirty men were sent by train that evening to guard the Marconi wireless stations at Glace Bay and Louisbourg.[62] On the evening of August 4, a naval brigade of forty-three personnel from the Halifax dockyard with two 12-pounder field guns and two machine guns was also dispatched to Glace Bay, where they joined the now thirty RCR troops already on duty there.[63] Among them were William Palmer and John Grant, who were each put in charge of a field gun and carried a pistol for the first time.[64] When the RCR men reached Table Head, the site of the Marconi towers, they threw up earthworks and built a gun emplacement "for the old Maxim gun." William Hayes later recalled the warm welcome the troops received from the local population. A few days after they arrived, for example, the nuns who operated St. Joseph's Hospital sent "a huge hamper of 'Comforts'" that Hayes thought was "probably the first hamper received by any Canadian troops during the War." The gift was "typical of the spirit of the civilian population of the district," he said, "and was very much appreciated. All kinds of facilities were placed at our disposal and everything possible was done by the people of the Sydney's [*sic*] to make us comfortable."[65]

Meanwhile, the 94th Regiment had mobilized eight companies of men totalling 377 all ranks under the command of Lieutenant J. D. McRae, and a special train set out from Orangedale on the morning of August 5 to pick up the men as it worked its way to Sydney. On arrival, they were quartered in the arena before being distributed among Sydney, North Sydney, Glace Bay, and Louisbourg. Dan MacQuarrie later recalled that he was working in the woods when he

> *got this letter, to report to Baddeck, and they sent us down to Marconi Towers in Glace Bay. We were guards. They had about 50 masts there then, and they had—oh, it was foolish, when you come to think of it—...men hoisted up in them, up in the tower in a kind of a basket, watching [to] see if the enemy'd be coming. They kept men there all through the war.... Vital to the country, you know, when the war was on. Whether they would be destroyed or not, I don't know.*[66]

These facilities were extremely important, especially in wartime, because they were the only high-speed communication links between England and North America. The Western Union station at North Sydney was so busy even before the war that a much larger facility had to be built, which opened only in December 1914. There were some 300 people employed there, processing 30,000 messages a day. On August 3 E. L. Gilpin was appointed telegraphic censor with a staff of ten men.[67]

Because Sydney's 17th Field Battery had been accepted for overseas service, a battery of the Prince Edward Island Heavy Brigade Canadian Garrison Artillery was sent to Cape Breton with four 4.7-inch guns on travelling carriages. Under the command of Major J. R. Darke, it travelled on the Dominion Coal Company's Black Diamond liner *Cacouna*, which landed half the unit and two of the guns at Port Hawkesbury for rail transport to North Sydney, and the other half with two guns for Canso.[68]

Their arrival may have reassured local people that their communities were being defended, but the 4.7-inch artillery pieces on travelling carriages that were employed in Nova Scotia and elsewhere were actually useless for coastal defence "and the gunners knew it."[69] The problem was that their wheeled carriages could not be levered about readily enough to track and engage a moving ship. Proper coast artillery guns sat on a perfectly balanced carriage on a heavy steel pivot set in concrete so that they could swing rapidly and precisely on a wide arc. A battery commander at Saint John complained early in 1915 that trying to fire on a hostile vessel with guns on travelling carriages would "aggravate the situation rather than better it." Gwatkin was well aware of this, of course, and only sent the 4.7-inch guns to Nova Scotia and New Brunswick during the panic in early August 1914 to "soothe the citizens."[70]

By the tenth, there were 707 men all ranks stationed in Cape Breton and at Canso. The garrison at Sydney included three companies and the staff of the 94th, comprising 169 men. Headquarters was established at 33 Charlotte Street. At North Sydney and Sydney Mines, the 94th had a company of forty-six men, the RCR had seventy men, and the PEI Heavy Brigade had sixty-six men with two 4.7-inch guns on travelling carriages.

The artillery was placed at Chapel Point in Sydney Mines—one of the sites identified in the pre-war defence scheme—because it overlooked the cable landing at Lloyd's Cove, but it was later moved to the ridge about 640 metres behind Chapel Point. A 94th contingent guarded the old Western Union cable office in North Sydney at the corner of Commercial and Union Streets about five kilometres away (and was connected by an underground landline) and from January 1915 the new office on Court Street, which was "generally considered to be the most modern telegraph office in the world."[71] The changing of the guard was accompanied by a piper.

The North Sydney detachment also supplied a detachment at Whitney Pier in Sydney, which was at the disposal of the customs officer to enforce his authority to examine ships and, if necessary, to detain them. At Glace Bay there were two companies of the 94th, comprising eighty-one men, and thirty men from the RCR. Another sixty-two men from the 94th were at Louisbourg, while there was a half battery of the PEI Heavy Brigade with seventy-four men and two 4.7-inch guns on travelling carriages, as well as a company of the 94th with fifty-nine men and fifty RCR men at Canso.[72]

Fig. 2.2: A detachment of troops from the 94th Regiment at the Marconi wireless station in Louisbourg, August 1914.

During the autumn the militia units began to dig in. In October the Bate McMahon Construction Company, whose managing director was the Halifax-born Robert Low, began building wooden barracks in the industrial area for the soldiers, who until then had been sleeping on the ground in tents. Bate McMahon, an Ottawa company, was obviously well connected because it had also built the camp at Valcartier, and went on to build Camp Borden in Ontario and Camp Hughes in Manitoba, and was in charge of reconstruction in Halifax after the 1917 explosion.

By the middle of November the buildings at North Sydney near the new cable office and at the cable landing at Sydney Mines were completed. Following an inspection visit by Low, now a colonel, extensive improvements were made, including the installation of water, sewer, and electric lights in the barracks that did not yet have them.[73] Barbed wire was strung around the main compounds, and Bate McMahon built what were described as blockhouses, presumably meaning that they were timber structures within the wire with rifle loopholes. At Louisbourg the militiamen assisted the contractor with the work and built earth-banked firing positions outside the wire, and at Hazel Hill there were extensive trench works behind an outer line of wire around much of the cable company site. The defences also included two blockhouses on the coast east and west of Canso. One of the 4.7-inch guns was removed in March 1915, when half of the artillery detachment was transferred to Halifax where there was a shortage of trained gunners.[74]

Gwatkin's policy towards Sydney was quite different from his policy towards Halifax. Because Halifax was an imperial naval base, it was necessary to defend the whole harbour. At Sydney, however, he thought only a few particular sites needed to be defended. Thus, when the RCR withdrew from the coastal garrisons to go to Bermuda late in August, he rejected Rutherford's proposal to expand the 94th Regiment. It remained at its limited establishment of about 500 men, and the only action taken was to call out a single company of sixty men from Pictou County's 78th Regiment for service at Canso.[75] In fact, Gwatkin proposed to reduce the size of the 94th Regiment's establishment but backed off in the face of a political firestorm. Rutherford did move one company of troops from Sydney to Canso and another to Louisbourg, and granted permission to men in the 94th to volunteer for overseas service.[76]

This appears to have provoked a movement to form a home guard unit. Bridgeport took the lead as early as September 1914 when, at the instigation of Dr. Marcus Dodd, about 150 men attended a meeting and sixty-eight signed the roll. "It is expected," the *Daily Post* optimistically reported, "that the neighboring mining towns will join Bridgeport in forming a full battalion."[77] A month later more than 300 people attended a meeting at the Empire Theatre in New Waterford to discuss the formation of a home guard battalion, and approximately 100 men signed up. It took another six weeks before Sydney, led by the irrepressible Walter Crowe, joined the movement, but on November 20 another meeting took place and about 120 men signed up.[78]

The Sydney Home Guard engaged enthusiastically in squad drills and special classes were even provided "for those who wish to have private tuition prior to their taking their place in the ranks."[79] The lack of rifles was a problem, but it was overcome to some extent when a local carpenter made "a very fair and quite useful imitation of the service rifle." This dummy rifle allegedly "called for the highest praise," and the *Daily Post* told its readers on December 7 that "it seems almost an assured fact that about fifty of them, or even more" would soon be available. By this time the Sydney Home Guard, comprising four companies, had been reconstituted as the Sydney Battalion of Home Guard. It's not clear just what happened, but the home guard movement seems to have fizzled out, especially as the need for more men to go overseas continued to increase.

Gwatkin had not given up on his determination to reduce the militia garrisons at home, however, but he knew he couldn't cut at

Halifax because of the Royal Navy's insistence on a high level of security. He therefore made cuts in Cape Breton, withdrawing the 4.7-inch guns from Sydney Mines and Canso for use at training camps for overseas artillery drafts. Towards the end of the year, Rutherford reduced all of the 94th Regiment's companies to an establishment of forty-four men all ranks and withdrew the company of the 78th that had been on duty at Canso. Again, the reduction appears to have been achieved through personnel volunteering for overseas service, in this case largely for the Highland Brigade that was then being raised.[80]

At the same time, troops were needed to guard the new Marconi wireless station at Birch Hill, near Barrington Passage, which was regarded as vulnerable because it was situated on the old Woods Harbour road. Construction took place during the winter of 1914–15 and when completed, the facility's two 300-foot towers were the tallest structures in Shelburne County and served as useful beacons to local fishermen at sea. There were also buildings to house the generators and accommodations for the station workers and the militiamen assigned to guard the facility.

The station was commanded by two British junior naval officers, who were allowed to have their wives with them, and was guarded by sixty militiamen, who were not, although Lieutenant Colonel Thomas Seeley, their commanding officer, was allowed to bring his horse for which he received an additional allowance. It is not clear why he needed a horse or, for that matter, why a detachment of sixty men needed a lieutenant colonel. One gets the impression, however, that Rutherford was trying to find a useful role for Seeley, who was publisher of the *Yarmouth Light* newspaper and a long-time officer in MD 6's militia artillery.

Seeley's troops consisted of Captain Wallace Ernst and twenty men from the No. 1 Siege Company of Mahone Bay, Lieutenant Glidden Campbell and twenty men from the 27th Battery at Weymouth and Digby, and Lieutenant Edgar Vickery with twenty men from the 29th Battery of Yarmouth.[81] Remarkably, the militiamen were paid $1.10 a day, the same rate as men serving overseas. As well, the men were allowed ploughing, seeding, haying, and harvesting furloughs at full pay. The situation began to change in November 1915 when fourteen men were transferred to garrison duties in St. Lucia, then changed dramatically in May 1917, when several men transferred into overseas battalions. That left just ten militiamen at the station, and they were mostly older married men. The reductions in personnel reflected the fact that home defence was not being taken very seriously by 1917.

The 63rd and 66th Regiments were allowed to send drafts as well, eventually supplying seventy officers and 815 men and fifty-four officers and 850 men, respectively, for overseas service.[82] Three of them were brothers: Cyril and Ray Colwell, both lieutenants in the 63rd, went overseas in September 1917 and August 1918 respectively, and Garnet was a lieutenant in the 66th when he went overseas in May 1918. All survived and returned home to run the family's Halifax clothing business.

Home service was not without its dangers. Two men died at the Barrington Passage wireless station, one from illness and one from being accidentally shot by another soldier. George Groves, a Newfoundlander who had enlisted in the militia in Mahone Bay in 1914, was shot by Stanley Lohnes, on June 3, 1915, during a bit of horseplay. Lohnes was also a member of the Mahone Bay detachment and reportedly Groves's best friend.

On a happier note, two men fell in love with local girls and were allowed to marry them.[83] Five other men returned after the war, settled in the area and married women they had courted while posted there.

Chapter 3

FOR KING AND COUNTRY

There's a regiment to the fore
From Nova Scotia's rugged shore,
And we go to fight for our country and our kin,
Whate'er the cost, we'll fight and win.[1]

As soon as war was declared, Canada offered the British government an infantry battalion and Sam Hughes called for 25,000 volunteers. Ignoring the 1912 mobilization plan that had assigned recruiting to the regional military districts, he sent telegrams directly to all 226 militia commanding officers across the country, inviting them to recruit the volunteers instead. Hughes wanted no more than a company—125 men—from each militia unit, however, because he thought overseas battalions that would be engaged in combat should be more broadly based.

Nova Scotia's militia consisted of nine militia infantry regiments, six artillery batteries, one cavalry unit, and one hospital unit. The infantry regiments were the 63rd (Halifax Rifles) and 66th (Princess Louise Fusiliers) based in Halifax, the 69th (Annapolis), 75th (Lunenburg), 76th (Colchester and Hants), 78th (Pictou), 93rd (Cumberland), and 94th (Victoria) Regiments. The artillery batteries were the 17th (Sydney), 18th (Antigonish), 27th (Digby), 28th (Pictou), and 29th (Yarmouth), and the 1st Regiment Canadian Garrison Artillery in Halifax. The cavalry unit was the 14th King's Hussars (Kings), and the medical unit was No. 2 Clearing Hospital (Queens).

All responded enthusiastically, but because of the limitation that Hughes had stipulated, only about 2,000 men were wanted from the province. At the same time, the 63rd, 66th, 69th, and 94th Regiments and the Canadian Garrison Artillery were called out for coastal and home defence duties and that accounted for another 2,200 men. It might have been expected that Hughes would build the overseas contingent around the Royal Canadian Regiment, the permanent force infantry regiment. He didn't, however, because he had little respect for professional soldiers and, as a long-time militiaman, he was convinced that civilian volunteers made the best soldiers after they were trained.[2] As recently as July 1913, he had taken the opportunity of a banquet in Halifax for Sir Ian Hamilton, inspector general of the British Army's Overseas Forces, to attack the permanent force in a speech in the presence of the RCR's officers. The regiment's historian later commented with admirable restraint only that his speech "added little to the amenities of the occasion" and "painfully embarrassed" the guest of honour.[3]

The RCR had provided the troops for the Halifax garrison since 1906. In 1914 it had six companies at Halifax, made up mostly of British soldiers who had chosen to remain when the fortress was taken over by Canada. At first it was not included in the proposed overseas contingent because of the importance attached to defending the port of Halifax. But when the War Office asked if Canada could send troops to Bermuda to enable the British garrison there to return home for service in Europe, Hughes immediately agreed and designated the Royal Canadian Regiment.

The RCR, therefore, had the honour of being the first Canadian troops to go overseas in 1914, although it got only as far as Bermuda, where there wasn't much of a threat from the enemy. It sailed from Halifax on the *Canada*, escorted by the *Niobe*, on September 14. The *Morning Chronicle* was clearly thrilled by the "impressive spectacle of Canadian military and naval forces starting off together on a joint operation...for the first time," an event that "held a deep significance for every one [*sic*] who witnessed the departure."[4]

This was no doubt true, but the Bermuda deployment was not a happy experience. The regiment spent eleven hot, boring, and frustrating months on the island, patrolling the towns, villages, and beaches, watching for enemy warships or submarines and guarding German prisoners who had been taken off a ship en route to Europe from New York.[5] By June 1915 Lieutenant General Sir George Mackworth Bullock, the British commander in chief in Bermuda, was reporting "insubordination and discontent" among the Canadians, so Hughes sent the regiment to Europe, replacing it with an overseas battalion from Ontario that he didn't want to send overseas for political reasons. The men of the RCR were so keen that seven men who had not been selected to go to Europe were discovered at sea as stowaways, and were signed up after they arrived in England. One of them was Frederick Laing of Halifax, who was only fourteen years old.

Meanwhile, the thousands of volunteers from across the country were summoned to gather not at Camp Petawawa but at a new training camp at Valcartier, a village near Quebec City, for basic training and to be organized into overseas battalions. The fact that Camp Valcartier did not actually exist did not deter Hughes. The

Militia Department had bought the land in the spring, planning to build a new camp there because its location close to a major port was more practical than one in the Ottawa Valley. But the department had not, of course, anticipated that the camp would be needed that summer.

Hughes did not see this as a problem. He called in William Price, a Quebec City lumberman and former Conservative Member of Parliament, to build the camp and to build it immediately. It seemed an irresponsible decision, but within three weeks the 12,000-acre site had been cleared and all the necessary buildings and facilities were completed, if not quite in time for the first arrivals, certainly in time for the later ones. The work was undertaken by Bate McMahon, whose managing director, Robert Low, told the *Halifax Herald* that he "had four hundred men driving ahead day and night on this work." Lieutenant John Cavanagh of the Royal Canadian Regiment, who came from Pictou, actually directed the construction work.[6]

What the *Herald* thought was "a somewhat ironical feature of the work" was that Germans and Austrians who had been detained because they were now enemy aliens "did much of it."[7] If this seemed very odd, and it did to many people at the time, the *Morning Chronicle* suggested, no doubt correctly, that these men were "quite content to remain in steady employment in Canada" and had "no desire to go back and help fight the battles of their military war lords."[8]

The men who volunteered in 1914 and later came from a variety of backgrounds, including professional men, doctors and dentists, office clerks, farmers and fishermen. The majority were recent British immigrants or men of British background but there were also men of various ethnic backgrounds, including Acadians, Mi'kmaq, and African Nova Scotians. In age, they ranged from teenagers to middle-aged men. Many had militia experience but many did not. Eighteen-year-old Jacob Burnstein of Glace Bay had served on the *Niobe* since 1911, which almost certainly made him the first Jewish man to serve in the Royal Canadian Navy. He resigned and went to Valcartier, making him the first Jewish Nova Scotian to enlist in the army as well.[9]

Not all Nova Scotian volunteers enlisted in the province. Hundreds if not thousands enlisted in other provinces because that's where they were in the summer of 1914. Enlistment records from all over the country show men who gave home addresses in Nova Scotia. For the most part, these were young men who had gone west seeking better opportunities but still considered themselves, and were considered by people at home, to be Nova Scotians. Charles Cantley of New Glasgow, for example, son of the general manager of the Nova Scotia Steel and Coal Company, enlisted in a Montreal battalion because he was studying engineering at McGill at the time. Charles Frost, although born in Argyle, enlisted in the Newfoundland Regiment in St. John's because he was employed there by the Bank of Nova Scotia.[10] Frank Iriam of Brazil Lake enlisted in Kenora, Ontario, because he was working there for the Canadian Pacific Railway. Daniel Cameron of Shelburne enlisted in Melbourne, Australia, because he was a sea captain and happened to be there.[11] Many more examples could be cited.

On the other hand, a number of men who came from other places enlisted in Nova Scotia. Some were Newfoundlanders who had moved to Cape Breton seeking work in the coal mines and steel mills. There were also European immigrants who had come to Nova Scotia in recent years for the same reason. They included a large Belgian community in Pictou County, brought in by Nova Scotia Steel and the Acadia Coal Company, which was owned by a Belgian company. In Cape Breton, there was a small Belgian community in New Waterford, and the Dominion Coal Company had brought in French and Greek miners, most of whom had settled in New Waterford and Birch Grove.[12] Several French miners worked in the Inverness mine as well. Many people identified as "Russians" and "Austrians," who were usually actually Poles or Ukrainians, also enlisted.

Most European countries had adopted conscription before the war, and men remained members of the army reserve after completing their service even if they immigrated to Canada or other countries. For this reason, and because the Militia Act stipulated that only British subjects could enlist, some recent immigrants returned home to rejoin their regiments. This was not a problem for British, French, or Belgian immigrants, but it was for Germans and Austrians, who were not allowed to board ships sailing from Canadian ports. Some made their way to the United States, which was neutral, and travelled to Europe from there.

Twenty Belgians from New Waterford left for home on August 15,[13] and others from the New Glasgow area soon followed. About 250 French reservists from the Sydney area returned home as well. This caught the attention of the *Morning Chronicle*, which organized a parade of those who stopped over in Halifax led by the bands of the 63rd and 66th Regiments. The enthusiastic Frenchmen carried "the Tricolor and the Union Jack" and sang "the national songs of the Triple Entente," to the delight of "fully fifteen thousand" people who turned out to cheer them.[14] Around the same time "about fifty" Russians living in Halifax volunteered to go home to fight for their country, and the *Halifax Echo* expected that number to rise to 300.[15]

Not all of the first volunteers were fighting men. There were doctors as well, six of whom were members of No. 2 Canadian Clearing Hospital, the militia unit from Liverpool. Perhaps because it had not occurred to Hughes that the troops would need dentists, only three volunteered in August 1914 but two of them were Nova Scotians: Dr. Bruce Kelley of Bridgewater and Dr. Bayard Neiley of New Glasgow. When they went overseas they were the only dental surgeons with the Canadian contingent, but by the end of the war there were more than 1,000 dental officers and personnel overseas.[16]

Similarly, Hughes had not planned to provide chaplains to the overseas battalions but was persuaded to change his mind and appointed the Reverend Richard Steacy to serve as director of the chaplaincy service. Steacy had three qualifications: he was Anglican, he was a friend of Hughes, and he shared his prejudices. As a result, most of the first thirty-three chaplains were Anglicans, even though most of the volunteers were not. Only six of the original chaplains were Catholic, which proved to be a problem, not just in Quebec but also in Nova Scotia where a high percentage of the volunteers were Catholic.

This became a serious problem that affected enlistments. It was not resolved until 1916, when both Steacy and Hughes were sacked. Steacy was replaced by the Reverend John Almond, who was also Anglican but more liberal and realistic. His appointment of the Reverend W. T. Workman, a Catholic priest, as assistant director of the service had a very positive impact on recruiting, especially in Nova Scotia.[17] Eventually, 524 clergymen served as chaplains in the war, 447 of them overseas. The enthusiasm of clergy to go to war reflected their very real sense of duty and their understanding that men risking their lives needed and deserved spiritual support.

Some, like the Reverend John Pringle, the sixty-two-year-old minister of St. Andrew's Presbyterian Church in Sydney, also were motivated by their belief that the war was a "righteous" one.[18] He served as chaplain of the 9th Battalion, the Edmonton-based unit in which his son had enlisted. His son was killed on the Somme in September 1916, but Pringle returned to Cape Breton and was a prominent Canadian churchman in the 1920s.

The volunteers in 1914 also included women because the Canadian Expeditionary Force—the official name of the overseas army—would definitely need nurses. When the war broke out there were only five nurses in the Canadian Army Nursing Corps. Their matron was Margaret Macdonald of Bailey's Brook, Pictou County, one of the founders of the service and the first woman in the British Empire to achieve the rank of major in the armed forces. She had already had a remarkable career by 1914, having served with the American Army in the Spanish-American War, in Panama during the construction of the canal, and then as one of twelve nurses with the Canadian contingent in the South African War.

Macdonald was authorized to recruit 100 more nurses and had no difficulty in doing so, as there was much enthusiasm among nurses to play a role. Like the men of the First Contingent, these 105 nurses proved to be only the first of the 2,504 who served overseas during the war. There were six nurses from Nova Scotia in the First Contingent. In addition to Macdonald, they included

Fig. 3.1: Nursing matron Margaret Macdonald, 1918, had a remarkable career even before she served overseas.

Ann Doctor Allan of Halifax, Pearl Fraser of New Glasgow,[19] Janet MacGregor of Big Island, Margaret MacLeod of Donkin, and Adruenna "Addie" Tupper, who was born in Yarmouth but lived in Bridgewater.

We often read about boys who lied about their age in order to get into the army. Addie Tupper lied about her age, but she shaved off an entire decade because she feared, probably correctly, that she would not be accepted if she admitted that she was forty-five years old. Her war proved to be a relatively short one. Her health began to fail under the workload and she was sent home in November 1915 to recuperate. She returned a month later but contracted pneumonia and died in England in December 1916.

While there was no difficulty raising recruits in Nova Scotia until 1916, one does get the impression that the armouries were not as flooded with eager volunteers as was the case elsewhere. The *Amherst Daily News* remarked on this as early as August 11, observing that "many, who would be perfectly willing" to enlist were unable to do so "owing to the numerous home ties that bind them to Amherst." They would, however, "immediately sign on for service in Canada."[20] Daniel Murray, the lieutenant colonel of the 93rd Regiment, complained of an ailment he called "better-halves," referring to the fact that married men had to produce written proof of their wife's consent before they could be accepted.[21] The problem was not serious enough to prevent every militia unit from raising the men required, however.

HAVING ENLISTED, THE VOLUNTEERS EAGERLY AWAITED THE call to proceed to Valcartier. It was not long in coming: the men from mainland Nova Scotia were ordered to travel together on the same train on August 20, and the men from Cape Breton followed a week later. While the Halifax units prepared themselves, the men of Liverpool's No. 2 Clearing Hospital mobilized on the eighth and went to the home in Milton of Major F. S. L. Ford, their commanding officer, to be issued their blue serge and khaki shirts and trousers, forage caps, straw hats, and kit bags. On the nineteenth, the unit's six officers and forty-one men paraded from the Mersey Hotel to the train station "through streets filled with cheering crowds, followed by hundreds of citizens and a long line of beautifully decorated automobiles and teams."[22]

According to local historian Janet Mullins, "so intent was the band on its music that it failed to turn down Market Street, and had nearly reached the Town Hall before Major Ford succeeded in turning the parade about." With the unit now leading the band, they had to march back to the starting point, "a maneuver that the public cheered as a fine piece of tactics," and made their way to the station.[23] There, "patriotic airs were played by the band and sung by the people. Tears were shed by the well-to-do and those in humbler life."[24]

Fig. 3.2: Major F. S. L. Ford and the men of No. 2 Casualty Clearing Station leave for Halifax.

No. 2 was travelling only as far as Halifax that day but it took the precaution of carrying its own stores, consisting of fifty loaves of bread and thirty-eight pounds of cheese. Friends and relatives also brought "a generous supply of food and other comforts" to the station. The unit arrived early in the evening, had supper at the Revere Hotel, across from the Intercolonial train station on North Street, then marched to the nearby Wellington Barracks where the NCOs and men were billeted for the night. The officers stayed at the King Edward Hotel, then one of the city's finest.[25]

The next morning, "nearly half" of the population of Halifax gathered at the station to bid farewell to the sixty-one officers and men from the 63rd Halifax Rifles and 66th Princess Louise Fusiliers and the Liverpool contingent. The troops marched from the Wellington Barracks to the station "through streets literally lined by thousands, and at times the stirring martial music" provided by the bands of the two regiments "was drowned by the thundering cheers that greeted the men all along the way."[26]

As the train pulled out of the station, the thousands of spectators cheered as the bands struck up "Soldiers of the King." The *Morning Chronicle*, while declaring that "the vast crowds, the enthusiasm expressed and the responses of the volunteers all combined to instill [*sic*] the spirit of Imperialism into the big throng," also recognized that the departure of these men brought home to those left behind that "there really is war in Europe and...these men were going to the firing line....They were Halifax's first offering to the War God and to many the last seen of them was through tear dimmed eyes."[27]

When the train stopped at Truro, more than 4,000 people crowded the streets as the 126 officers and men from Pictou County's 78th Regiment, the ninety-nine officers and men of the 76th Colchester and Hants Rifles, forty-four volunteers from Antigonish, eleven men from the 14th King's Hussars, "and a sprinkling from other parts of the Province" paraded from the armoury to the station, led by the 76th's regimental band. "Flags and decorations were everywhere in profusion and the enthusiasm was unbounded."[28]

When the train reached Springhill, it stopped to pick up that community's volunteers. In "one of the biggest demonstrations ever held" in the town, they marched from the armoury to the train station through streets "thronged with thousands," led by a band and several schoolchildren.[29] They were accompanied by the fourteen recruits from Parrsboro led by Captain T. C. Choisnet of the 93rd Regiment,[30] who had also been given "a stirring and thrilling" send-off by "probably 1,000" people when they boarded the train for Springhill.[31] At the same time, however, two men got off the train at Springhill: Lieutenant James Simpson of Amherst, "who could not come to an understanding as to his rank, and Private Allen Kennedy whose complaint was 'My Wife Won't Let me.'"[32]

The volunteers from Cape Breton followed a week later. Actually, they weren't all Cape Bretoners because Sydney's 17th Battery had been reinforced with twenty men from the 29th Battery in Yarmouth, raising its total strength to 141 officers and men. The Yarmouth contingent had travelled to Sydney on the

Fig. 3.3: 29th Battery volunteers leaving Yarmouth for Sydney, August 22, 1914.

twenty-second, led by Captain Fletcher Pickles of Hebron, but not before it had been treated to an official farewell supper in Churchill's Café. Needless to say, the meal was accompanied by speeches, all of which, the *Yarmouth Herald* claimed, "were enthusiastic, snappy and full of patriotic sentiments and were warmly applauded."[33] When the men marched to the train station led by the town band, the town "was gaily dressed with flags, the automobiles and carriages being similarly decorated, and Main street [*sic*]...took on a holiday appearance, both sidewalks being lined with interested spectators." As the train pulled out of the station, the crowd sang "God Save the King."[34]

The people of Sydney and surrounding communities gave their volunteers a tremendous send-off. "The whole city was at a high tension of excitement" that day, and "everywhere...from housetop to button hole, the Union Jack was in evidence." The *Daily Post* claimed that "tens of thousands...thronged the streets" to watch the men march up George Street from Victoria Park and down Dodd Street to the train station. This may have been an exaggeration, but there were certainly thousands. In addition to the local population, the North Sydney ferry had brought "close upon two thousand people from the towns across the harbor" and the "special half hour" train service from Glace Bay "was taxed to capacity." At the request of Mayor Arthur Richardson, all city stores closed at three o'clock so that everyone could see their boys off to war.

Shortly after two o'clock, a company of the 94th, led by a pipe band, marched from Whitney Pier to Victoria Park, where it was joined by the regiment's 100-man honour guard. At 3:30 the Sydney Mines and 94th bands arrived and entertained the crowd until the speakers arrived in carriages escorted by the Sydney City Band. Following the speeches, the men marched to the station where "many stirring scenes were witnessed."[35] Yarmouth's Wilfred Doane reported that they "were all crazy to give us something. One old fellow gave me four packages of tobacco and wanted to fill me up on whiskey."[36] Mixed with the patriotic excitement, however, was the realization that some "might never return, but find instead a grave beneath the sod of some bloody European battlefield," so "there was scarcely a dry eye in the vast multitude...as the troop train slowly pulled away....But all joined in a mighty cheer which echoed and re-echoed till the long train of coaches vanished in the dim distance."[37]

When the train reached Point Tupper, where it had to be loaded onto the ferry *Scotia* to cross the Strait of Canso, the town's powerhouse emitted "a screech which seemed to rend the heavens," to which the engine responded with its whistle. "It was," the *Daily Post*'s reporter said, "a very effective sendoff and it was augmented by very brilliant lights, from some shipping and from points along the shore." On the men's arrival at Mulgrave, a crowd had gathered to greet them with "a splendid selection of songs and patriotic airs."[38]

Another "crowd of hundreds" and the town band met the train at Antigonish even though it was 2:30 in the morning. Then, having had "to undergo quite an amount of good natured chaff from his brother officers," Lieutenant Colonel Harvey MacLeod got off the train and drove by automobile to Wine Harbour, where he married his sweetheart, Margaret Irwin. They then rushed back to Antigonish, arriving just in time to catch the noon train, which travelled much faster than the troop train that had to operate more slowly because it was carrying the artillery unit's horses, and was able to overtake it at Campbellton, New Brunswick.[39] Thus it was that MacLeod arrived at Valcartier with not only a field battery and 123 horses, but a bride as well.

When the first Nova Scotians arrived at Valcartier on the evening of August 23, they were impressed by the camp. Charles Holden, an electrician from Liverpool who served in the hospital unit, thought it resembled "a good big city, with its traffic and hustle." It wasn't quite completed, but "they have about 3,000 carpenters and other tradesmen constructing buildings, putting in water works and laying sewers. It will soon be in A1 shape."[40] Arthur Chute compared Valcartier with gold-rush cities like San Francisco in 1849 and Dawson City in 1898 because "here was the same spontaneous and sudden springing up, and here was the same restless blood of a new country, bringing with it an air of imminence and adventure."[41]

Wilfred Doane was struck by the great variety of men: "There are educated, smart men, ex-imperial army men, men who have seen active service, prize-fighters, booze-fighters, toughs, and some mighty fine fellows. There are some fine specimens of manhood up here—the very best." But he was learning

> *a lot about the ways of men that I did not know before. They have no use for the man who is polite or gives in to them. It is the man who can push and put the bluff and carry it through. It's every man for himself here and I think it is going to make a man of me. I can curse them and look out for myself with any of them now.*[42]

Doane wasn't too impressed by the food which, not surprisingly, wasn't "the same as I got home, I can tell you. For breakfast we have a piece of bacon, about 3 by 1½, two pieces of bread, a mug of tea or coffee, no milk. For dinner we have meat, either stewed or fried, a mug of tea and two pieces of bread. For supper, a mug of tea, a piece of bread and jam and a piece of cheese, but we get along somehow." On the other hand, the YMCA had a canteen where the men could purchase "soda water, ice cream, fruit and different things. We have newspapers given us free, and moving pictures are open air on a great big sheet; we can see them for a great distance. About 10,000 soldiers were down to see them the other night; very good pictures too."[43]

Sam Hughes, who was a strict teetotaller, would allow no alcohol in the camp. Needless to say, this did not please some men but others thought it a wise policy. "If liquor ever got into this camp, it would be bad," Doane thought.[44] He was probably right. In 1914 the widespread availability of cheap alcohol, which was still 100 proof, was a generally recognized social problem. In fact, there was an incident a couple of days later that confirmed the wisdom of banning alcohol from the camp. It began when "a general alarm was sounded at about nine o'clock for an attack on one of the moving picture shows. It appears that a body of men thinking that the price being charged was too exorbitant, took the law in their own hands and as a result, considerable damage was done the tent, and the money box."[45]

It requires little imagination to appreciate how ugly this affair might have been if the men had been drinking. But this was not the last time the troops would display their frustration and anger with inflated prices in the camps or in nearby towns.

Many of the volunteers, including twenty men from New Glasgow, were sent home in September, most because they failed their medical examination, but some "for imbibing too freely of the ardent."[46] One of them was John Dan Brown, a well-known character in New Glasgow, who almost certainly was the unidentified subject of the following anecdote published in the *Eastern Chronicle.* On the day the Pictou volunteers left for Valcartier, one of them, described as a "burly cabman, popular in the town and a general good fellow," had

> *gathered a rather generous jag. At the depot was an immense throng, among them the ex-cabbie's wife. She naturally felt badly at her husband's departure; sobbing, she threw her arms around his neck. "John when you reach there you will write me, won't you?" In a loud voice John replied, "never a line, woman, never a line until I reach Berlin."*[47]

Not surprisingly, Brown was one of those who had imbibed "too freely" and given "the police of Quebec city, an example of rough house." Dr. Neiley intervened on his behalf, however, and he was allowed back and went overseas with the 17th Battalion.

The major task at Valcartier was to organize the volunteers into overseas battalions. This proved to be problematic with respect to the men from Nova Scotia. First, the 17th Battery was broken up. Part of it was combined with detachments from the 3rd Regiment Garrison Artillery from Saint John and the 19th Battery from Moncton to form the 6th Field Battery, which in turn was joined with two batteries from Quebec to form the 2nd Brigade. The good news was that the 6th would be commanded by Major Harvey MacLeod. Because of that, and the fact that so many of the men in the 6th were from the 17th, Cape Bretoners identified with the 6th Battery, at least until MacLeod's untimely death in December 1915. The Cape Breton connection was also gradually weakened as casualties were replaced by men from all over Canada and a section was detached to the 48th (Howitzer) Battery. As Peter Moogk has said, "The 6th was not so much a Cape Breton battery as an artillery unit containing a large number of Cape Bretoners."[48]

Meanwhile, other men from the 17th were combined with Montreal's 21st Battery to form the new 5th Battery. Among them was Captain "Johnnie Angus" MacDonald, who has been described as "Cape Breton's best known gunner."[49] He had joined the 17th in 1896 and served in the South African War, during which he was awarded the Queen's Medal with three clasps. He went on to command the 7th Battery, then was promoted to lieutenant colonel and commanded the 3rd Brigade. By war's end he had received the Distinguished Service Order with bar and had been mentioned in dispatches four times.

Yet others from the 17th were assigned to the 1st Brigade Ammunition Column, which was commanded by Captain A. A. Durkee. Born in Yarmouth, Durkee owned a shoe factory there before moving it to Truro, and had been an officer in MD 6's 11th Brigade. Wilfred Doane was posted to the column and seems to have enjoyed the experience. He was appointed bugler even though he had never played the instrument, but then he had no experience with horses either. He learned to ride at Valcartier. "It's a case of stick on or get killed, because up here when a battery moves it moves on the dead gallop, and if you fall off, one of those guns will run right over your neck."[50]

Liverpool's Clearing Hospital was designated the camp hospital at Valcartier. With a staff of five physicians, several medical students, and "one of the finest bodies of men in camp," it occupied "a fine commodious building."[51] Even so, it was unable to save Adolphe Gallant of Sydney, who fell ill and died on September 12. He was, Wilfrid Hearn wrote, "one of the most popular members of the 'old 17'" and his death was "a severe blow to his comrades in camp."[52] Gallant may have been the first Nova Scotia–born serviceman to die in the war. Over the years, there would be many more who died from illness or accidents before leaving Canada.

After absorbing personnel from Toronto's No. 1 Casualty Clearing Hospital, No. 2 was designated the clearing hospital for the First Contingent with Ford, now promoted to lieutenant colonel, in command.[53] This was, as the *Liverpool Advance* rightly pointed out, a significant honour, which reflected its "efficiency and trustworthiness."[54]

No doubt this was true, but No. 2 was the only distinctively Nova Scotian unit in the First Contingent that emerged at Valcartier. As we have already seen, the 17th Battery was merged into a new more broadly based battery, and that was the plan for Nova Scotia's infantrymen as well. The fact that none of the sixteen infantry battalions in the First Contingent represented Nova Scotia aroused concern in the province and outright anger on the part of the senior militia officers who had raised the volunteers and led them to Valcartier. Those officers—Lieutenant Colonels Daniel Cameron and Daniel Murray, Majors Struan Robertson and Charles Andrews, and Captains C. E. Bent and L. R. Cutten—had agreed while travelling to Valcartier that there should be a Nova Scotian battalion and that its commanding officer should come from the 78th Regiment. Cameron, the 78th's commanding officer, had even agreed to step down because he was a well-known Liberal, and be replaced by Robertson, who had preceded him as lieutenant colonel and was a well-known Conservative.

But only about 500 officers and men had volunteered from Nova Scotia, not enough to make up a battalion. It was thought that there were another 300 Nova Scotians at Valcartier who had enlisted in other provinces, but they were being allocated to battalions associated with those provinces. Even if they had been transferred to join the Nova Scotian volunteers, there were still not enough. The explanation for this apparently weak showing was that Hughes had only accepted a company from each militia unit and 2,200 militiamen had been called out in Nova Scotia for coastal defence purposes.

Undeterred by facts, Robertson and the other senior officers naturally applied political pressure on the Militia Department and, when Hughes remained firm, went over his head to Borden, who was, of course, a Nova Scotian. They accused Hughes and Lieutenant Colonel Victor Williams, the commanding officer of Valcartier, of discrimination and charged that both men were, "by reason of their unfairness, partiality and proneness to use profanity, quite unfitted to organize or command forces made up of patriotic Canadians whose only desire is to serve their beloved empire as best they can."[55]

Then they leaked their letter to the press, enabling Nova Scotian Liberal politicians to join the attack. This obviously placed Borden in a very difficult position, especially because the accusations against Hughes and Williams were credible, even if not true. Borden therefore intervened, ordering Hughes to authorize a Nova Scotia battalion, which became the 17th. Hughes did so but it was still well under strength, despite Stuart Hunt's unfounded claim that it took only three days to recruit "sufficient men...in Cape Breton, Pictou, Colchester and Cumberland Counties practically to complete the strength of a Regiment."[56]

The 17th went overseas with a full complement of officers but only 773 other ranks, but two of the fourteen captains and seven of the sixteen lieutenants were not Nova Scotians. Of the 773 other ranks, most but not all of the men in the first three companies were from Nova Scotia but the entire fourth company—140 men—had no connection with the province. In other words, whatever Robertson and his colleagues thought of Hughes and whatever he thought of Nova Scotia, he had bolstered its weak numbers to make it at least appear viable.[57]

THE FIRST CONTINGENT WENT OVERSEAS AT THE END OF September, just six weeks after gathering at Valcartier. Wilfred Doane reported on the twenty-third that their horses were all saddled and they were leaving "in a few hours. We will leave about midnight, and march mounted to Quebec, about 28 miles—a nice little jog before breakfast."[58] Like many still naïve Canadians, Doane assured his father that he would be "back soon" because "I don't think things are going to last so very long."[59] The infantry battalions did not leave until morning but only had to march to the Valcartier train station. If Lester Wile, a tailor from Bridgewater in the 17th Battalion, is to be believed, the journey somehow took six hours.[60] According to Dr. Neiley, before they boarded their transport that afternoon, the captain of 3 Company "halted them and asked if John Dan was still with them, and someone answered 'yes,' then said the Captain, 'Let the war begin.'"[61]

The First Contingent sailed in a convoy of thirty-three transports with a Royal Navy escort. Unfortunately, the *Niobe* was unable to participate in the historic journey because it had developed mechanical problems two weeks earlier. The fourteen days at sea were uneventful and increasingly boring to most men, and were not a happy experience for those who suffered from seasickness. Dubious food, which caused "a lot of our fellows" to get "very sick" from ptomaine poisoning, and serious overcrowding among the enlisted men also spoiled the adventure for many men. Lester Wile was one of the lucky ones: "I did not mind it at all.... I was as happy as a lark."[62]

The journey was not entirely uneventful. A sailor on the *Royal Edward* fell overboard but was rescued, two Germans who had enlisted were arrested on the *Megantic*, and a soldier on the *Ruthenia* died from heart failure. According to Kenneth Clarke of Bridgewater, the *Ruthenia* "nearly ran us down the other night but we put on full speed and got away from her."[63]

Originally destined for Southampton, the convoy was redirected to Plymouth because of concerns about German submarine activity. The Canadians, being the first troops to arrive from any of the overseas dominions, received a warm welcome. Captain Fletcher Pickles of Hebron described their reception:

> *At last we are in Plymouth harbor and as we pass up we are greeted with cheer after cheer from the training ships which line the shore. Bugles call for the general salute and we who are arriving answer back, the men with hearty, deep-throated cheers, the officers with a stand at attention and salute. It means rather more than one can put on paper.*

Pickles added, perceptively, that "to a large percentage of our men it means coming back to the land that gave them birth to fight for it. To the native-born Canadian it means the first glimpse, in a great many cases, of the Motherland, which we one and all have always held in reverence and which we have offered our all to defend."[64]

The nurses disembarked the day after arrival and proceeded to St. Thomas' Hospital in London for orientation but, because of the huge numbers involved, the troops had to remain on board the ships for up to seven days while trains were organized to transport them to Salisbury Plain. As frustrating and tedious as the delay must have been for the men, "thousands of people came to see us," Lester Wile reported, "and they brought us all kinds of nice things...I tell you I was never treated better in my life than I was at Devonport [the naval base adjacent to Plymouth]. They just gave us everything that we wanted, and we could hardly get them to take our money."[65]

Russell Harlow, a fireman from Caledonia, reported that when they finally disembarked, "the English soldiers came and marched us up from our boat with their band playing the 'Maple Leaf' and 'Oh, Canada.'"[66] When the Canadians got their first look at "a train load" of German prisoners at the Plymouth railway station, Harlow thought they were "certainly a fine lot of men; they have a fine uniform, too, but not as nice as ours, of course."[67]

Because Sam Hughes had not allowed any alcohol at Valcartier, the sudden temptation of public houses and friendly women was just too much for some. Captain J. F. C. Fuller, then the British Army's deputy assistant director of railway transport, later recalled that it was difficult to get the troops onto the trains because they were "assaulted by every young and old harlot in the dual city. Men fell out or were pulled out of the ranks to vanish down side streets. A few reached the railway station, but the remainder painted Devonport and Plymouth pink, red, and purple."[68] Bruce Donald of Pictou, a lieutenant in the 17th Battalion, said only that Plymouth "is famous for its large number of good looking girls, and...they gave us a great send-off to Salisbury, but nuff said, or I'll be putting my foot in it."[69]

By the time city officials closed the pubs early the next day, Plymouth was "swarming with drunks."[70] Fuller requisitioned an empty building and turned it into a prison in which drunken Canadians were locked for twenty-four hours while they dried out, and each morning a train informally labelled Drunkard's Special left for Salisbury Plain, site of the Canadian training camp. Even so, a few went AWOL and only showed up days later.[71]

When they arrived at the train stations nearest to their positions at Salisbury Plain, the troops had to march several kilometres to their camps, carrying a full backpack weighing between forty-five and fifty-seven kilograms. They arrived to find tents that had been erected but not secured. And it was raining, as it continued to do for most of the time they remained on Salisbury Plain. Arthur Chute described it as "the vilest winter climate on earth."[72]

That was bad enough, of course, but Harold Suttie compared the canvas of their tents to "Mexican mosquito netting, for it leaks in heavy rainstorms."[73] To be fair, the British could not control their weather, and the army camp on Salisbury Plain, like Valcartier, was only intended for use as a summer camp, which is why there were no huts or barracks. Chute added, somewhat improbably but apparently truthfully, that despite the vile weather and hard training, "no matter how gloomily the day began, dinner always found us gay, masters of our spirits. Hard exercise and ceaseless training prevented repining, and brought forth strong bodies and brave spirits."[74] Keith Rogers echoed this perception. "What strikes one very forcibly," he said,

> *is the splendid spirit in which the men meet all the discomforts they have. No amount of frost, rain or mud, nor wet clothes and cold tents, seems in any way to dishearten them, and at night after the day's work is done, singing and laughter from the lines show that they are by no means as miserable as one might think, judging by the outside surroundings.*[75]

When the Canadians arrived at Salisbury Plain they learned that Major General Edwin Alderson would be their commanding officer. He seemed an appropriate choice because he had served as a young man in the Halifax garrison and later commanded Canadian troops in South Africa. He quickly earned the respect of the Canadians by dismissing the most obviously unsuitable officers and trying—unsuccessfully—to replace the Ross rifle. He trained the men hard but also managed by December to move many of them out of the tents to nearby camps that had wooden huts, which Lieutenant Thomas Carter of Antigonish reported were "quite warm and much nicer than the tents."[76]

But that awful winter in inadequate housing—combined, no doubt, with the problems inevitable when thousands of men are crowded together for several months—took its toll. Pneumonia and meningitis swept through the camp, making many men ill and killing some. Chute later claimed that 400 men died, adding that "every day I could look out of my tent in the melancholic blur of mist and rain and see the draped gun-carriage moving to the 'Dead March' from Saul, while one battalion or another slowly followed their comrade to his grave."[77] He exaggerated. According to Dr. Bruce Kelley, who worked at the camp hospital, 400 men were hospitalized, which he considered "a small percentage,"[78] and only twenty-eight died. Among them was John MacDonald of Westville, who thus became the first soldier from Pictou County to die in the war.

Even so, the situation became so serious that Major Waldorf Astor, the New York millionaire who had moved to England, offered the grounds of his estate at nearby Cliveden to establish a hospital. No 2 Clearing Hospital was given the assignment, and the facility developed in time into the Duchess of Connaught's Canadian Red Cross Hospital. Two of its beds were endowed by the Wolfville Red Cross.[79]

Unsurprisingly, many men, having never been away from home before, soon felt homesick. "How I would like to be home just for Saturday night and go away Monday morning," Russell Harlow wrote his wife on November 11, "but I hope to be home some day to stay longer than that." The good news was that "I had my fortune told yesterday, and they said I was going to live through this war, but I would go to the next war and be killed, but we cannot put any faith in that. Some were told they were going to be killed, and they believed it, and it nearly set them crazy."[80]

The Canadians generally found the British people friendly and welcoming, and many reported receiving invitations to private homes for meals, especially during the Christmas holiday season. Lester Wile and four others were invited to dinner by a local family not long after their arrival, "and they certainly treated us fine." The meal included roast lamb with vegetables, a Christmas pudding with "a fine piece of holly stuck in the centre" and mince pies.[81]

Getting used to British money posed a challenge because it was not a decimal system like Canadian money. Kenneth Clarke thought getting used to it was "great fun"[82] but others didn't, especially when British shopkeepers and taxi drivers sometimes overcharged or cheated soldiers when making change. The Canadians often thought a one-pound note was the equivalent of a dollar, when in those days it was actually worth five dollars. Some were also confused about the value of a half-crown or shilling, coins that resembled quarters and fifty-cent pieces.[83] If this wasn't bad enough, Wilfred Doane bitterly complained that the local merchants "steal from us" because they charged the soldiers higher prices than the local people. In his view, "we should get things half-price.... I tell you they know how to rob us in their slow way."[84]

These problems were offset to some extent when Alderson announced on October 22 that wet canteens would be allowed in camp. This naturally outraged Sam Hughes and the temperance advocates in Canada, but Lieutenant Victor Tupper, grandson of Nova Scotia's Sir Charles Tupper, no doubt spoke for most of the troops when he said that Alderson "won the hearts of all ranks by fighting Sam Hughes" and saying that "we had been treated as schoolboys long enough, and in the future we should be handled like men."[85]

Alderson was actually trying to solve a problem because the Canadians, having been denied alcohol since they reported to Valcartier in August, were proving to be somewhat disruptive when they visited village pubs in the area around the camp. This behaviour continued despite the wet canteens and the dry social club and concerts provided by the YMCA. Willard Allen of Yarmouth claimed that the pubs in the area were doing "a flourishing trade, especially with the Canadians, who are able to get drunk very cheaply."[86]

Part of the problem, of course, was that many of the soldiers were young men who had never been exposed to alcohol. The Reverend T. W. Hancox, a British Methodist chaplain, reported that when he spoke to some Nova Scotian soldiers whose "boisterous and tipsy" behaviour was drawing attention, they told him that "they had never tasted drink prior to coming to England," provoking him to denounce the "cruel and brutal" liquor interests which in his view were growing rich on sin and war.[87]

Meanwhile, Struan Robertson kept up his complaints about discrimination until January 11, when Alderson, who had little regard for him, suggested that he resign because "the authorities were down on me...[and] they would get me sooner or later."[88] When Robertson refused to resign, he was sacked, prompting him to fire off a letter to F. B. McCurdy, the Conservative MP who was Robert Borden's chief organizer in Nova Scotia, that was leaked to the press and revived the controversy. It is difficult to determine if Robertson's complaints about how the 17th was treated in England were unique or if they applied to other battalions that also suffered through that appalling winter in a freezing sea of mud. But when some of the 17th's men were transferred into the 14th Battalion less than a month later, its war diary recorded that "their clothing was in as bad shape as their documents."[89]

Was this the fault of Alderson or Hughes or the inexperience and ineffectiveness of Robertson and his senior officers? In any event, another round of political warfare ensued, and when it petered out the *Amherst Daily News* concluded that "not a single useful end has been served" by it.[90] That was true, and as James Cameron said, it "left a bitter taste" in Nova Scotia, "felt a little more keenly in Pictou County because of the leading part Pictonians had played in the dispute."[91]

On February 4 the Canadians were inspected by the king and Lord Kitchener, the most famous British general of his time who was now secretary of state for war, and the next day they headed for France. But not Nova Scotia's 17th Battalion. Hughes had reportedly sworn that "Borden's Beauties" would never get to France and they didn't. The 17th was one of the battalions kept behind as a reserve unit, to provide reinforcements and train new arrivals.

Indeed, that was how it spent the rest of the war. It was commanded briefly by Lieutenant Colonel Edward Worthington, a cavalryman from Sherbrooke, Quebec. Then Daniel Cameron, who had posted a sign inscribed "Politically Unfit" on his tent during the controversy, was promoted much to his own surprise, to command the battalion until May 1917, when he returned home.

The First Contingent arrived at Hazebrouck, headquarters of Lieutenant General Sir Horace Smith-Dorrien's 2nd British Army, on February 7. It was placed under his command because, like Alderson, he had commanded Canadian troops in South Africa. A few days later, the Canadians marched the thirty-five kilometres to Armentières, just behind the front line at Ypres. It was a historic moment. As Arthur Chute observed, "the first of the New World troops had come to take their place on the firing line."[92]

Chapter 4

MEN AT WAR 1915–1916

These men will be heard from when their turn comes and Nova Scotia in general will echo with their names.[1]

ACTUALLY, THEY WEREN'T THE FIRST. THE FIRST CANADIAN combat unit to go to France was Princess Patricia's Canadian Light Infantry, which was there FOUR months before the First Contingent because it was made up almost entirely of British veterans. There were some Canadians among them, though, including at least seven Nova Scotians.[2] But the first Canadian unit to go to France was actually No. 2 Canadian Stationary Hospital, a Montreal unit that arrived on November 8, well before the PPCLI. It established itself in the Hôtel du Golf on the dunes at Paris Plage in Le Touquet, a resort community on the English Channel.

This 320-bed hospital treated British soldiers initially, of course, then Canadians as well. Among its thirty-five nurses were three from Pictou County—Harriet Graham, Pearl Fraser, and Myrtle Gratton—and one, Annie Strong, from Canning.

Harriet Graham reported in December that they were "simply proud of ourselves, for [being] the FIRST Canadian Hospital to be in France." They had been "awfully busy" reconfiguring the hotel as a hospital and cleaning it, but "we all love it. We have a dandy crowd of girls and a very nice crowd of officers, and our men are as willing as can be, though most of them are untrained." Each ward was named after a province and Nova Scotia got "the prettiest ward, with seventy-five beds and the most important place. We all were extremely pleased."[3]

Their introduction to war came very quickly because of the heavy losses being sustained by the British Army as it tried to stop the German invasion of northeastern France. Ambulances usually arrived at night, so that was the busiest time. Writing at ten o'clock on Christmas Eve while waiting for them, Graham reported that she had been on duty all day, but "I see where we don't get to bed tonight. By the time we get the poor souls into bed and half way clean, and a dressing done, its [*sic*] morning before you know it."[4]

Wartime nursing was very different from what they had done at home, of course. The "poor creatures...are so filthy, and many times just alive with vermin." Fraser commented, "Isn't it funny, in our hospitals we despised men who were dirty, and here the worse they are, the better we like them. When they say, 'keep away sister, I'm so dirty, but I have been in the trenches and I haven't had a bath for so many weeks,' I just feel like saying, 'I honor your dirt.'"[5]

The PPCLI went into the trenches at Vierstraat in early January. In its first offensive action—a raid on a German position on February 28—it sustained the first Canadian battle casualties of the war when five men were killed and several others were wounded. Among them was John William "Jack" Tate of Melrose, Guysborough County.[6]

Tate is sometimes described as the first Nova Scotian soldier to be killed in the war. Whether or not this is true depends on what we mean by "Nova Scotian" and "soldier." Tate had left Nova Scotia years before and never returned. Meanwhile, Anatole Descamps, a French coal miner who had immigrated to New Waterford, returned home at the outbreak of the war and died on September 25, 1914, while serving in the French Army. If recent immigrants are considered Nova Scotians, he was the first to be killed in the war. The *Sydney Daily Post*, not usually a broad-minded newspaper, described him as "one of Cape Breton's heroes" and "the first to fall in the field in the defence of his country."[7]

But if we include sailors as soldiers in the broad sense of servicemen, the first native-born Nova Scotians to be killed in action were Malcolm Cann, John Hatheway, William Palmer, and Arthur Silver, all of whom died together on November 1, 1914. Cann was from Yarmouth, Hatheway was from Granville although his family had moved to Fredericton, and Palmer and Silver were from

Fig. 4.1: HMS *Good Hope* at Halifax, August 1914. When the ship was destroyed at Coronel three months later, four young Nova Scotian midshipmen were among the 919 officers and men who lost their lives.

Halifax. They had just graduated from the Canadian Naval College and joined HMS *Suffolk* when it came into Halifax in August 1914. They were later transferred to HMS *Good Hope* and died along with its entire crew, including Rear Admiral Sir Christopher Cradock, when it was sunk in the battle of Coronel.

The first Nova Scotian unit to go to France was Liverpool's No. 2 Casualty Clearing Hospital (soon redesignated No. 1 Casualty Clearing Station), which accompanied the 1st Division to France in early February. It established itself at Aire-sur-la-Lys, near St. Omer, the headquarters of the British 1st Army. This was in preparation for what became known as the Second Battle of Ypres, the 1st Division's introduction to modern warfare.

It began when the Germans launched a strong attack on Ypres, preceded by a week-long artillery bombardment of the city. Then a heavy, low-lying, greyish-yellow cloud was observed drifting westerly from the German lines. It was chlorine gas, which the Germans were using for the first time, despite having signed the 1907 Hague Convention banning the use of such weapons. The gas was aimed mainly at French and Algerian troops, but it hit the Canadians as well because they were holding the line on the right flank of the French, at St. Julien. Wilfred Doane, who was about 730 metres behind the front line with the divisional ammunition column, said that the Algerians "lost their nerve and beat it,"[8] creating a six-kilometre gap in the line. That meant the road to Ypres was open, with only the newly arrived and inexperienced Canadians in the way. Remarkably, they stood their ground despite the gas and stopped the German attack. British military leaders were properly impressed, if somewhat surprised, that inexperienced amateur colonials could be so reliable.

The first Canadian offensive operation of the war followed. The goal was to retake Hill 60, the only high ground in the area, which overlooked St. Julien. This meant that they would have to attack uphill. Norman Rogers of Amherst took part in the charge and later said, "Never in my life will I forget the moment when the Germans opened fire on us. It was awful—bullets hitting human flesh all around me with a sickening smack, and about every second man going down; but we kept right on with a cheer for old Canada, and drove them back. Afterwards we had time to realize how awful it had been."[9]

He wasn't exaggerating: two thirds of the Canadian officers and men involved in the battle were casualties. The Germans naturally counterattacked, again using gas aimed now directly at the Canadians. This time they had cotton bandoliers which, when soaked in tubs of water that had been placed along the line and held to the nostrils, provided some protection. Even so, David Shand, a British soldier in the area, later reported seeing between 200 and 300 Canadian soldiers at a casualty clearing station, some of them "still writhing on the ground, their tongues hanging out."[10]

Most of the Canadian wounded and many others from the fighting at St. Julien were treated at No. 1 Canadian Clearing Station. Dr. Morris MacKinnon later reported "that several thousand cases passed through our station" but that many of the gas victims died before they could be moved to a hospital.[11] No. 1 CCS performed so well that Major Ford was appointed a Companion of the Order of St. Michael and St. George (CMG), the first Canadian to be awarded this honour in the field. In June 1916 he was promoted to deputy assistant medical director of the Canadian Corps, then assistant medical director of the 1st Division. He was succeeded at No. 1 CCS by Dr. Charles Young of Pictou.

When the ferocious battle ended on May 25, the Germans had lost 35,000 men but they had reduced the size of the salient. The Allies had lost more than 70,000 men, including 2,000 killed, 4,000 wounded, and 1,400 taken prisoner. The loss of 7,400 of the division's 17,000 officers and men in one battle shocked not only the troops themselves but people at home, who had not anticipated slaughter on this scale. As the *Amherst Daily News* said, the casulaties brought home the harsh reality of what being at war actually meant and was "not wholly dispelled by the reflection that the Canadians behaved heroically, that they won the admiration of the best armies in Europe, and that they exalted the name of Canada."[12] It was during the Second Battle of Ypres that Dr. John McCrae, the medical officer of the 2nd Brigade Artillery, wrote "In Flanders Fields," the poem that quickly gained such extraordinary fame throughout the English-speaking world.

MEANWHILE, THE MILITIA DEPARTMENT HAD BEGUN RECRUITING for a second division, and this time there would be a Nova Scotian battalion. The 25th, commanded by Lieutenant Colonel George Augustus LeCain of Round Hill, easily raised the necessary 1,000 men, perhaps because they knew that the 25th was going to represent Nova Scotia on the front lines. The *Amherst Daily News* actually claimed that when the recruiting officer arrived in "many sections" of Cumberland County, "the men were awaiting his appearance, eager for the fray."[13] Fifty men volunteered during "the biggest meeting ever held" in New Waterford on November 23, and Sydney's *Daily Post* declared that it had been "informed on the very best of authority" that that number would rise to "at least two hundred."[14] Smaller communities contributed fewer men, of course, but as the *Yarmouth Herald* pointed out, the town's fifteen volunteers meant a lot to a community of its size because these men were "among the cream of our junior citizens" and it would be "a hard pill to swallow" when they left.[15]

The 2nd Division differed from the 1st in that the majority of its officers and men were Canadian-born. This was certainly true of the 25th: thirty-nine of its forty-two officers and 915 of its men were born in Canada and most, although not all, were Nova Scotians. Men enlisted from all over the province but more than half of its officers and men came from Cape Breton. For that reason and because many of them spoke Gaelic, they thought of the 25th as a Highland battalion, although the Militia Department refused to grant it that status, allegedly because of the additional cost.[16] Sometimes brothers enlisted together, or even fathers and sons: the three Livingstone brothers from Big Bras d'Or—William, Harrison, and Daniel—for example, while Ezra Etchells, a miner in New Waterford, enlisted with his three sons, Frederick, Peter, and Joseph.

The 25th mobilized at Halifax and was housed in the armoury and in tents on the Common. Even then, 350 men had to be moved in February to the federal immigration building at the Deep Water Terminal because of overcrowding in the armoury. The battalion trained daily on the Common and on the slopes of nearby Citadel Hill, while daily musketry training took place at McNab's Island. There were also route marches and manoeuvres around the North West Arm, at Chain Lake, and across the harbour in Dartmouth.

Ralph Lewis, a Newfoundlander, recalled how they "strutted about, proud of our khaki uniforms, hugging the fond thought that

Fig. 4.2: Yarmouth volunteers for the 25th Battalion leaving Yarmouth, November 1914. Second from the right in the front row is Robert Clements, who later wrote a fascinating account of the battalion's experiences in the war.

we were real soldiers." Robert Clements, a nineteen-year-old from Yarmouth, recalled the hijinks that some of the men inevitably got into, usually involving liquor, which he reminded modern readers had not yet been diluted to 40 proof alcohol.[17] Alcohol was not allowed inside the armoury except for weak beer sold at an inflated price, but some of the men discovered that they could place a bottle near an open window at ground level before entering the building, then recover it once inside. Unfortunately, the provost sergeant found out what was going on and alerted the guards at the entrance. Thereafter, when the sergeant of the guard saw a bottle being deposited by the window he quickly removed it, leaving the poor soldier perplexed and not very happy. Needless to say, the guards enjoyed the alcohol themselves for several weeks and "an improved degree of nocturnal peace prevailed from then on."[18]

The 2nd Division did not cross the Atlantic in a dramatic convoy as the 1st had done. Instead, the battalions sailed separately on fast ocean liners, but not until May 1915. When the 25th marched from the armoury down to Pier 2 on the twentieth to board the *Saxonia*, "bands of children from the various schools were massed" on the Common "and the route...was crowded with spectators." By now people had a more realistic sense of what lay ahead for their fathers, sons, and brothers and some broke into the ranks "for a last farewell, a kiss or a handshake" and men and women "sobbed openly and without shame."[19]

Before the ship left the wharf, Brigadier General Rutherford called for three cheers for the king, the 25th Battalion, and the 22nd, which was sailing on the same ship, "and the crowd responded with vim." But then, as Georges Vanier, an officer in the 22nd, observed, "a quiet descended as we left the wharf, the people silently waving flags, handkerchiefs and hats."[20] As the *Saxonia* slowly moved down the harbour, three men who had been left behind "chased us in a tugboat and...arrived on board five miles [eight kilometres] off the harbour about eight o'clock in a somewhat nervous frame of mind."[21]

The 25th was not the only unit recruited in Nova Scotia during the winter of 1914–15. Lieutenant Colonel T. M. Seeley, publisher of the *Yarmouth Light* newspaper and commanding officer of the 11th Artillery Brigade, MD 6's artillery militia, was authorized to recruit the 23rd Battery for overseas service. Seeley raised so many men that he was authorized to form the 24th Battery to take the surplus. Bruce Ingraham of Sydney, who had brought "a large detachment of fine men" from Cape Breton, was appointed its commanding officer.[22] More than half of the men in the 23rd were Nova Scotians recruited from the 18th, 28th, and 29th militia batteries, but figures are not available for the 24th. Much to Seeley's chagrin, he was replaced as commanding officer by Captain John Keiller MacKay of Plainfield when the 23rd Battery went overseas in February 1915 because, like many long-serving militiamen, he was too old for service in the field. It didn't really matter, however, because when they got to England, both batteries were placed in a reserve brigade to provide reinforcements for other artillery units.

Meanwhile, Walter Crowe, who had to be one of the most energetic men in Sydney, was authorized to recruit the 36th Battery, which was made up entirely of Cape Bretoners. According to Hunt there were so many applications that "over one hundred [men] had to be turned away."[23] Crowe trained the unit and took it overseas but, like Seeley, he was considered too old for combat at the age of fifty-three and Major D. A. MacKinnon of Charlottetown took the 36th to France. It served throughout the war with distinction but no attempt was made to maintain its regional character as reinforcement drafts took the places of the Cape Bretoners and other Nova Scotians as they were killed or wounded.

By now tunnelling to plant explosives under enemy trenches had emerged as a useful part of major offensives and Nova Scotia contributed many men to No. 1 Tunnelling Company. It was recruited in mining communities in central and eastern Canada in the autumn of 1915 but miners who had already enlisted in infantry battalions were transferred into it as well. When it sailed for England in January 1916, its 284 officers and men included at least seventy-two Nova Scotians: Lieutenant Donald Murray of Springhill and seventy-one sappers. Sam Glode, a Mi'kmaw man from Liverpool, subsequently transferred into it from the 64th Battalion.[24]

The 6th Canadian Mounted Rifles (CMR) Battalion was also recruited in 1915 from the three Maritime provinces but was built around the 14th King's Hussars, the cavalry militia unit based at Canning commanded by Lieutenant Colonel R. H. Ryan of Kentville. It had offered its services in August 1914 but had been held back for possible home defence duties, but now it provided ten of the 6th CMR's officers and 209 of its men. Like the other CMR battalions, when it went overseas, it went dismounted, in other words as infantry units, although they took their horses with them just in case.

The 6th sailed from Quebec City on July 18 but not before James Johnson of Truro took an unofficial leave to visit his girlfriend in Manganese Mines, knowing it would be his last chance to see her. He left on Saturday and arrived back very early on Monday morning, managing to sneak into camp and crawl into bed. When the unit paraded later that morning, the sergeant asked if he had had a nice weekend. Johnson responded honestly that he had. Three days later the sergeant returned and said, "'You did not have a pass last weekend, did you?' I said, 'No.' 'Oh well, lucky for you it's too late to have you up as I would be in as much trouble as you for not reporting your absence.'"[25]

Johnson paid for his little escapade on the voyage to England. He was one of the men detailed to look after the horses while at sea. The animals had to be fed and watered and have their stalls cleaned daily. That meant that "all the cleanings were forked into a large wicker basket, hoisted up and dumped overboard," an unpleasant task because the air on the bottom deck where the horses were quartered "was foul and hot." Conditions weren't much better on the second deck where the men slept in hammocks strung up over the mess tables. "I didn't mind the hammocks," Johnson recalled, "but with eight hundred men sleeping in one compartment the air was not good." One day Johnson and a friend discovered a large box that was open on one side on the ship's deck and got permission to sleep in it for the rest of the journey. "An officer walked by one evening after we had retired. He stopped and said, 'Sorry I have no peanuts.'"[26]

Upon arrival in England, the 2nd Division did not go to Salisbury Plain as the 1st had done, but to the large British Army camp at Shorncliffe in the hills overlooking Folkestone, and to other smaller camps nearby. These camps had proper housing for troops and were very close to London and the channel ports. The Canadians were generally happy there, despite "plenty of drill, lots of road marching, and especially a hell of a lot of bayonet exercise."[27] They did, however, object to being overcharged for goods, including diluted beer, at the camp canteens, which were operated by a private company. To make matters worse, the canteen manager, according to Robert Clements, was "loud mouthed, insolent and just plain ignorant." The situation was a ticking time bomb and one night it exploded. Some of the men "escorted" the canteen's manager and staff to the camp gates, then burned down the building with all its contents. Needless to say, this caught the attention of the officers, who investigated the situation and remedied it.[28]

There were also problems in nearby Folkestone, where the soldiers spent their short leaves, because some shopkeepers overcharged for goods and took advantage of the fact that many Canadian soldiers did not understand the sterling currency. As with the canteen problem, a crisis was not long in coming. It came on the weekend after the 2nd Division arrived in Shorncliffe, when all of the men were allowed into town. It began in a fish-and-chip shop on Tontine Street in the lower part of town, when a Canadian soldier paid with a one-pound note and was given change for a ten-shilling note (i.e., half of a pound). When the soldier pointed out the error and asked for the correct change, an argument resulted and "the

Canadian and his friends took the shop apart and distributed its contents, including the shopkeeper, in the street. This citizen called on his friends for support," and soon a major riot was taking place. The Canadians naturally rallied to the support of their friends and not only "took charge of the whole street" but also "badly damaged" several shop fronts, and "some looting took place." Eventually two British cavalry regiments had to be called in to restore order.[29]

Seventy soldiers were arrested, many of them one suspects from the 25th Battalion, which Major Arthur Jarvis, the assistant provost marshal, claimed was undisciplined and had a "very unsavoury reputation."[30] It is hard to know if this was a fair observation, although Wilfred Doane, who was at Shorncliffe at the time, told his father that "the Canadians fight the booze just as savage as they fight Germans.... The English say they are abnormal."[31]

Problems at Shorncliffe weren't always caused by dishonest British shopkeepers or drunken Canadians. Lieutenant Colonel Ryan, the commanding officer of the 6th CMR Battalion, was court-martialled and sent home in October after a dust-up with Brigadier General C. A. Smart, who briefly commanded the 2nd Brigade Canadian Mounted Rifles, over the treatment of his men. According to Johnson, Ryan's men returned from a long hard march on a hot summer day with blisters on their feet, and the next day's orders called for another long march. Ryan cancelled it and sent his men down to the beach at Hythe with orders "to take off our shoes and socks and wade in the salt water. We spent most of the forenoon taking it easy." When Smart found out, he "severely reprimanded" Ryan, who perhaps unwisely "told the Brigadier a few things." Smart had him court-martialled "for disobeying an order and insolence to a superior officer."[32] It is gratifying to know that the 2nd Brigade was subsequently merged with the 1st to form the 8th Infantry Brigade, leaving Smart a brigadier general without a brigade. He spent his war commanding training camps.

THE 2ND DIVISION CROSSED OVER FROM ENGLAND IN SEPTEMBER 1915 to join the badly mauled 1st Division at Locre, near Ypres. The two divisions, plus the PPCLI and the Royal Canadian Regiment, were now brought together to form the Canadian Corps, a fighting unit of 1,354 officers and 36,522 men. Alderson was promoted to corps commander, Arthur Currie was given command of the 1st Division, and Richard Turner was given command of the 2nd Division.

Almost immediately it was discovered that the 25th Battalion, which went into the lines at the beginning of October, was not quite ready. On the early evening of the eighth, after a quiet day, the Germans surprised it by exploding several mines, following up with an artillery bombardment. The *Morning Chronicle*'s front-page story loyally reported that the 25th had "fought like seasoned veterans and saved the situation,"[33] but the facts were otherwise. Because the men had no combat experience, many were badly shaken, and in the absence of effective leadership from their officers, some even fled to the rear. According to Ralph Lewis, the battalion's front-line officers—MacRae, Logan, MacKenzie, Tupper, Roberts and Johnstone—performed well, but "we never saw the colonel at all that night" and the major only showed up "about four the next morning...when we had a new parapet built."[34]

The battalion was immediately pulled back to rest billets and Alderson showed up a week later to deliver "a pretty severe lecture" to both officers and men.[35] It was, he bluntly informed them, their duty "to die in the trenches" if necessary to prevent the enemy from breaking through their lines. Indeed, it was their duty "to shoot those who retire without orders." That seemed a bit strong, but he knew that the problem lay with the officers, who had not provided the necessary leadership. By their "determination and force of character," he told them, "they *must* get a real grip of their men."[36]

To reinforce the point, he sacked both LeCain and Major William Conrod. LeCain was replaced by Edward Hilliam, an experienced

British officer who had moved to Canada, and he replaced Conrod with Major Duncan Bauld, a member of a prominent Halifax merchant family.[37] He also sent home Majors James Grant MacKenzie and Alfred Jones. This was tough medicine but it worked. Because Hilliam was personally fearless and had the common touch, he quickly earned the respect of both officers and men. "It was truly wonderful the confidence we placed in him," Lewis wrote, "and he never disappointed us."[38]

The winter of 1915–16 was relatively quiet, the main enemy being the rain and mud, which, as Lewis recalled, were "something awful. The mud was waist deep and of such a nature that once a fellow got stuck it took another chap to get him out."[39] That meant that men "doing front line work" had to endure twenty-four-hour shifts without any hot food and rations consisted of bully-beef, hard-tack, and water. Not surprisingly, the daily rum ration was welcomed, even by men who had not previously drunk alcohol. According to Frank MacGregor, dry tea was issued along with "tommy-cookers," small cans of fuel that could boil water, and tea leaves were saved and "boiled over and over. We had no milk, butter, sugar or any change until we were relieved in about two weeks [*sic*] time."[40] As a result, men scrounged the countryside in search of vegetables and livestock, which they purchased or "appropriated," according to circumstances, and looked forward to their return to rest billets where they could purchase meals in local estaminets (cafés).

That Christmas there was a modest ceasefire, one that is much less-well-known than the famous one in 1914. William Mahoney of Margaree was pleased that he was able to attend midnight mass, celebrated in a barn with three priests on the altar, two of them Canadian. "It is a great comfort to me," he said, "to be able to practice, even occasionally, the religious devotions so faithfully taught me at home."[41] Edward Greenough of Canard reported that in the morning the men not in the front lines opened presents sent by different organizations at home, then had the day off. They also enjoyed a good dinner that included plum pudding and peaches, "but we all missed our Xmas skate and sleigh drive."[42] Osborne Perry of Carleton commented on how childlike the men were on Christmas morning: "We all got a pair of socks from Canada, each pair filled with tobacco, chewing gum, etc. When the boys got those socks it put me in mind of a bunch of kids going through their stockings on Christmas morning and each one decided the stuff in his sock was the best.[43]

James Johnson, who was recovering from bronchial pneumonia at No. 1 Canadian General Hospital, was somewhat surprised, though not unpleasantly, on Christmas morning when Nursing Sister Annie Jones gave him a job. She had acquired a supply of wine and brandy and asked him to "see that everyone in the ward has an appetizer, and you may have one or two if you wish." He did and reported that "we were served a very nice dinner considering the hospital was generally filled to capacity."[44]

Battalions normally served six-day tours successively in the support trenches, in the front line, and then in reserve. At their rest billets in the battered little towns behind the lines the weary, muddied men from the trenches enjoyed the luxury of hot showers, albeit brief ones, and laundry facilities improvised by the engineers. Some enterprising commanding officers contrived to have occasional showings of films, but what the men really came to love were the divisional concert parties that entertained them with music and comedy.

They originated, allegedly, with Gitz Rice, who was from New Glasgow but had moved to Montreal. A musician who could sing and play the piano, he formed the 1st Division's concert party. Alistair Fraser attended one of its minstrel shows in October 1915 and thought it "simply great. I do not mean for here, but for anywhere." The star of the show was "the piano player" who could play "the most wonderful harmonies along with any song the mandolin band and seventeen minstrels started." Fraser was from New Glasgow and "all through the play I was trying to place the pianist, when suddenly it dawned on me. Gitz Rice! Can you believe it?" The concerts were not entirely upbeat and humorous. As Fraser reported, the men "laughed till they shook," but then,

> *in the twinkling of an eye it would all change and to the strains of... many of* [the] *old darky favorites, the men would fall silent and I am afraid we were a little wistful, and saw visions and dreamed a dream or two.... It was a privilege given to few to hear the thousand men sing, and somehow or other it was all so wonderfully big and clean and thrilling.*[45]

Rice became the best-known individual entertainer in the Canadian Corps, partly because he wrote several tunes that became very popular. One was "Dear Old Pal of Mine," which was made famous by John McCormack, the leading Irish tenor of the day. Another was "Mademoiselle from Armentières," although debate continues over the authorship of this enormously popular song which immortalized a barmaid in a town near Ypres frequented by Canadian troops.[46]

There were other divisional concert parties, of course, the best-known of them being the 3rd Division's Dumbells. Their two best-known performers were Merton (Mert) Plunkett, who founded the group, and Ross Hamilton. Originally from Pugwash, Hamilton became hugely popular for his female impersonation act, which he introduced during the group's first show at Gouy-Servins, near Passchendaele, in August 1917. "Marjorie" became an audience favourite. After the war the Dumbells enjoyed a successful entertainment career in both Canada and the United States.

MEANWHILE, IN PREPARATION FOR THEIR VERDUN OFFENSIVE, the Germans had launched a series of diversionary attacks, one of them in the sector held by the British 5th Corps, which resulted in the creation of a salient at St. Eloi. The 5th Corps launched its counterattack on March 27 with the explosion of a series of enormous mines, which shook the country for kilometres around like an earthquake. Those mines were planted by No. 1 Tunnelling Company, which had just arrived at the front a month earlier. When the Canadian Corps relieved the exhausted and depleted British troops a week later, it was the first time that an entire corps had attempted to relieve another, and it was done on an active battlefront. Unfortunately, the Germans chose this moment to counterattack.

The so-called battle of the St. Eloi craters was a disaster, partly because the weather, which had improved somewhat during March, reverted to its usual shocking state, so it was fought in "one big sea of mud and water" with very low visibility caused by a thick fog.[47] Trenches no longer existed in the area, nor did any landmarks for that matter and, as Clements recalled, "the conditions could not possibly have been worse."[48] Meanwhile, the heavy shelling had severed the telephone wires, so the officers back at divisional headquarters, whose intelligence reports turned out to be inaccurate, also lost contact with what was going on.

The slaughter was heavy on both sides, and the 25th Battalion was hit especially hard. Gerald McElhenney of Truro later described the battle as "beyond a doubt the most trying experience" the 25th ever endured, suggesting that "the situation may better be imagined than described."[49] Lieutenant Howard Johnstone and his men beat off "no less than five attacks in four hours."[50] It finally came to an end on April 19 with both sides exhausted. The Canadians had sustained 1,373 casualties, three times those of the Germans, and as one historian later said, "the slaughter had all been over the ownership of seven holes in the mud."[51]

News reports at home praised the Canadians and particularly the Nova Scotians for their bravery, prompting Premier George Murray and Conservative leader Charles Tanner to pay public tribute to their "great gallantry."[52] The praise was certainly well deserved but the battle was a fiasco and there were bound to be repercussions. This time Sir Douglas Haig, who commanded the British Expeditionary Force, sacked Alderson and replaced him with Sir Julian Byng, a British cavalry officer.

A quiet spell followed, while the senior officers planned their next attack and the men rested and recuperated. This was when Frederick Laing of Halifax was killed by shellfire. Laing had joined the Royal Canadian Regiment at the age of fourteen and served in Bermuda but was one of those left behind when it sailed for England. In fact, he sailed with it as a stowaway and was attested at Folkestone upon arrival. The military authorities knew he was under age but thought he was seventeen. He didn't go the front until March 1916 and was killed two months later on May 11. He wasn't the youngest Nova Scotian to enlist but he was almost certainly the youngest Nova Scotian soldier killed in the war.[53]

Byng's first test came with the battle for Mount Sorrel in June. The Canadian Corps held the southern part of the Ypres salient at that point, including Mount Sorrel, which was the last high ground still in British hands. The Germans sought to capture it and also to divert Allied resources from the large offensive they knew was being prepared on the Somme.

After a massive artillery bombardment that killed large numbers of Canadians, the German infantry captured Mount Sorrel and two surrounding hills. This meant that the road to Ypres was open and undefended. Byng counterattacked unsuccessfully on June 3, then tried again on the thirteenth and managed to recapture much of the lost ground. Nothing had been achieved by either side but the Canadians had incurred 8,000 casualties. Among those killed was Lieutenant Colonel Frank Creighton of Dartmouth, who commanded the 1st Battalion. Morale was high, however. Joseph McKenzie of Rear Christmas Island told his father that he was not sorry he had gone overseas, and "if I am destined to die here, it is where many a good fellow has fought and died that freedom and civilization might live."[54]

It was during this fighting that John Dan Brown of New Glasgow distinguished himself. He had been transferred from the 17th Battalion into the 15th and, according to Dr. Neiley, he went out in front of the Canadian trenches to assist three of his injured comrades who were lying there. He "threw himself on top of them and shielded them with his own body" during the shelling, even though he himself was badly wounded. Then, "when the stretcher bearers arrived he used some strong language to them because they wanted to put him on a stretcher, telling them to take care of the other three fellows and he would look after John Dan Brown himself." Neiley reported that Brown had been recommended for a decoration, "and everybody here thinks and hopes it will be nothing less than a VC." He also hoped that "those at home who have been ready to shun him or give him a knock will now be as ready to acknowledge his bravery and devotedness as a soldier. He has at least justified the opinion of some of the officers in the 78th Battalion [sic], who were often laughed at for taking him to a training camp."[55] It was true but John Dan's war was over. He was awarded the Military Medal and was invalided home to Nova Scotia.

MEANWHILE, THE EASE WITH WHICH THE 25TH BATTALION HAD been recruited led to the formation of a second Nova Scotian battalion, the 40th. The response to it was less than enthusiastic, at least in the first few months, so a recruiting drive was undertaken, using returned veterans and men who had already signed up to speak at meetings. Lieutenant John Anderson of Halifax, who had been wounded in the spring while serving with the 23rd Battalion, was very likely the officer who visited McNab's Island to encourage members of the 63rd Regiment training there to sign up for overseas service. "Winnie" McClare of Mount Uniacke reported that an officer—he thought he was a captain—came and told them "that the men at the 'front' are happy as can be. He made a long

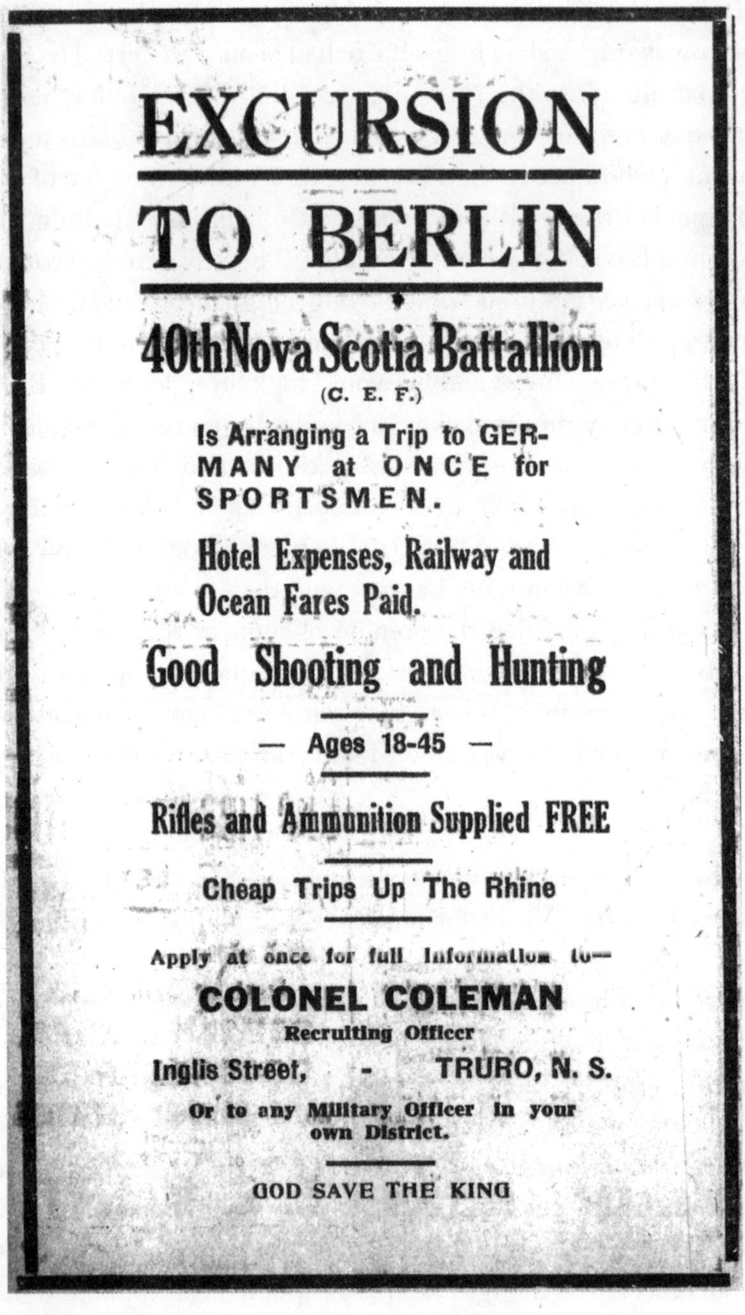

Fig. 4.3: "Excursion to Berlin," *Truro Daily News*, August 9, 1915. This unusual ad was part of a recruitment drive.

speech, told us how they live and everything about them. Said they had a Jolly time."[56]

If that was misleading, an advertising campaign that was either remarkably dishonest or was just attempting a light-hearted approach published full-page ads in newspapers headlined "GOOD PAY Honorable Work," offering $1.10 a day with "all Board and Clothing, Transportation and every necessity of living supplied absolutely free." No experience was necessary, it declared, and "all will have a chance of visiting Great Britain and Europe and seeing the sights of a life time." Another ad announced that the 40th Battalion was arranging an "EXCURSION TO BERLIN...for SPORTSMEN," promising "Good Shooting and Hunting," "Rifles and Ammunition Supplied FREE," and with "Hotel Expenses, Railway and Ocean Fares Paid."[57]

The campaign was so successful that the 40th ended up with 1,540 men, far more than were needed. As was the case with the 25th, some families contributed more than others. Oscar Bennett of Halifax enlisted, for example, even though he had three brothers—Charles, Edgar, and Harold—serving in the 25th.[58] Three Purcell brothers, also from Halifax—Reginald, Elwood, and Lawrence—joined the 40th, even though Elwood was only seventeen.[59] Another underage volunteer was seventeen-year-old Keith Crosby of Carleton. He was transferred into Montreal's 24th Battalion and was killed at Ypres in April 1916, four days after going to the front.

Perhaps the most interesting recruit to the 40th, at least in retrospect, was Archibald Belaney, who enlisted at Digby in May, claiming that he was born in Montreal and was a trapper. In fact, he was born near Hastings, England, and had immigrated to Canada in 1906. He lived mostly in Indigenous communities in northern Canada but had spent the winter of 1914–15 in Digby for reasons unknown. Belaney later became famous as Grey Owl, who claimed to be an Indian and probably wanted to be one, and achieved considerable fame as a spokesman for First Nations peoples and an early conservationist, publishing four bestselling books before his premature death in 1938.

The 64th Battalion, commanded by Lieutenant Colonel Henry Montgomery-Campbell of Fredericton, was also recruiting in all three Maritime provinces in 1915. It raised 1,863 men, far more than it needed, so more than 700 were transferred to other units. The 64th was not a Nova Scotian battalion, but when it went overseas 431 of its 1,250 officers and men were Nova Scotians. The 64th spent the winter of 1915–16 on the second floor of the Pier 2 building in Halifax and trained on the Common and on Citadel Hill. Perhaps unfortunately, depending on one's point of view, Water Street was "right outside the door of the guard-room and every second door-way on the Street was an entrance to a dispensary of everything that was missing in Sussex. The memory of weeks of 'drought' in New Brunswick must be buried or rather drowned. It took a week to do it properly."[60]

Pier 2 was a "cold, miserable" place during the winter months, and the battalion endured an epidemic of diphtheria and meningitis that killed a number of men. But there were hockey games at the old South End rink, basketball games against the sailors of the *Niobe* and men of the 85th Battalion at the YMCA, boxing matches and weekly entertainments put on by the men, church socials, route marches out along Quinpool Road, and one long cold day when they had to stand at attention along the route from the church to the cemetery for Sir Charles Tupper's funeral. Like so many other soldiers in Halifax, they enjoyed eating at the Green Lantern Restaurant on Barrington Street, "a great rendez-vous for romance" according to Machum, and marching in the weekly church parades on Barrington, "with one eye on the man in front of us and the other on the girls on the sidewalk."[61]

In September 1915 the Militia Department authorized the formation of another Nova Scotian hospital unit. No. 7 Canadian Stationary Hospital was organized by the medical school of

Dalhousie University. Dr. John Stewart, a prominent Halifax physician who had gone overseas with Liverpool's No. 2 Canadian Clearing Hospital, was appointed its commanding officer despite being sixty-seven years of age. Laura Hubley of St. Margaret's Bay was appointed matron. Most of the doctors came from the Dalhousie medical school, but for nurses preference was given to graduates of the Victoria General Hospital in Halifax and St. Joseph's Hospital in Glace Bay because they "were the only general hospitals in the Province with the necessary number of beds to meet the requirements of the Military Service in the matter of training."[62]

While undergoing initial training, the unit was billeted in the old Medical College building on the corner of Robie and College Streets, with its mess in the Maritime Business College next door. When No. 7 Canadian Stationary Hospital sailed for England in January 1916, it included twelve doctors, one dentist, twenty-seven nurses, and 121 other ranks, almost all of them from Nova Scotia. After a few months in England, it moved to Arques, on the edge of St. Omer, just in time for the Battle of the Somme, in which the Canadian Corps would play a major role.

Even though Dalhousie was the only university in the Maritimes with a medical school, it was not the only university to send a hospital unit overseas. Rather oddly, St. Francis Xavier University also offered one, which became No. 9 Canadian Stationary Hospital. The idea apparently originated with Dr. J. Stewart Carruthers, a graduate of St. FX who was medical officer at the marine hospital in Pubnico.[63] Perhaps more importantly, he was also the son-in-law of Adam Crosby, a prominent Halifax businessman who had served as mayor, represented the county in Parliament from 1908 to 1911, and was appointed to the Senate in January 1917.

Why would a small university without a medical school offer a medical unit? The Reverend Hugh MacPherson, St. FX's president, thought it should do so because it was the major English-speaking Catholic university in the country. His vice-president, the Reverend

J. J. Tompkins, reportedly "rejoiced that the government would pay all expenses, while St. FX got 'all the glory' and its name 'blazed' from the Atlantic to the Pacific."[64] The university's historian, James Cameron, asserts that there was more to it than that: participating in a St. FX hospital unit would protect Catholic youth from the "grave moral and physical dangers" to which they would be exposed if they served in combat battalions.[65]

A serious effort was made to recruit doctors and nurses who were Catholic alumni of St. FX. Dr. Roderick MacLeod, a native of Dunvegan who practised in North Sydney, was appointed commanding officer, Dr. Stewart Carruthers was appointed adjutant,[66] and Sarah MacIsaac of Joggins was appointed matron. MacLeod's second in command, however, was Dr. Henry Kendall, a Protestant from Sydney and an alumnus of Mount Allison University. The men trained in the Dalhousie medical building in May and June before sailing for England on June 19, 1916, with fourteen medical

Fig. 4.4: Officers and nurses of No. 9 (St. Francis Xavier University) Canadian Stationary Hospital, Bramshott, England, 1916.

officers, twenty-seven nurses, and 118 men, only about sixty of whom were St. FX students or alumni.

As Cameron acknowledges, the hospital's overseas experience "was not entirely satisfactory."[67] Because its personnel did not come from a medical school, they were dispersed to various hospitals in England for several months before going to France. Then MacLeod contracted anthrax and died, which meant that Kendall assumed command and took the unit to France in February 1917. It seems to have been relatively inactive until the spring of 1918, when it was established at Etaples, just in time for the infamous German air raid on the town in May. Three men, including Dr. William Fielding McIsaac of Antigonish and Horace MacMillan of Isaac's Harbour, were killed, and twelve were wounded.[68]

In August Dr. Ronald St. J. Macdonald—a St. FX alumnus and brother of Margaret Macdonald, the chief matron of the Canadian Army Nursing Service—succeeded Kendall in command. But then, in what must have been an intensely embarrassing development—at least for MacPherson, Tompkins, and other clergy back home—No. 9 was assigned to manage a "special" hospital that treated men with venereal disease. There certainly was a need. The Canadian Corps had the highest rate of venereal disease among the Allied armies. By the end of the war, 66,083 cases of venereal disease had been treated. Putting this in context, the number of men infected with venereal disease was virtually the same as the number of men who died in the war, and the 5th Brigade, a majority of whose troops were Catholics from Quebec, Nova Scotia, and New Brunswick, had the highest rate of infection in the Canadian Corps.[69]

The response of doctors and nurses to the need for medical services was not limited to those who served in No. 1 Casualty Clearing Station or No. 7 and No. 9 Stationary Hospitals. Precise figures don't exist, but more than 100 Nova Scotian doctors served overseas, most with the Canadian Corps but a few with the British Army, and four of them died.[70] Of the 2,411 Canadian nurses who served overseas, about 200 were Nova Scotians,[71] not counting a few who went to England and joined Queen Alexandra's Imperial Military Nursing Service, the nursing corps of the British Army. At least ten Nova Scotian nurses joined the Canadian Army Nursing Corps after having served in the medical unit sponsored by Harvard University in 1915.[72] Nova Scotia provided at least seven nursing matrons. Margaret Macdonald was matron of the CAMC nursing service, and six others were hospital matrons.[73] Fifty-three Canadian nurses died overseas during the war from enemy action or illnesses, including four Nova Scotians.[74]

HAIG UNWITTINGLY CELEBRATED DOMINION DAY ON JULY 1, 1916, by launching the massive Somme offensive—the largest and bloodiest Allied offensive of the entire war—which he hoped would shatter the German Army and end the war. The Canadian Corps was not involved until September, when the 2nd Division was assigned to capture Courcelette and Regina Trench, a major German defensive position that lay just beyond the village. The attack began on the fifteenth with what Lieutenant Harry Hiltz of Kingsport described as "some of the greatness of England, thousands of guns of all caliber belching out tons of steel per minute on the German defences."[75] Arthur Chute, whose ammunition column delivered shells to the artillery during the barrage, was momentarily "dazed by the awful shock of noises," which he described somewhat melodramatically as "England's answer to the Hun, our voice to the Beast."[76]

The attack on Courcelette marked the first use of "queer looking objects,"[77] as Ralph Lewis described the first tanks. Frank Ferguson described them as "buckets of bolts lumbering along the road, snorting and shooting fire from their nostrils like blooming dragons."[78] Impressive no doubt, but their impact was insignificant because only thirteen actually participated in the battle, and of the seven allotted to the Canadians, only one got through! Even so,

Lewis was undoubtedly right when he concluded that "the moral effect was just as terrible as the real."[79]

The 25th and 22nd Battalions jointly led the attack on Courcelette. Hiltz claimed that "it was simply wonderful to see the men advancing over that mile and a half of shell swept country, never hesitating and with a smile on every face,"[80] which reads suspiciously like he was trying to reassure the folks at home that all was well. The battle for Courcelette was in fact brutal, involving house-to-house fighting over two days, during which the Germans counterattacked eleven times. After the village was taken, other battalions carried on for two weeks before capturing Regina Trench.

The capture of Courcelette and Regina Trench was not only the 25th Battalion's first victory; it was the only major Allied achievement in the Somme offensive. Hilliam, who was himself wounded in the assault, later declared, "I have the honour of commanding the finest body of men I have ever seen."[81] He even cabled Premier Murray to "let Nova Scotians know that all [of the] Canadian Corps is proud of [the] Nova Scotian Battalion's magnificent work."[82]

This was high praise and it was merited, but there weren't a lot of men left to appreciate it. The battalion suffered 304 casualties, including thirty-six killed in just the first three days. They were among the 24,000 Canadians who died in the Somme offensive, a modest number when we realize the total casualties on both sides were more than a million men. It was, as Desmond Morton and J. L. Granatstein have said, "mass butchery."[83] Howard Johnstone, who survived Courcelette only to be killed at Regina Trench, found it "hard to know which of two feelings is upper most in my mind, pride in the glorious achievement of the regiment or sorrow at the loss of so many old comrades."[84] Robert Clements didn't have such mixed feelings. "This," he later wrote, "was the price the people of Nova Scotia, through their senior battalion on active service, paid for half a broken-down small French town and a few acres of muddy clay."[85]

Clements and other members of the 25th were bitter on another score as well: press coverage in Canada seemed to give all or at least most of the credit for the costly victory to Quebec's 22nd Battalion, and a brief history published in 1921 also asserted that the 22nd "won the honors at Courcelette."[86] Men in the 25th were aware of this and resented it. Writing on September 30, for example, Percy Willmot of Sydney said, "The FC's [French Canadians] get the most credit but this unit was the one that *did* the business."[87] Certainly the 22nd shared in the assault and deserved its full share of the credit, but Clements suspected that the press had been "encouraged or instructed" to focus on the 22nd in a misguided effort to encourage recruiting in Quebec.[88]

To be fair, more than twenty Canadian battalions participated in the battle, and there were Nova Scotians scattered among them as well. John Chipman Kerr of Fox River was one of them. He had gone west and was farming in northern Alberta, so he served in the 49th Battalion. He was awarded the Victoria Cross for single-handedly attacking an enemy trench at Courcelette, leading to

Fig. 4.5: John Chipman Kerr (right), with unidentified friend, was awarded the Victoria Cross for his heroics at Courcelette.

the capture of sixty-two prisoners. He was the first Nova Scotian to be awarded the Victoria Cross in the war.

Unfortunately, there was one member of the 25th Battalion who did not contribute to the victory. Elsworth Young, a nineteen-year-old miner from Glace Bay, had enlisted with his brother Calvin in November 1914 and served until the fighting at Courcelette, when he went missing. When found by the military police some distance behind the lines, dressed in the uniform of a corporal in an artillery unit, he was charged with desertion. Found guilty, he was executed by firing squad early on the morning of October 29. Harrison Livingstone, who knew Young, believed that he went AWOL because he had "gone sweet" on a French girl. Livingstone was a member of the firing party and the experience haunted him for the rest of his life.

Young was the only Nova Scotian among the twenty-five Canadian soldiers executed during the war. But another Nova Scotian soldier was court-martialled and executed while serving as an officer in the British Army. Eric Skeffington Poole was a son of Henry Skeffington Poole, the Stellarton-born mining engineer who managed the General Mining Association's coal mines, was inspector of mines in the 1870s, then manager of the Acadia Coal Company, and finally served with the Geological Survey of Canada until moving to England in 1905. Eric Poole grew up in Halifax and served in the 63rd Regiment for two years before moving to England with his family. When the war broke out, he joined the 11th Battalion West Yorkshire Regiment as a second lieutenant. In October 1916 he wandered away from his platoon during the fighting near Flers and was charged with desertion. He was convicted and executed on December 10, even though there was reason to believe that he was suffering from shell shock and possible brain damage from an artillery barrage in July. He was one of only three British officers executed during the war.[89]

Chapter 5

THE WORST YEAR 1916–17

Our present honor will lose some of its lustre if it can ever be said that in this great cataclysmic struggle Canada did not do all that she could.[1]

THE SOMME FIASCO MADE CLEAR THAT NO ONE QUITE knew how to break the stalemate of trench warfare on the Western Front. It also made clear that more men were needed to keep up the effort. Borden therefore announced on New Year's Day 1916 that he was doubling Canada's commitment to 500,000 men. By that time about 5,000 men had enlisted in Nova Scotia, not counting another 3,500 engaged in coastal and home defence, those serving in the navy, or those who had enlisted outside the province.

Public opinion was beginning to divide on the issue of enlistments. As early as November 1915 the *Halifax Herald* claimed that "strapping young fellows" along the South Shore were attending recruitment meetings and listening "most attentively and respectfully to all that was said," but then "turned their backs and went home!"[2] There is no evidence to suggest that the rate of enlistments was lower on the South Shore than in other areas, but the *Herald* was hinting at something more serious. It actually wondered if low enlistments on the South Shore suggested that people there were "indifferent to the call of the blood."[3] Put simply, it was asking if Lunenburgers, because of their German ancestry, were not responding to the visceral Anglo-Saxon and Celtic call to rally behind king and empire. This was a disturbing warning of how ugly the manpower question might become if the war dragged on.

Meanwhile, with the 2nd Division fully engaged alongside the 1st Division, casualties were inevitably higher in 1916 than in 1915. That meant, as Borden had indicated, that more men were needed. Seven new battalions—the 85th, 106th, 112th, 193rd, 219th, 246th, and No. 2 Construction—were recruited in Nova Scotia and that meant more than 7,000 men just to form them. Remarkably, most had no difficulty in raising them even though recruiting officers were now competing with employers in a thriving wartime economy.

In August 1916 the Militia Department organized what it hoped would be a more effective recruiting system. Provincial recruiting associations were created, with local branches in each county. The first chairman of the Nova Scotia Recruiting Association was Sir Frederick Fraser, the superintendent of the Halifax School for the Blind,[4] but he was soon replaced by George Campbell, a prominent Halifax businessman. Campbell's son, also named George, was killed in May 1916 while serving with the Canadian Pioneers. In his last letter home, his son had pleaded that "every available man must come over or it will never end."[5] Campbell resigned only a few months later, however, and was replaced by W. B. A. Ritchie,[6] a Halifax lawyer who in turn was shortly replaced by George Cutten, the Baptist minister and president of Acadia University, who took a leave of absence from the university. Cutten also joined the 219th Battalion so he was able to tour the province in uniform, appealing—some would say preaching—to men, women, and certainly university students to enlist or at least to fully support the war effort in some other way. His travelling road show included military bands, returned soldiers, and a skilful blending of patriotism and religious fervour that drew large audiences.

He was not the only clergyman who combined patriotism with religion in support of the war effort. As Stuart Hunt readily acknowledged, pulpits were "commandeered" in the 1916 recruitment campaign, as "military uniforms appeared in the pulpit and unwonted martial strains, even from the bagpipes, were heard in sacred precincts."[7] By 1916 the Protestant churches had all linked the war effort with the pre-war social gospel movement and identified Christianity with the values allegedly represented by the British Empire. Thus, the conflict had become a struggle between good and evil. Reading the church newspapers in the war years is an increasingly disturbing experience, as they compared death in a righteous war with crucifixion and assured people that the war was "a testing ordeal from which a better world would emerge."[8] US President Woodrow Wilson's oft-repeated declaration that this war would end war as a means of settling future disputes was built on this kind of thinking.

Fig. 5.1: Rev. Dr. George Cutten in uniform, 1916, led recruiting campaigns.

Like Cutten, the Reverend Clarence Mackinnon, principal of Pine Hill Divinity Hall, took a leave of absence and joined the 112th Battalion as chaplain but was soon brought home to employ his considerable oratorical skills in the cause. The Reverend E. Watering Florence, rector of the historic St. George's Anglican Church in Sydney, justified the war on religious grounds from the outset and became an effective recruiting officer in Cape Breton. The Baptist Reverend William White played a major role in recruiting black men for No. 2 Construction Battalion and served as its chaplain. Another Baptist minister, the Reverend C. W. Corey, joined the 246th Battalion as chaplain and campaigned for conscription during the 1917 election.

Many clergymen joined the army, most to serve as chaplains but some as combat officers. Lieutenant Colonel William Muirhead claimed that fourteen clergymen enlisted in the 219th Battalion.[9] Whether or not that was true, we do know that the Reverend E. J. Brooks, a Baptist, joined the 25th Battalion and the Reverend Rod Jackson, a Presbyterian, joined the 85th, both as combat officers. No doubt there were more.

If appealing to patriotism and denouncing the Germans as anti-Christian barbarians did not work, recruiters were not above trying to shame men into enlisting. Many followed the lead of Lieutenant Governor David MacKeen, who kicked off the 1916 campaign by asking young men to respond to "the cry that comes back to us from the blood-stained trenches of Flanders…so that the sons of Nova Scotia who have already made the supreme sacrifice, shall not have died in vain."[10] One wonders if this was inspired by John McCrae's poem, "In Flanders Fields," which achieved almost instant popularity following its publication in *Punch* magazine in December 1915. Its last verse reads:

Take up our quarrel with the foe:
To you from failing hands we throw

The Torch; be yours to hold it high! If ye break faith with us who die
We shall not sleep, though poppies grow
In Flanders fields.

Recruiters also urged mothers who were discouraging their sons from enlisting to "consider how those sons will remember them, when they have to tell their children in years to come that they failed in their plain duty to our great British Brotherhood because 'Mother Forbade.'" As for employers who discouraged their workers from enlisting, their motives were "so sordid that they only need to be suggested to arouse universal contempt."[11]

There were female recruiters as well. Grace McLeod Rogers of Amherst became a popular speaker on the recruiting circuit. The wife of a prominent lawyer and author of a successful book about the Annapolis Valley, she had three sons in the army. She started with a week-long speaking tour of Cumberland County in December 1916, after which she received "requests…from different parts of the Province for her services at meetings to be held in future days."[12]

Without a doubt, however, the most outrageous attempt to shame men into enlisting was a letter written by Allison Borden, recruiting men for the Highland Brigade, which was distributed to all Nova Scotian schoolchildren. Borden told them that the king had asked him to raise 3,500 men "who are willing to…go across the Atlantic with me to help beat the cruel Germans who are trying to destroy our Empire," and warned that "if the Nova Scotia men do not cross the sea to fight the Germans in France, the Germans may come to Nova Scotia and take or destroy our farms and houses. So you see…you must help me to raise these 3,500 men." How? "Well, you can carry this letter home and show it to your father and big brothers and you can ask them to come with me and other grown up Nova Scotia school boys," and "ask them to write to their friends and relatives not now living at home, to return to Nova

Scotia and enlist with us in this great cause.…Boys and girls of Nova Scotia, I am depending on you to help fill up the three Nova Scotia Battalions."[13]

Stuart Hunt believed that this letter "converted every child into an irrepressible recruiting agent among his big brothers at home."[14]

Fig. 5.2: Lieutenant Colonel Allison Borden tried to shame men into enlisting.

That was certainly its aim, but it is hard not to agree with Murray Angus when he describes it as "a chilling, Orwellian approach to recruitment."[15] What the letter demonstrates in a highly disturbing fashion is that by 1916 the war had become a crusade, at least in the minds of its protagonists. What it also illustrated was that effective salesmanship produced results because five of the seven battalions being recruited reached their quotas, and men were raised for the 165th Battalion, the Royal Canadian Regiment, and No. 10 Halifax Siege Battery as well.[16]

NO. 10 HALIFAX SIEGE BATTERY WAS AUTHORIZED IN OCTOBER 1916 as a depot battery to provide drafts for overseas units. It was commanded by Major James Slayter of Halifax, who had fifteen years' experience in the garrison artillery, four of them in the permanent force. No. 10 sent 385 officers and men to England during 1917 and trained nearly 800 conscripted men, sending drafts overseas as needed.

Meanwhile, the 11th Brigade—the junior artillery brigade in Military District 6—was mobilized and redesignated the 14th Brigade, and recruited men during this period as well. Commanded by Lieutenant Colonel John Lauchlin MacKinnon of Antigonish, its 58th Battery was recruited in New Brunswick and Nova Scotia, and its ammunition column, commanded by Captain Fred Burns of Halifax, was recruited entirely in Nova Scotia. In addition to MacKinnon, the headquarters staff included Captain George Oland of Halifax whose brother, Captain Sidney Oland, commanded the Montreal battery.[17] Dr. Charles Trites of Liverpool served as medical officer.

More significant were the new battalions. The 106th, authorized in November 1915, was commanded by Walter Allen, a carriage maker in Truro who had been active in the pre-war militia and had joined the 17th Battalion as a captain in 1914. When the 17th became a reserve unit, he was promoted to major and transferred into the 15th Battalion but lasted less than a month before being wounded. He was sent home, then was appointed commanding officer of the 106th, presumably on the basis of his brief battlefield experience. His unusual wounds were under investigation, however, and two months later he was court-martialled for "behaving in a scandalous manner, unbecoming the character of an officer and a gentleman."[18] His improbable replacement was Robert Innes, a twenty-four-year-old major from Coldbrook then living in Ottawa, who had militia experience but also, it would appear, Conservative party connections.

The 106th recruited three companies in Colchester, Cumberland, Pictou, and Antigonish Counties and the fourth in Cape Breton. Like the 40th and 64th Battalions, however, when it arrived in England it was broken up to provide reinforcements for battalions already in the field. This, in fact, was the fate of almost all of the battalions raised across the country from 1916. Innes naturally complained that the Militia Department was discriminating against Nova Scotians, a charge likely based on his awareness that almost all of the 106th's men were used to reinforce significantly under strength English-speaking battalions from Quebec.[19] It made no difference and he, to his credit, eventually reverted in rank to lieutenant and served with the 87th Canadian Grenadier Guards until being wounded and invalided home to Canada in 1917.

The 112th Battalion was authorized in December 1915. Based in Windsor, it was commanded by Hadley Brown Tremain,[20] a Windsor lawyer who represented Hants in Parliament and also claimed to have a PhD. The 112th recruited in the eight western counties and by late March 1916 was over strength. It trained initially at Fort Edward in Windsor and went to England in July but got no further. It was used to supply reinforcements until January 1917, when it was absorbed by the 26th Reserve Battalion.

Meanwhile, the Moncton-based 165th Battalion had been authorized late in 1915 under the command of Lieutenant Colonel Louis-Cyriaque D'Aigle to recruit Acadians from throughout the

Maritime provinces. It succeeded in enlisting 170 Nova Scotians from Acadian communities throughout the province; forty-five came from Chéticamp and Isle Madame in Cape Breton, and forty-four from the Meteghan area, who had enlisted in the 112th but were transferred to the 165th. Among them were four Saulnier brothers.[21] C Company consisted of fifty-eight men, commanded by Major Emile Stehelin of Church Point. Charles Deveau of Mavillette was probably the youngest Acadian to serve in the war. He was undoubtedly the youngest Nova Scotian and may well have been the youngest Canadian. He was only thirteen years old when he enlisted in January 1915 but served throughout the war, returning home at the age of eighteen. The 165th was only able to raise 658 officers and men by the time it went overseas and, like the other battalions, it was broken up in England. Some men were drafted into existing battalions, while others were transferred into the Forestry Corps. We should bear in mind, of course, that many Acadians enlisted in other local battalions and artillery batteries, and some enlisted in other provinces.

Without a doubt the major recruiting success in 1916 was the 85th Battalion. Authorized in September 1915, it was commanded by Allison Borden of Guysborough, a distant cousin of the prime minister. Its success was largely attributable to the fact that it was designated a Scottish Highland battalion, an idea that had enormous appeal to Nova Scotians. When the 85th was recruited over strength within a month, the Militia Department eagerly accepted Borden's proposal to expand it into a brigade, i.e., four battalions. If this seemed overly ambitious, it was not. The three additional battalions—the 185th, 193rd, and 219th—were all designated "Nova Scotia Highlanders" and filled their quotas within three weeks.

The 185th was recruited entirely in Cape Breton by its company commanders under the supervision of Gordon Harrington, a Glace Bay lawyer and mayor from 1913 to 1915.[22] Even though the 85th had raised a full company on the island, the 185th quickly and easily raised the required men and mobilized at Broughton, a recently abandoned mining town near Glace Bay. Somewhat oddly, Frank Parker Day was appointed its lieutenant colonel, even though he wasn't of Scottish descent and had no connection with Cape Breton.[23]

The 193rd was recruited in the six northeastern counties of mainland Nova Scotia and mobilized at Truro. It was commanded by John Stanfield, a member of the prominent Truro textile family and the Conservative Member of Parliament for Colchester.

The 219th was recruited in Halifax and the western counties and was commanded by William Muirhead, a Halifax stockbroker and close associate of F. B. McCurdy, a Conservative MP and the party's chief fundraiser in Nova Scotia. Muirhead's appointment was blatantly political and caused much controversy because he had been charged with bribery and forgery in relation to a Conservative victory in a provincial by-election in staunchly Liberal Victoria County.[24] By the time the case went to court, Muirhead had joined New Brunswick's 12th Battalion and was in England, prompting

Fig. 5.3: The Guysborough detachment of the 193rd Battalion marches to the dock to board a ship en route to Camp Aldershot, 1916.

D. D. McKenzie, the Liberal MP for Victoria County, to quip that he had "fled the country on the pretext that he was going to war."[25]

Although the 12th Battalion was kept in England as a reserve unit when the 2nd Division went to France in February 1915, McCurdy later claimed that Muirhead had "been in the trenches... in charge of a bombing party."[26] In any event, he was back in Nova Scotia by January 1916 and was transferred as a major into Hadley Tremain's 112th Battalion. Within four months, at the age of thirty-nine and with virtually no military experience, he was appointed lieutenant colonel of the 219th.

A tremendous recruiting campaign travelled the province in the summer of 1916, promoting enlistment in the Highland Brigade. "Every available medium was used to attract men to the colours—pulpit, press, platform speakers, parades...and finally, a tour of the province by a speakers' team," headed by Allison Borden and the popular band of the 85th Battalion.[27] When the brigade raised more men than it needed, another battalion, the 246th, was created to serve as a reserve, and officers and men who "were temporarily unfit for service at the Front" were transferred into it.[28] One might have thought that Norval Parsons, its commanding officer, fit into that category because he was a forty-eight-year-old Wolfville merchant with no military experience beyond his membership in the pre-war militia. The 246th alone failed to achieve its quota and sailed to England with only sixteen officers and 375 men.[29]

The brigade trained at Aldershot that summer of 1916, generating considerable public interest. This was exploited, of course, most notably when the camp "was thrown open to the public" for two days in late August so that people could observe the unprecedented spectacle of 6,000 men, mostly Nova Scotians, training for war. Special trains were organized and 8,000 people showed up. So too did the governor general, who inspected the brigade, which Hunt claimed "excelled itself in its manoeuvres, and especially in the March Past."[30]

Departure for overseas was imminent by the middle of September. But the men were "fairly stunned" when all leaves were cancelled on the twenty-sixth because this meant they would have no opportunity to visit their homes and families before shipping out. Many went home anyway, but they "came streaming back... ready to do their duty in facing the foe."[31] Some 10,000 people flooded into Halifax from all over the province to bid them farewell and watch them parade to Pier 2 to board the *Olympic*. Much to the distress of the men of the 85th and 185th, and their families, they were marched directly from the North Street train station to the pier and immediately boarded the ship, even though they had been assured that they would march first to the Common to say farewell to relatives and friends.

This foolish error was remedied for the 193rd and 219th, whose men were allowed to mingle with their families, while "some who did not have anyone there to greet them assumed an indifference they did not feel." When "the bugle sounded ranks...mothers and sisters and fathers and brothers walked with their lads;" military discipline "was for a time forgotten and all gave themselves over to those emotions that move one most deeply. There was no cheering."[32]

When the brigade arrived in England, Borden was there to meet it because he had gone ahead to gain some practical experience in the field with the Royal Canadian Regiment. He probably gained rather more than he had hoped for, because he was wounded and was back in England recovering from the experience. Meanwhile, the English were amused by the brigade's appearance, according to Lyman Totten of Truro, and called them "red Indians and some other names" at first because they wore a feather in their cap.[33] Actually, they wore traditional Scottish Balmoral military caps with a feather that was dark grey but had a distinctive colouring for each battalion: red for the 85th, green for the 185th, blue for the 193rd, and purple for the 219th.

Alas, the Highland Brigade proved to be another victim of the Militia Department's duplicity. Even though Sam Hughes had boasted in March about how quickly it had been recruited and claimed that "these men who speak Gaelic are the finest fighters in the world,"[34] the Highland Brigade was disbanded to provide reinforcements for existing battalions. Only the 85th survived to become the second Nova Scotian battalion in the field. Many of the men from the other battalions served in the 25th and 85th Battalions, but others went to different battalions. More than 800 men were drafted to Montreal regiments alone. Clarence Mackinnon later recalled the day when they were taken:

> *No soldier will likely ever forget the early morning when the first draft left for France. Dawn was just breaking in a cloudless sky. The morning star of hope was still shining brilliantly as we passed down the excited lines bidding our last adieu. Then came the sharp command, "shun!" We stepped back. The Highland pipes broke into a military strain and they were gone.*[35]

To describe this betrayal as a major disappointment to Nova Scotians, who had invested so much pride in the brigade and what it symbolized because of the province's rich and treasured Scottish heritage, would be a gross understatement. The abolition of the 185th caused the most disappointment, at least in Cape Breton, where it had been recruited in villages throughout the island and aroused enormous enthusiasm and pride, which it retains to this day.

It is worth noting, however, that despite all the romantic talk about the brigade being comprised of "Highland Laddies" and the frequent references to New Scotland and so on, not everyone who served in the 85th or the other battalions was of Scottish descent. Acadians, Mik'maw, blacks, and European immigrants all enlisted in the brigade and, judging from photographs, wore their kilts and feathered caps with pride.

Faced with the understandable anger of the general public, Conservative politicians and other prominent men tried to get the decision reversed, warning Prime Minister Borden that breaking up the brigade would be considered a breach of faith and would damage future enlistments in the province.[36] James Maddin went further, bluntly telling Borden that the brigade's destruction would "never be forgiven by Nova Scotia,"[37] a serious consideration because an election was almost certainly going to take place in 1917.

It was all in vain, but Borden knew he had a mess on his hands and finally took action, firing Sam Hughes and turning to solid managers like George Perley and A. E. Kemp to sort out the Militia Department. He also made another difficult decision that he had been avoiding: he broke up the 5th Division, which was sitting in England tying up 20,000 troops who could be used to reinforce the four divisions in the field.

The idea of the Highland Brigade endured, as newspapers continued through the rest of the war to refer to the 85th Battalion as the Highland Brigade, perhaps out of ignorance or because they wanted to believe that it still existed. And, despite the warnings, it is not clear that breaking up the brigade had a negative effect on enlistments in Nova Scotia. Enlistments did decline in 1917, but not at a greater rate than elsewhere.

There may have been a political impact, however. Despite the call in August 1914 for a political truce, this was too much to hope for, especially when the war did not come to a speedy conclusion. There were bound to be disagreements, but they were certainly aggravated by the Borden government's policy of carrying on with patronage, including the awarding of contracts and the appointment of senior army officers, as if it were still 1913.

This was especially so in the Militia Department as long as Sam Hughes was in charge. Contracts tended to go to men with Conservative connections and preference was given to Conservatives in appointments of all kinds. It was claimed, for example, that even the local doctors appointed to carry out the physical examinations of volunteers were Conservatives unless there was no Conservative physician in the area.

More significantly, battalion commanders were too often active Conservatives. Walter Allen, Hadley Tremain, John Stanfield, and W. H. Muirhead were all well-known Conservatives, and Tremain and Stanfield were actually Conservative MPs. Liberals noted that Tremain drew both his MP's pay and his military pay while recruiting the 112th, although Stanfield, to his credit, declined his military pay. There was also a widespread perception dating back to before the outbreak of war that Borden was a weak leader and that there was a great deal of mismanagement in high places. Had the war not broken out in 1914, it is quite possible that the government would have lost the next election, expected to take place in 1915.

There was no federal election in sight, but the 1916 provincial election provided an opportunity for testing the popularity of the Borden government and its management of the war. The election was fought on provincial issues, of course, but politics do not always observe the divisions of a federal system, and the provincial Conservatives thought they had a good chance of defeating the thirty-four-year-old Murray government, especially with the patronage of the federal Conservative government behind them. They were wrong. The Murray government was re-elected with a larger majority.

THE GOVERNMENT WAS NOT ONLY SEEKING MORE RECRUITS, IT was also trying to enlarge the pool of men who would be accepted into the army. Indigenous men, whom the government had previously rejected because this was "a white man's war," were now welcomed and more than 4,000—approximately 35% of all status males of military age—enlisted, a figure that does not include non-status First Nations, Métis, or Inuit men for whom there are no records. The Mi'kmaw population of Nova Scotia, according to the 1911 census, was 1,758. Precise records do not appear to exist, but one historian has reported that "nearly half of eligible Mi'kmaq and Maliseet men in Atlantic Canada enlisted," including "every eligible male from the Mi'kmaq reserve near Sydney."[38] Don Julien, executive director of the Confederacy of Mainland Mi'kmaq, more precisely claims that ninety Nova Scotia Mi'kmaq men enlisted.[39] While this number appears to be lower than the national average, it remains impressive when we realize that status First Nations men who enlisted lost their status and could not return to their reserves.[40]

The government even agreed in 1916 to accept African Canadians. This marked a significant change in policy. Until now the Militia Department had left the decision on which volunteers to accept to the commanding officers of the units doing the recruiting. Because racial discrimination was normal in Canadian society at the time, few black volunteers were accepted, although one notable one in Nova Scotia was Roy Fells of Yarmouth, who was accepted by the 25th Battalion in November 1914 and was even promoted to the rank of sergeant.

In Nova Scotia, which had the largest black population in the country, there may have been a local factor as well. Haligonians at least were exposed to black soldiers that year when the ship on which the British West Indies Regiment was sailing from Jamaica to England in March, ran into a blizzard. Because the troops wore only lightweight tropical uniforms and the ship was unheated, most of them were suffering from frostbite when it pulled into Halifax. Some were able to carry on after minor treatment, but 106 men required more serious treatment and remained in Halifax.

No provision was made for that treatment, however, so the Local Council of Women got involved under the leadership of May Sexton, an influential social activist in the Red Cross and the wife of Frederic Sexton, the first principal of the Nova Scotia Technical College. She co-chaired a committee with J. L. Hetherington, a prominent Halifax businessman, which established what became known as the

Clayton Convalescent Hospital because it was funded by William Clayton of the Clayton & Sons clothing factory. According to Lois Yorke, it was "the first institution to be established in Canada for the express purpose of the educational, vocational, and physical training of disabled soldiers."[41] The IODE got involved as well, providing comforts and outings, and at Christmas presented a tree "loaded down with smokes, candy and fruit," plus "gifts for everyone [*sic*] of the gallant fellows" and "a programme of music and recitations."[42] Following their recovery, which involved acquiring artificial limbs in many cases, the Jamaican soldiers returned home.

Fig. 5.4: This appeal to African Nova Scotians to enlist appeared in the *Atlantic Advocate*, a newspaper published by leaders of Halifax's black community during the war years, in January 1917.

This episode certainly stimulated interest in Nova Scotia's black community and may have convinced some whites that black men could—and perhaps should—contribute to the war effort. When the Reverend Joseph Freeman Tupper, an Anglican priest from Kentville who had joined the 193rd Battalion as chaplain, learned that as many as 100 black volunteers had been rejected, he offered to raise an integrated battalion. This drew no response but when Walter Allen, the commanding officer of the 106th Battalion, asked the Reverend William White, the black minister of Truro's Zion Baptist Church, to recruit a segregated company for his battalion, he was told by the Militia Department that black recruits could not be segregated.[43] The result was that when the 106th went overseas in July 1916, its 1,009 men included sixteen black Nova Scotians.

Among them were the two Ash brothers of Guysborough County, both of whom were transferred into the 26th Battalion when the 106th was disbanded. Rollie Ash may well have been the first African Canadian soldier to have been killed in action when he died on January 16, 1917. His brother, Norman Ash, was killed seven months later, on August 15, 1917.[44] Also among the sixteen blacks who went overseas with the 106th was Jeremiah Jones of Truro, who at fifty-eight must have been the oldest enlisted man in the army when he signed up, claiming to be only thirty-nine. He served overseas in the Royal Canadian Regiment and distinguished himself at Vimy Ridge. His nephew, Sydney Jones, also served in the Royal Canadian Regiment and when he died in 1993 he was Nova Scotia's last surviving black veteran of the war.

Even so, Gwatkin made no secret of his personal view that blacks were good workers but not likely to be good fighters.[45] He recommended the creation of a segregated labour battalion and No. 2 Construction Battalion was the result.[46] As Gwatkin had expected, there was some difficulty in finding a white officer who would agree to command it, the assumption being that it could not be a black man. Borden intervened and Daniel Sutherland, a railway contractor from River John who had just joined the 193rd Battalion, agreed to take on the job.[47]

The battalion was mobilized at Pictou and all of its officers were white except for the Reverend William White, its chaplain, although Dr. Clement Ligoure, a Halifax physician from Trinidad who spent seven months helping to recruit the battalion, very nearly became its medical officer. He was initially appointed but then was rejected when it was "discovered" that due to a calculation error, he had not actually passed the medical board exam for Nova Scotia, even though he had earned his degree at Queen's University and had been practising medicine in Halifax for some time. Instead, the battalion's medical officer was Dr. Dan Murray, whose son Dr. Carson Murray was the father of Ann Murray.[48]

It is generally believed that when the Reverend William White was appointed chaplain of the battalion with the rank of captain he became the only commissioned officer of African descent in any of the British Empire's armed forces during the war. This is actually not correct. While his appointment was obviously a significant and well-deserved honour for White and a breakthrough in the struggle for racial equality, it was also an acceptable exception at a time when most whites were not yet ready to accept racial equality because chaplains were not actually commissioned officers. Their rank of captain was "honorary," meaning that they enjoyed the status, privileges, and salary of commissioned rank but lacked any command authority. It was a technical distinction to be sure, but an important one.[49]

Unfortunately, the battalion had great difficulty in raising men, even though prominent figures like F. B. McCurdy and John Stanfield promoted it and its brass band accompanied recruiters as they toured the province, giving concerts that included a minstrel show that "was no end of fun and received loud applause."[50] Recruiting was no doubt hindered by rumours—largely true—that the military establishment was "less than enthusiastic" about a black battalion, that it "had been imposed on them for political reasons," and that its members were only going to be used as trench diggers.[51] One has to assume also that some men saw no reason why they should go to war to defend an empire in which they were second-class citizens and were discriminated against in terms of jobs, recreation, and schools. The bottom line, however, was that the black population just wasn't large enough to support a battalion.

The result was that when the battalion went to England, it was seriously under strength, with nineteen officers but only 605 men, 500 of them from Nova Scotia. This was not viable, so it was reduced to company status and spent the rest of the war attached to the Canadian Forestry Corps. Lieutenant Colonel Sutherland, to his credit, accepted a reduction in rank to major so that he could serve with his men.

Although the men of No. 2 worked alongside white soldiers in their forestry work, their accommodations and recreation facilities were segregated. The white soldiers even refused to accept the Reverend William White as their chaplain and a white chaplain had to be brought in for them. It should also be recognized that, while working in a forestry unit was obviously safer than serving at the Front, it was hard labour and not without its dangers and some died from illnesses. The first to do so was nineteen-year-old Chester Pannell of Yarmouth, who fell ill on the voyage to England and died of pneumonia in April 1917.

Ironically, when conscription was introduced, it applied to black men, and Sutherland proposed that conscripted blacks be sent to No. 2 so that it could be restored to battalion status. Sydney Mewburn, the new minister of militia, agreed and all battalion commanders were instructed to do so. But only about 100 black men were conscripted, at least four of whom were Nova Scotians: Alexander and William Carvery, both of Africville, Wilfred Borden of New Glasgow, and Isaac Phills of Sydney, who had only arrived in the country from St. Vincent in 1916.[52]

When the British Canadian Recruiting Mission in New York reported that about 2,000 black British subjects living in the United States had volunteered and could be transferred into No. 2, the Militia Department's response was a terse "none required."[53] And when the Reverend William White appealed directly to Borden to reinforce No. 2, his letter was referred to Major Everett Bristol, the private secretary of Sir Edward Kemp, the minister of overseas forces. His response was that "these Niggers do well in a Forestry Corps and other Labour units."[54]

Meanwhile, despite the prevalent racial prejudice but possibly because of the Militia Department's order to recruiting officers to accept black volunteers, several black men did serve in infantry battalions. In addition to Roy Fells, mentioned earlier, Lester Ince, a Barbadian living in Halifax, who had three years' experience in the Royal Navy, was accepted in the 60th Battalion. Twelve black men from Digby reportedly enlisted in the 112th, and Robin Winks claims that sixty-six black men served in the 85th Battalion.[55] This figure is questionable, but some black men certainly served in the 85th. Some, like Isaac Phills, later reported that they were assigned to menial tasks and were segregated.

Black Nova Scotians take great pride in the contribution to the war made by the men who served in No. 2, and white Nova Scotians appear to be proud that their ancestors displayed such progressive thinking. But one has to question why people today think that allowing men of colour to serve only in a segregated labour unit marked a step forward in the struggle for racial equality. One also has to question why a segregated battalion was even created at the very same time that the Militia Department was ordering battalion commanders to accept black men, a dramatic change of policy that really did signify progress. The answer to the first question, based on a reading of media treatment of the subject, appears to be that people do not notice the contradiction. As for the Militia Department's contradictory policies, the records offer no explanation. The fact that Hughes and Gwatkin appear to have disagreed on the matter may also help to explain the inconsistency.

WHEN HAIG FINALLY ABANDONED THE FUTILE SOMME OFFENSIVE in November 1916, the Allies began planning for a spring offensive. This time the French would attack along the Aisne River to secure a breakthrough between Reims and Soissons, while the British attacked further north at Arras, in order to outflank the Hindenburg Line and advance towards Cambrai.

The primary task of the Canadian Corps was to form a strong defensive flank for the British effort. This involved capturing Vimy Ridge, which overlooked the industrial area of Lille and the coalfields of Lens and the Scarpe and Souchez Rivers. Tactically one of the most important features on the entire Western Front, it was the keystone of the defences linking the Hindenburg system to the main German lines leading north to the Belgian coast. In short, Vimy Ridge was a position the Germans could not afford to lose, and they had successfully repulsed three previous Allied assaults on it.

This would, therefore, be a major challenge, and for the first time the four divisions of the Canadian Corps went into battle together. Sir Julian Byng, the corps commander, planned the assault in exceptional detail, training the troops on a full-scale mock-up of the battlefield built behind the lines so that all officers and even the men knew the terrain and understood precisely what was expected of them. Instead of attacking in line in successive waves—the usual practice—they would attack in platoons, moving at their own rate. Tramways and plank roads were built to carry ammunition, other supplies, and equipment to the front line and when the day of battle came, the men got to the attack point through underground caves and tunnels instead of having to slog through the mud.[56]

The story of the Canadian victory at Vimy Ridge is well known. It began with a two-week artillery barrage of more than a million shells and nightly raids by the Canadians to learn as much as possible about the defences. Lieutenant Alex O'Brien of Antigonish said that "the guns spoke in one prolonged roar and the air seemed alive with hissing shells." It was "a gruesome but fantastic sight," according to James Johnson, who claimed rightly that "never before had any of us seen such a barrage put up by our artillery."[57]

The infantry attacked in driving wind, snow, and sleet at dawn on April 9. The "position of honour"—i.e., the most difficult position, in the centre of the line—was assigned to the 2nd Division's 5th Brigade, with the 24th and 26th Battalions leading the assault. They were followed closely by the 25th, which passed through their lines to carry the attack further, while the 22nd was held in reserve to carry out mopping-up operations.

Major J. A. De Lancey of Middleton led the 25th Battalion in the assault, while two of the battalion's pipers "played the boys over the top."[58] When De Lancey was killed, Major A. O. Blois took over. According to Alex O'Brien, the ground "was churned beyond imagination" and the German lines "were distinguishable only by the dead bodies, dugouts and broken fragments of wood." The fighting was fierce, however, and the carnage was profound:

> *Some of the wounded were crawling on all fours, but the seriously wounded remained where they fell, and suffered untold agonies, and all the while stretcher bearers wading knee deep in mud worked pluckily carrying them off the field.... [T]he dead lay thick on all sides, Germans and Canadians side by side peaceful in their last sleep, some completely submerged in pools of blood.*[59]

James Johnson was struck by the realization that, in the midst of such a savage and nightmarish situation, German prisoners were helping the stretcher bearers:

> *Here were men striving to save the lives of men they had tried to destroy a few hours before. The Germans worked hand in hand with*

> *us, dressing wounds, [and] carrying stretchers over muddy soaked ground.... There was not a trace of hate in the heart of any of the men I worked with that day, friend or foe. Oh the futility of war! Some of the Germans were killed or wounded by their own guns that day.*[60]

Only the 4th Division, which was responsible for taking and holding Hill 145, the highest and most important point on the ridge, encountered problems. But by mid-afternoon on the tenth it had succeeded as well, thanks largely to an assault without artillery support by two companies of the newly arrived and totally inexperienced 85th Battalion, who had only been brought in to help with trenching and carrying up supplies.

The 85th's assault on Hill 145 was led by Major Percy Anderson of Baddeck, leading D Company, which was made up mostly of Cape Bretoners. They distinguished themselves in fierce hand-to-hand fighting and Anderson rescued one of his men despite being wounded, an extraordinary action for which he was awarded the Military Cross. Another "Highlander" who distinguished himself at Vimy Ridge was Steven Toney, a Mi'kmaw from Pictou Landing who served as a sniper and reportedly killed fourteen Germans at Vimy Ridge.[61] Jeremiah Jones also distinguished himself by single-handedly destroying a German machine-gun post and taking several prisoners, despite being wounded. Jones was reportedly recommended for the Distinguished Conduct Medal but never received it, perhaps because of his race. In 2010 the government finally recognized him, awarding him posthumously the Canadian Forces Medallion for Distinguished Service. It was accepted on behalf of his family by his grandson, Rocky Jones, Halifax lawyer and prominent civil rights activist.

Philip Gibbs, the best-known British war correspondent, described the Canadian assault as "astoundingly successful"[62] and actually singled out the Nova Scotian troops, describing how, when the battle was over,

> *the boys of Nova Scotia came slowly, dragging one foot after the other in sheer exhaustion, stumbling over loose stones and bits of sandbags and strands of old wire, caked with clay from head to foot. Even their faces had masks of clay, and they were spent and done, but through that whitish mud their eyes were steel blue and struck fire like steel when they told me of the great victory they had shared in and of the enemy's flight before them—all this without a touch of brag, with fine and sweet simplicity, and with manly frankness. They had suffered tragic hardships for five days since the Battle of Arras began, but there was no wail in them.*[63]

British military historian Robin Neillands has described the battle of Vimy Ridge as "that rare thing, a Great War battle that went according to plan."[64] John Keegan, the most respected British historian of the war, described the victory as "sensational," noting also that it was "the first major offensive effort by a Dominion contingent on the western front."[65] This was true, but it was a good deal more than that. It was the first major Allied *victory* on the Western Front since 1914. As Canadian Corps historian Tim Cook has pointed out, the Canadians "had captured more ground, more prisoners, and more guns than any previous operation, all of which had been done against the heaviest of odds."[66]

The Canadian triumph at Vimy Ridge was not, as some think, the turning point in the war but it was "the turning point…for the Canadian Corps: the point where it moved from an amateur to a professional warfighting force." From this point on, the Canadians "never lost another set-piece or major engagement, delivering victory after victory, and often against the most formidable of defensive positions."[67]

Vimy Ridge was also significant because all four divisions fought together for the first time, which meant that men from all regions of Canada contributed to the victory. For this reason it immediately assumed a profound symbolic significance for Canadians. Percy

Willmot of Sydney wrote that "as the guns spoke, over the bags they went—men of CB [Cape Breton], sons of NS [Nova Scotia] & NB [New Brunswick]—FC's [French Canadians] & westerns—all Canucks."[68] Even eighteen-year-old Winnie McClare, who went into combat for the first time at Vimy Ridge with the 24th Battalion, recognized that the victory "will be one of the biggest things in Canadian history."[69] "Are you not proud to be a Canadian?" asked the *Truro Daily News*.[70] The *Victoria News* was, predicting that April 9 "will be in Canada's history one of the great days, a day of glory to furnish inspiration to her sons for generations."[71]

The cost of glory came high: more than 10,500 casualties, 3,598 of them fatal. According to Tim Cook, the battle of Vimy Ridge was "far more intense and costly than the slaughter on the Somme" and was in fact not only "the single bloodiest day of the entire war for the Canadian Corps" but also the "bloodiest in all of Canadian military history."[72] The cost to Nova Scotia cannot readily be calculated, but it appears to have contributed about 10% to the fatal casualties.[73] As Ralph Lewis said, "The empire bore no braver sons and history will chronicle no greater sacrifices than those of the men of Nova Scotia."[74]

Chapter 6

CONSCRIPTION

Our first duty is to win, at any cost... in order that we may continue to do our part in winning the War and that Canada not be disgraced.[1]

THE SUCCESS OF THE CANADIAN CORPS AT VIMY RIDGE AROUSED enormous pride among Canadians, but it also triggered the manpower crisis that sharply divided the country for the rest of the war. It wasn't just that Vimy Ridge cost more than 14,000 casualties. The problem was that enlistments had been plummeting since the spring of 1916. From 30,000 men per month at the beginning of the year, they were down to fewer than 8,000 by July, and they continued to decline to about 3,000 a month.

Not a single battalion raised anywhere in Canada after July 1916 reached full strength.[2] Casualties for April 1917 totalled almost

24,000 men, against only 4,761 enlistments. In other words, the rate of enlistments was so low that it took more than four months to replace one normal month's losses. That meant that battalions were going into action with as few as 600 or 700 men instead of the nominal 1,000, and wounded men were being returned to their units before they had fully recuperated.

Most Nova Scotians accepted that the war was a necessary and righteous one, but many thought the Borden government's management of it had been partisan and less than competent. Even when it set about to find out how many men were potentially available, it went about it in a less than helpful way. It formed the National Registration Board, appealing to all men to register, but appointed the brilliant but heavy-handed R. B. Bennett of Calgary as its chairman. Thus, the Trades and Labour Council, the national organization that represented organized labour, was neither given representation on the board nor consulted while Bennett called on unions to co-operate, knowing that the TLC opposed conscription unless action was also taken to reign in the large profits being made by businesses engaged in war production.

The government did not strengthen its position when it agreed in September 1916 to provide up to 5,000 men, many of whom would likely come from the Maritime provinces, for service in the Royal Navy. The government had also authorized the Royal Flying Corps and the Royal Naval Air Service to recruit men in Canada and thousands were responding. Meanwhile, the Royal Canadian Navy was advertising in Nova Scotia for "experienced men…and boys" to serve in its coastal patrol vessels.[3] The government seems to have had a problem with prioritization.

The Militia Department then came up with a scheme to create the Canadian Defence Force, inviting men to "serve Canada at home if you cannot go overseas." The goal was to raise forty-seven battalions—50,000 men—among those unwilling or unable to go overseas. Replacing troops engaged in coastal or home defence would enable them to volunteer for overseas service.[4] Despite a vigorous advertising campaign in the newspapers, the scheme was a complete failure: only 1,858 men responded and it was quietly abandoned.

In Nova Scotia, and in other provinces, a Farm Labour Exchange program was developed to encourage men and women in the urban

Fig. 6.1: This unsuccessful appeal for home defence volunteers was published in newspapers on April 9, 1917, the day the Canadian Corps stormed Vimy Ridge.

centres to help the farmers with their harvests. "A few weeks of such work will prove of benefit to the health," the government optimistically claimed.[5] Again, there was not a strong response, although some high-school students did volunteer, assuming that summer jobs were being offered. They weren't, according to young Thomas Raddall, who did respond; he worked hard and returned home with nothing more than the thanks of the farmer for whom he had worked.

Meanwhile, George Campbell was publishing notices in the provincial press urging coal miners to stop enlisting because "the production of coal is so vital to the successful prosecution of the war." He acknowledged that miners had been "among the first to respond to the call for men," but "it was just because of their readiness to drop their picks and go out to fight for their country that such a serious coal situation faces the country to-day." The "most important war service" a miner could provide was to stay home and help to increase coal production, because "every ton of coal you help to raise is helping us to shorten the war and save thousands of lives."[6]

Clearly, there was a manpower crisis, especially since the government was determined to maintain the size of the Canadian Corps. After consulting with British political and military leaders and Arthur Currie, Borden returned home in the spring of 1917 convinced that conscription had become necessary. He made the announcement in the House of Commons on May 18, the same day that the US Congress approved a selective service act. The United States had entered the war a month earlier.

Borden did not justify conscription on the grounds of supporting Britain. Instead, he exploited the public response to the Canadian victory at Vimy Ridge, appealing to Canadian nationalism and the moral imperative to support the men already in the field. "The battle for Canadian liberty and autonomy is being fought today on the plains of France and Belgium," he proclaimed, and conscription was needed not just to maintain the strength of the Canadian Corps but also to keep faith with its members. If they returned to Canada "with fierce resentment in their hearts," feeling that they had been "deserted and betrayed," he asked, "how shall we meet them when they ask the reason?"[7]

Borden knew that conscription would be highly controversial and, therefore, invited the Liberal party to join the Conservatives in a coalition government. He even offered to defer conscription until after the new government was formed. Sir Wilfrid Laurier, the Liberal leader and former prime minister, pondered the dilemma for two weeks before rejecting both conscription and a coalition. His primary concern was the impact on Quebec and national unity, but he also spoke for many Canadians when he argued that conscription might be acceptable if Canada were under attack—actual or threatened—but it was not acceptable to use it to raise troops for an overseas war.

Thus, Laurier and his Quebec followers stayed out of the new "Union" government, which became a coalition of Conservatives and Liberals from English Canada. The new cabinet consisted of fifteen Conservatives, nine Liberals, and one tame labour representative, despite Borden's initial promise to balance the party representation in it. This wasn't necessarily because he didn't want more Liberals.

In Nova Scotia, Borden hoped that Premier Murray would join the government, but he was cautious as always. Murray had two sons overseas and supported both conscription and the coalition but sensed that Union government would be very divisive in Nova Scotia and stayed out.[8] Borden also hoped that W. S. Fielding, who had been premier of Nova Scotia from 1884 to 1896 and Laurier's minister of finance from 1896 to 1911, would join the government. He too refused, although he publicly supported conscription. The result was that Nova Scotia's representation in the government remained what it had been: Borden carried on as prime minister and F. B. McCurdy carried on as parliamentary secretary to the minister of militia and defence. The only change was that A. K. Maclean, a Halifax lawyer, former attorney general in Murray's government, and MP for Halifax since 1911, joined the government as a minister without portfolio.

Murray's political instincts, as usual, were sound. Conscription was highly controversial in Nova Scotia. When the Military Service Act was passed, all of its eight Conservative MPs—Robert Borden, Avard Davidson, Clarence Jameson, F. B. McCurdy, Edgar Rhodes, John Stanfield, Dugald Stewart, and Hadley Tremain—supported it, but only two of its eight Liberal MPs—A. K. Maclean and J. H. Sinclair—did so, while the other six— William F. Carroll, A. W. Chisholm, William Chisholm, George Kyte, E. M. Macdonald, and D. D. McKenzie—opposed it.[9] They remained loyal to Laurier, declaring that they supported the war but not conscription, and especially not any form of coalition with the Conservative party.

There was, as they knew, widespread opposition to conscription in Nova Scotia and many if not most Liberals would never support any kind of union with the Borden Conservatives. Farmers had enlisted at a lower rate than others, and farmers were generally opposed to having their sons conscripted because they were essential labour at a time when the government was appealing to them to boost food production.[10] There is some evidence to suggest that fishermen felt the same way, although historians interested in the conscription issue ignore them. Similarly, organized labour opposed conscription unless wealth was conscripted as well. As James Watters, the president of the Trades and Labour Council, declared, "We…refuse to be sent to the Front to protect profiteers."[11] It was the beginning of a new militancy that would have profound political implications after the war.

Nobody has ever examined the attitude of Nova Scotia's Acadians towards the war and there was no francophone newspaper in the province. A study of New Brunswick Acadians concluded that they generally endorsed Laurier's policy of supporting the war but only on the basis of voluntary enlistment.[12] Neither of that province's two Acadian newspapers supported conscription. *L'Evangeline,* which had the larger circulation and was read by many Nova Scotian Acadians, expressed pride in Acadian enlistments and advised its readers to obey the Military Service Act as they would any other law. Moncton's more outspoken *L'Acadien* opposed conscription even though its owner, P. J. Veniot, had two sons serving overseas.[13]

The situation in Nova Scotia appears to have been very similar. As we have already seen, many of its Acadians enlisted in Nova Scotian and New Brunswick battalions, and they made up a quarter of the 165th Battalion, but they opposed conscription. None of the province's members of Parliament was Acadian and the only prominent Nova Scotian Acadian who supported it was Edward Girroir, a Halifax lawyer who had worked in Robert Borden's law office and briefly represented Antigonish County in the House of Assembly from 1911 to 1912 before being appointed to the Senate. Only one Acadian ran in the 1917 federal election in support of Union government and conscription, and that was Thomas Gallant in Inverness. He was defeated by the Liberal Alex Chisholm, as he had been in 1911.

The Mi'kmaq were largely irrelevant politically because they did not have the franchise unless they had left their reserve and given up their status under the Indian Act. As we have seen, some had volunteered but when it came to conscription, Indigenous leaders across the country believed that their treaties guaranteed they could never be compelled to take up arms against their will. The Military Service Act included them, but under intense pressure the government later recognized their position and exempted them.[14] It is not known how Nova Scotia's black community felt about conscription, but they must have enjoyed appreciated the irony that, not being welcome until 1916, they were now being forced into the army.

The formation of the Union government was followed by an election because the Liberals had already made it clear that they would not agree to a second extension of the life of the Parliament elected in 1911. In Nova Scotia, the election was largely fought on traditional party lines because most Liberals remained loyal to Laurier. At the same time, the formation of a coalition government created "chaos" in the Conservative Party, according to Senator William Dennis. T. P. Calkin, a party organizer agreed with him, warning Borden that "some of our people will go against us."[15] That was because most Conservatives didn't want to coalesce with the Liberals any more than the Liberals wanted to coalesce with them. J. H. Tuck, the only scholar who has seriously examined the 1917 election in Nova Scotia, rightly concluded that instead of uniting men of both parties in a common cause, the formation of the Union government "added another divisive issue to an already long list.... Partyism was as strong as ever."[16]

The Unionist position in the election was clear-cut. The war must be won because of what was at stake and that meant more men were needed. Since not enough were volunteering, they must be conscripted. Anyone who disagreed was disloyal or at best irresponsible. The Liberal position was more complicated and certainly less clear-cut. Most Liberals did not oppose conscription in principle, but they were not yet convinced that the voluntary system had failed. Some were not even convinced that there was a manpower shortage, in view of the thousands of officers and men sitting in England. They blamed declining enlistments on the incompetent management of recruiting and the government's highly partisan management of the whole war effort. As the *Acadian Recorder*, one of the less strident newspapers of the day, said, "there is nothing wrong in principle in compelling the manhood of the nation to defend the nation, but in a democratic state like this, it is incumbent upon those in power to show that the voluntary system has failed. This has not been done."[17] Tuck summed up Liberal policy well when he compared it to Prime Minister W. L. Mackenzie King's position in the Second World War: "conscription if necessary but not necessarily conscription," with the corollary that if it was necessary a Liberal government could manage it more effectively than the Conservatives.[18]

The government knew that it would have difficulty winning an election fought over conscription. Convinced, however, that "our first duty is to win, at any cost,"[19] it rewrote the country's electoral laws to ensure victory. Women were allowed to vote for the first time, but only those with a direct connection to a man who was serving or had served in the armed forces. This was very controversial in Nova Scotia, not just because of the obvious bias, but also because the House of Assembly had just voted down a bill enfranchising women. Enemy aliens who had been naturalized since 1902 were disfranchised except those who had a son serving overseas with the Allies. And anyone exempted from conscription, such as conscientious objectors and members of pacifist churches (Mennonites, for example), were disfranchised.

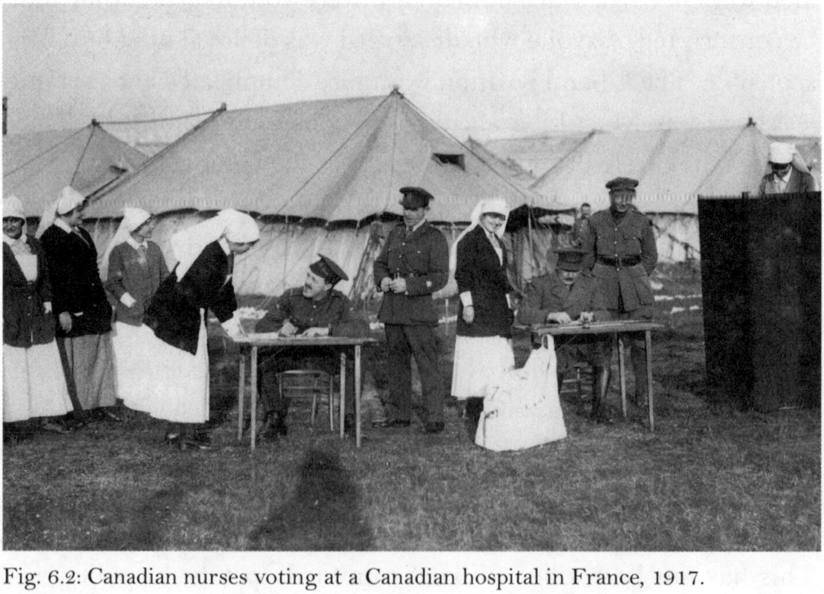

Fig. 6.2: Canadian nurses voting at a Canadian hospital in France, 1917.

At the same time, confident that most of the overseas soldiers favoured conscription, they were given the franchise, even those who didn't normally qualify for it. This included women (nurses), men under the age of twenty-one, and even First Nations soldiers. Overseas soldiers were also given the option of having their votes counted in their home constituency, or if they did not know their constituency they could name any constituency. This meant in effect that they could be influenced by officers to designate their ballots for constituencies in which the government thought they were needed. As the *Antigonish Casket* observed as early as June 1917, the election was beginning to look like "a crooked horse-race."[20]

The campaign began in October and quickly degenerated into increasingly hysterical flag-waving and accusations of disloyalty and cowardice by Conservative politicians and newspapers. They also appealed to anti-Quebec prejudice, blaming the shortage of manpower on disloyal French Canadians, enemy aliens, and so-called slackers. The *Sydney Daily Post*, for example, charged somewhat irrationally that the Liberals were engaged in a "conspiracy against the honor of Canada at the expense of the Canadian soldiers on the firing line" because they sought "to seize the reins of office with the aid of a solid Quebec, of the Germans and Austrians who hold the balance of power in scores of Western constituencies, and of other alien and slacker elements in the community."[21] The *Bridgewater Bulletin*, now displaying a Union Jack on its editorial page, agreed, arguing that disenfranchising "newly naturalized Huns" was reasonable because "the character of the average alien enemy is well-known and he may be depended on to do all in his power to assist the Central Powers and injure the Allies."[22] Other Conservative newspapers expressed similar views.

The Liberal *Lunenburg Progress Enterprise* reminded those who blamed the whole manpower problem on Quebec that conscription would apply to the young men of all provinces, including Nova Scotia, and the *Richmond County Record* suggested that if French

Canadians objected to conscription "it may not be because they are disloyal citizens, but because compulsion in any form is as distasteful to them as it is to hundreds of others in Richmond county, as elsewhere, who are not Frenchmen."[23]

The Unionists had the strong support of the Protestant churches, which denounced Quebec and "the cowards and slackers" in English

THE KAISER—"Well, that just suits me."

THE WAR POLICY SNAIL—SPECIES PARADOXIBUS

Fig. 6.3: "The Kaiser," *Sydney Daily Post*, November 30, 1917. Emotions ran high in Nova Scotia, as elsewhere, over conscription.

Canada.[24] To be fair, the Methodist and Presbyterian churches also called for "the conscription of money and labor and the nationalization of all our national resources and of our public utilities."[25] The Catholic Church held back, endorsing conscription but expressing concern about its impact on national unity. As the Reverend Charles Brewer put it in his study of the Diocese of Antigonish in the war, conscription was "simply the duty of all able Canadian men," although "it would be senseless to win the war...but lose our own country by increasing hatred and prejudice."[26] There were exceptions, however. The Reverend D. M. MacAdam, the priest at Sacred Heart Church in Sydney, asked his parishioners just before voting day how any "intelligent and patriotic Canadian" could not believe that voting against Union government was "a vote against the best interests of Canada and the Empire."[27]

The Unionist campaign was conveniently reinforced by the highly publicized activities of the Win the War League, a women's organization. Formed officially to support the war effort, its members actually campaigned for the Unionists and the extension of the franchise to female relatives of soldiers. A meeting held in Baddeck on November 16, for example, adopted a resolution approving the extension of the franchise "to the mothers, wives, sisters and daughters of those who have placed their services on the altar of their country's need" and welcoming to the meeting "those representatives of their sex who by their presence here indicate that they intend taking up the fiery cross and carrying on the good work so nobly begun by their dear ones overseas."[28] The use of terms like "altar" and "fiery cross" resonated powerfully in Celtic communities.

The Unionist campaign benefited also by the fact that the annual Victory Bond sales campaign was taking place at the same time. This resulted in patriotic ads in all the newspapers—paid for by the government, of course—and supportive editorials reminding people that "every Victory Bond you buy is a blow struck for freedom."[29] Meanwhile, the Red Cross, IODE, and Canadian Patriotic Fund were all engaged in fundraising for their war work.

Another significant factor in the election that tends to be ignored was the presence by late 1917 of large numbers of returned veterans. There were so many, indeed, that they had formed the Great War Veterans' Association in April 1917 to represent them in dealing with government. Its first president was Willard Purney, a Conservative lawyer from Liverpool who had joined the 25th Battalion as a captain but soon came home. Not surprisingly, the GWVA pledged its full support for Union government. The Halifax branch of the GWVA, which had hundreds of members, appealed to voters to vote only for those candidates "whose pledge is to send immediate reinforcements to their comrades in the trenches."[30] Norman McLeod Rogers, a returned soldier, reminded people that "as we vote on election day the Canadian Corps is watching; and over in France remember there are those who will not sleep if you break faith with those who die."[31] Similarly, some one hundred veterans being treated at the Nova Scotia Sanatorium in Kentville, a tuberculosis hospital used to treat soldiers whose lungs had been badly damaged by poison gas, issued an appeal "to all parties to drop politics and to get together to win the war and to send reinforcements immediately."[32]

Some overseas soldiers did what they could to influence the election as well. Major J. L. Ralston of the 85th Battalion sent a telegram expressing the hope that Nova Scotians would "heavily support" conscription.[33] This was significant because Ralston, an Amherst lawyer, was also a Liberal member of the House of Assembly. Major Arthur Léger, the commanding officer of the 165th (Acadian) Battalion, also publicly endorsed conscription.[34] More impressively, thirty-one overseas soldiers from Victoria County sent a telegram to the *Victoria News* of Baddeck, stating that "we rely on our friends at home to back our bullets with their ballots."[35]

There was no doubt that they represented the views of most of the soldiers serving overseas. They had been complaining since as early as November 1914 about how many men they knew who should and could be overseas. Keith Rogers of Yarmouth, for example, acknowledged that "no doubt many of the men at home cannot come to the front, but there are unquestionably many...whose duty is to be here."[36] Manley Rafuse hoped in July 1915 that more Yarmouth boys would "get up courage and come. If we all got afraid and stayed at home what would become of us?"[37] Harold Aulenback of Maitland, Lunenburg County, wondered "what they will be able to say when this great war is over and somebody asks them what they did in the great war. I think it is the place of every young man who is fit to go to the front to volunteer right away."[38] Gerald Cragg, son of the owner of the *Bridgewater Bulletin*, hoped in November 1915 that conscription would not be necessary in Canada, "although I know of plenty that could come and they certainly will feel ashamed of themselves afterwards or when it is too late."[39]

When conscription was introduced, Patrick Whyte of North Sydney wondered sarcastically "if the boys who attend the dances" realized that there was a war on. "I'm not one who would ever ask anybody to enlist," he said, but "we would appreciate a rest just now" and "surely they must hear the cry of their schoolmates 'Come and help us hold the line.'"[40] Others like Winnie McClare of Mount Uniacke wrote to relatives and friends privately, telling them how wounded men were being returned to the front before they were fully recuperated.[41]

Wilburn Wallace of Truro felt the same way, noting that "there are some boys...that could come, but won't, [so] this new law will make them take notice."[42] Ira Moore of Oxford complained that "there are so many slackers hanging around Nova Scotia. It ought to bring shame to some fellows [*sic*] *faces to think they are not here helping to push these half human devils back.*"[43] Clarence Smith of Lunenburg hoped the Union government would "have a victory from shore to shore, and then the Kaiser will tremble and get scared when he knows that the Allies have men and money and that Canada has the best men from both sides of Politics with her."[44] Frank McGregor of Baddeck told his father that all the men overseas thought conscription was "a good thing" because "some of the able bodied chaps who are winning the war with their mouths will get a chance to come and see what it looks like in France."[45]

Others, however, struggled with the issue. Donald Reid of Middle Musquodoboit confessed he didn't know how to vote. He thought conscription was necessary "but I hope it will not touch any of our family....I hate to see any more boys come over but I guess it is the only way."[46] Two days later, Reid confirmed that he would vote for conscription, "but if I thought Gow or Ken would have to come I would not because I think there have been enough of us over here. This is just right to rout out the slackers as I think there are quite a number."[47]

George MacKinlay of Berwick did not believe in conscription, "but still I have voted for the Government. In one sense we don't want it as it is taking away the greatest thing we have, in fact what we are fighting for, our Liberty." But "we want reinforcements[48] and the more we get the easier it will be on us; the more leave we will get and above all the more rest." Besides, "any man with any reasonable excuse can get exemption, so it will only serve to root out a lot of slackers who should have come anyway."[49] Eighteen-year-old Ludlow Weeks of Wolfville, who was at Witley with the artillery, was more cynical. Writing on December 6, he told his sister they had been "very well fed" during the "the last couple of weeks...but the reason was simple. This week is election week and the gov't wanted every one to vote for it. I guess about everybody did. I did anyway."[50]

IT UNDOUBTEDLY DID NOT HURT THE UNIONIST CAUSE EITHER that the Canadian Corps was engaged in the horrendous fighting at Passchendaele during the election campaign. This battle was part of what was officially known as the Third Battle of Ypres but was actually a series of battles in which the British sought control of the ridges south and east of Ypres. The Germans were pushed back to Passchendaele Ridge, where Eric Bent earned the Victoria Cross at Polygon Wood. Bent was born in Halifax but had moved to Scotland as a child with his parents. When the war broke out, he joined the Leicestershire Regiment and was commanding its 9th Battalion as a temporary lieutenant colonel when he was killed on October 1 while leading his men. A few days later, the Canadian and Australian Corps were brought in to capture both the ridge and the village. Their starting point was virtually the same line the Canadians had defended more than two years earlier, before the first gas attacks at the Second Battle of Ypres in April 1915.

Arthur Currie questioned the wisdom of the assault, calculating that it would cost 16,000 casualties for an objective that was not very important. Haig—who had not even sent any of his staff officers to evaluate the situation—overruled him, of course. Currie, therefore, planned carefully as he had done at Vimy Ridge, making sure that he had ample supplies and enough artillery support, and preparing his troops thoroughly.

Even so, Will Bird of Amherst, who was there with the 42nd Battalion, complained that "the whole affair was cockeyed. We were new in the sector. None knew the terrain. None knew what defences the German had or his strength. The place after dark was a swampy wilderness with nothing to use as a guide."[51] And it rained continuously. John Angus MacNeil of Inverness later recalled that "it wasn't raining—it was pouring down," and "more people drowned in the shell-holes than were killed by the bullets."[52] John William MacVicar of Glace Bay later recalled that "we were in bog to our knees, and the machine gun fire and shelling was something awful."[53]

Part of the horror at Passchendaele was that the Germans used mustard gas for the first time. Of the three forms of poison gas used during the war—chlorine, phosgene, and mustard—it was the most insidious and excruciating because it caused terrible pain and could take as long as a month to kill its victims. Elkanah Clements of Yarmouth told his father that the 85th "walked through nearly three miles [five kilometres] of gas with our gas masks on," and "I...got some gas in my lungs...and it left me with a bad cough and I have lost quite a few pounds since."[54] Clements was soon sent home, developed tuberculosis in his damaged lungs, and died in the Kentville sanatorium in July 1918.

After two weeks of ferocious fighting, Passchendaele was taken on November 6. James Peter Robertson earned his Victoria Cross that day. Born in Stellarton, he had moved with his family to Medicine Hat, Alberta, where he was a miner. He had enlisted in June 1915 and served overseas in the 27th Battalion. On November 6, when his platoon was being held up by barbed wire and a German machine gun, he found an opening on the flank and rushed the gun. He killed four of its crew, then turned the gun on the others, enabling his platoon to continue its advance. Later, when two of his unit's snipers were wounded in front of their trench, he went out and carried one of them in while under fire. He went back and brought in the other man as well, but was killed by a bursting shell.

By the tenth, the Canadians held all the high ground northeast of the town. Newspapers at home hailed the achievement as yet another triumph of the Canadian Corps, confirming that it had become "much the most effective in the BEF," and Currie was emerging as "the most effective commander in the British Army."[55] The overall offensive had failed, however, and as Denis Winter has pointed out, the British and German forces had sustained a half million casualties on a front just seven miles [about eleven kilometres] wide, more killing per square metre than any other battle in the entire war.[56]

Among them were nearly 16,000 Canadians, including about seventy-four killed and an estimated 130 wounded in the 25th Battalion. The 85th sustained 148 killed and another 280 wounded, including Major Percy Anderson, the battalion's hero of Vimy Ridge, and Robert Borden, a young cousin of the prime minister.

The 85th's entire pipe band, whose members had gone in as stretcher bearers, was wiped out.

William Ross, one of those who did survive, described the scene when Lieutenant Colonel Allison Borden arrived the next day to find there were only sixty-five survivors to greet him. "Where are the rest of them?" he asked. "This is all of them, Colonel, this is all that is left of the 85th," Major Ralston replied "in a voice that was

Fig. 6.4: James Peter Robertson earned the Victoria Cross at Passchendaele, rushing a German machine gun and rescuing wounded men before being killed.

not too steady. For a few minutes Borden sat frozen in his saddle, speechless. Without a word he turned his horse's head around, and moved off at a walk."[57]

Canadians celebrated Passchendaele as another great victory, and in view of the fact that the overall Ypres offensive was a disastrous failure, it was. But as Robert Clements later recalled, "there was not any feeling of glorious achievement or particular satisfaction among the men."[58] Will Bird added that no man who survived Passchendaele would ever be the same.[59] Nor did they forget. The survivors of the 85th built a monument at Passchendaele to commemorate their fallen comrades but, more poignantly, the community around Dominion No. 3 and No. 11 collieries on the edge of Glace Bay was renamed Passchendaele.

British Prime Minister David Lloyd George, who had no respect for Haig and had opposed the offensive, described the Ypres offensive as a "senseless campaign" and "one of the greatest disasters of the war."[60] It was worse than that: it was the inevitable result of misinformation and poor planning. When Haig's chief of staff, Lieutenant General Launcelot Kiggell, visited the area after the battle he was genuinely appalled by the sea of mud littered with corpses and is reported to have burst into tears, asking "Good God, did we really send men to fight in that?"[61]

Undeterred, the ever-confident Haig launched another offensive on November 20, this one against Cambrai, a French city just west of Arras and about seventy-two kilometres south of Ypres. It was a key supply centre for the German Hindenburg Line, which the Allies could threaten by capturing the nearby Bourlon Ridge, and unlike the Ypres sector it was not a mass of mud. This was significant because Haig intended the infantry to be supported by more than 400 tanks and hundreds of aircraft, in addition to the usual artillery bombardment.

The attack on Cambrai was also ill conceived, because tanks alone could not win a battle and Haig had only five infantry divisions available. He knew they were not enough, however, and planned to use the Cavalry Corps if necessary. This meant that, while most of the Canadian Corps did not participate in the battle, the Canadian Cavalry Brigade—made up of the Royal Canadian Dragoons, Lord Strathcona's Horse, and the Fort Garry Horse—did because it was part of the British 5th Cavalry Division.

The assault began well as the tanks crushed the barbed wire and reached the German trenches, but by the end of the first day about half of them were out of commission from shellfire or mechanical problems. The British did succeed in taking Bourlon Ridge and Bourlon Wood, but the Germans naturally counterattacked. At this point the Cavalry Corps launched an old-fashioned cavalry charge against entrenched German machine guns and artillery. The Fort Garry Horse participated in this remarkable if foolhardy episode and paid a high price for the honour: of the 133 cavalrymen who took part in it, only forty-six lived to tell the tale. One of those who did not survive was John Gould of Steam Mill Village. He had enlisted in the 40th Battalion at the age of seventeen, then for some reason was transferred into the Fort Garry Horse. The sacrifice was not only foolish; it was ultimately pointless as well because the British were unable to capture Cambrai, although they did gain some ground. The effort cost them 44,000 men, to the Germans' 41,000. An offensive intended to restore confidence in Haig's leadership actually was a costly failure that "devastated British morale like no other setback of the war."[62]

THE BREATHLESS NEWSPAPER REPORTS OF THE GALLANTRY AND sacrifices of the Canadian Corps that autumn were hugely beneficial to the Unionist election campaign. The almost hysterical call to support the troops became more shrill and Liberals were denounced with ever greater vigour. Even so, in the final weeks of the campaign, the government recognized that opposition to conscription remained deep-seated in rural areas, so the minister of militia and defence announced that farmers' sons and experienced farm labourers would not be conscripted. He also promised to review the cases of farmers whose applications for exemption had been denied.

It has been claimed that the exemption extended to fishermen as well. Certainly the *Lunenburg Progress Enterprise* argued that it should because fishermen were just as important as farmers to the production of food. The conscription of fishermen "would mean disaster for those for whom it would be intended to help."[63] Some Unionist politicians in Nova Scotia claimed that the exemption for farmers did apply to fishermen as well but Mewburn made no reference to fishermen and there is no evidence to indicate that it applied to them.

The Unionists initially hoped Conservatives and pro-conscription Liberals would join together and agree on common candidates so that they could be elected by acclamation. This was vital in Nova Scotia because in the 1911 election the two parties had evenly split the province's seats in Parliament and the provincial government had been Liberal since 1882. A complicating factor was that parliamentary seats had been redistributed since 1911, and Nova Scotia's representation had been reduced from eighteen members representing sixteen constituencies to sixteen members representing fourteen constituencies.[64]

Acclamations were achieved in Shelburne and Queens and Colchester Counties, both of which had been won by Conservatives in 1911. Shelburne and Queens was Fielding's old seat, but he had been defeated in 1911 by F. B. McCurdy, Borden's chief organizer in Nova Scotia. Fielding was prepared to return to Parliament as an independent supporter of conscription, but only if he could have his old seat back. McCurdy naturally didn't want to step down, however, and Borden had to intervene personally. McCurdy was persuaded to yield to Fielding, and since the local Liberals regarded his support for the new government as lukewarm at best, they joined with the Conservatives to give him the seat by acclamation. John Stanfield now stood down in Colchester, making his seat available to McCurdy.[65] A Laurier Liberal did run against McCurdy but withdrew just before polling day, giving McCurdy his acclamation.

The other fourteen seats were contested. Most—Antigonish-Guysborough, Cumberland, Digby-Annapolis, Hants, Inverness, Lunenburg, Kings, North Cape Breton and Victoria, Pictou, and Yarmouth and Clare—were relatively straightforward contests between Unionists and Liberals. Others, however, were more complicated. In Halifax, a two-seat constituency, the Unionists ran a Conservative and a Unionist Liberal against an anti-conscriptionist Liberal and a labour candidate. In Cape Breton South-Richmond, also a two-seat constituency, the Unionists ran J. C. Douglas and R. H. Butts, both of whom were Conservative members of the House of Assembly, against the two Liberal incumbents, William Carroll and George Kyte, but the miners ran two labour candidates as well.

One constituency of particular interest was Yarmouth and Clare, which was the old Yarmouth constituency with the addition of Clare, formerly part of the Digby constituency. Combining Digby and Annapolis benefited the Unionists as both had elected Conservatives in 1911. Adding Clare to Yarmouth made no difference because Yarmouth had elected Liberals since 1869, and Clare was expected to vote Liberal because it was an Acadian community. The seat had been vacant since Bowman Law's death in 1916 and the Unionists sensibly agreed to support Edgar Spinney, a pro-conscription Liberal. But the Liberals in Clare ran J. W. Comeau, an Acadian who was a Laurier Liberal, so Yarmouth and Clare had the unique experience of a contest between two Liberals.

In the end, the Unionists won two seats in Nova Scotia by acclamation but only three of the twelve contested seats: Digby-Annapolis, Kings, and Yarmouth and Clare. In other words, while the Conservatives had won nine of eighteen seats in 1911, the

Unionists won only five of fourteen. They received two more by acclamation when the results came in from Halifax in January, where voting had been postponed because of the explosion. There the two Liberals stood down, allowing A. K. Maclean and Peter Martin, who was already mayor of Halifax, to be acclaimed. That gave the Unionists half of the province's fourteen seats, precisely what they had won in 1911, i.e., nine of eighteen.

But their share of the popular vote fell from 49% in 1911 to 44%, while the Liberal share rose to 49%. Clearly, Nova Scotians were not overwhelmingly in favour of Union government and conscription. As Laurier told E. M. Macdonald, "In the long list of disasters, Nova Scotia is the bright spot and, indeed, our success in your Province constitutes the sheet anchor upon which we must build our future hopes."[66]

He spoke too soon, because the overseas soldiers' votes still had to be counted, and everyone knew that most of them would be in favour of conscription. The government wasn't about to take any chances, however. It went to considerable lengths to make sure those who would vote the right way did vote, while trying to discourage from voting those who might not vote the right way. There was no pretence at impartiality. Clarence Mackinnon later recalled that "in spite of an agreement that no propaganda should be used on either side" among the overseas soldiers, he saw "a large placard" in a YMCA tent proclaiming, "'A vote for the Government means that another man will take your place. A vote for the Opposition means that you stay here for the rest of your life.'"[67]

Borden initially delegated Sir George Perley, the London-based minister of overseas forces, to manage the overseas soldiers' vote, but when he displayed little initiative Borden assigned the task to Willard Purney, the Conservative lawyer from Liverpool who was now president of the Great War Veterans' Association. Purney was promoted to lieutenant colonel and sent back to Europe to help manage the election in Britain and Flanders.

Borden also designated Hector McInnes, the prominent Halifax corporation lawyer who had organized the Conservative election campaign in Nova Scotia in 1911, to manage the voting among the province's overseas soldiers. McInnes found willing assistants among the many surplus Canadian officers in England, most of whom were Conservatives. Prominent among them was Dr. Joseph Hayes, a Halifax physician better known as an active Conservative organizer who had run in the 1916 provincial election even though he had already joined the 85th Battalion as its medical officer. His assignment was to organize the Nova Scotian soldiers' vote in England.

To make their task a little easier, the government promised to maintain the 5th Division, which had been sitting in England since February 1917 despite the shortage of recruits, promised a furlough to Canada for all soldiers who had gone overseas in the First Contingent, and guaranteed exemption from conscription to brothers or sons of men serving overseas.

If overseas soldiers did not designate the constituency to which their vote should be assigned, their officers or returning officers in Ottawa could allocate their ballots on their behalf. Needless to say, these would be distributed to constituencies in which the Unionist candidate needed help. Hayes was confident that he could deliver a couple of hundred votes to each of the seven Nova Scotian constituencies expected to need help, and frankly explained to F. B. McCurdy how it was done: "Many OC's [commanding officers] lined their men up and told them plainly what they wanted them to do as a matter of duty....Also many of the Chaplains took the stump and gave 10 minute addresses before the curtain at the shows each night."[68] There is evidence that in at least some cases officers actually voted on behalf of their men. When some of the bags containing the ballots of overseas soldiers were opened by the scrutineers in London, they were found to contain "tightly rolled bundles of envelopes," indicating that they had been packed en masse.[69]

Unionist candidates were counting on these votes. Edgar Rhodes did not expect to win the civilian vote in Cumberland but knew that the overseas vote would give him "a substantial majority."[70] Six days before the election he sent a telegram to Major Harold Daly at Unionist election headquarters, asking him to "try to arrange three hundred undesignated votes for Cumberland, Urgently needed."[71] According to W. T. R. Preston, admittedly a highly partisan Liberal party organizer, a bag of ballots from the Canadian ordnance depot at Ashford, England, was "wholly directed" to Cumberland County. Rhodes's brother-in-law allegedly commanded the depot.[72]

Hayes later told Rhodes that McInnes had only designated Digby-Annapolis, Hants, Lunenburg, and Pictou as constituencies needing attention.

> *The inference, of course, was that all the other seats were sure or hopeless. I knew, however, that the contest would be close in Cape Breton South and Richmond, and before getting any definite word, I lined up a number of units to turn their loose votes in to that constituency.*[73]

The overseas soldiers' votes changed the results in four Nova Scotian constituencies involving five seats: Cape Breton South-Richmond (two seats), Cumberland, Hants, and Pictou. That doubled the Unionist victories from five seats to ten and reduced the Liberals from nine to four. When the Halifax results came in, giving those two seats by acclamation, the Unionists ended up with twelve seats, compared to four for the Liberals. As Desmond Morton has said, "McCurdy, McInnes, and Hayes had not laboured in vain."[74]

Although there is no doubt that the overseas soldiers' votes were manipulated to improve the election results, it seems impossible to grasp the rationale behind how they were distributed. Some Unionist candidates, like Borden in Kings, A. L. Davidson in Digby-Annapolis, and Edgar Spinney in Yarmouth and Clare didn't need any extra votes but received 566, 805, and 541 respectively. Others, like J. C. Douglas and R. H. Butts in Cape Breton South-Richmond, Edgar Rhodes in Cumberland, and Alex McGregor in Pictou, were given far more votes than they needed. Yet others—J. A. Wells in Antigonish-Guysborough, John McCormick in North Cape Breton and Victoria, and J. W. Margeson in Lunenburg—received hundreds of soldier votes but not enough to affect the results.[75]

J. H. Tuck was probably correct when he concluded that the allocation of the soldiers' votes "was conducted on a hit or miss basis, which seems to have depended as much on the apprehensions, influence or dislikes of Conservative Unionist politicians as upon any accurate appraisal of need."[76] In any event, the end result was that, even including the soldiers' votes, traditional voting patterns "were largely followed in 1917," at least in Nova Scotia.

The Unionist victory—152 seats to 82 for the Laurier Liberals—did not end the conscription crisis. Those most affected by the application of the Military Service Act—the men being conscripted—very quickly made clear their opposition to the legislation. As was the case elsewhere in the country, the vast majority of those called up applied for exemption.[77] This led the pro-conscription *Sydney Daily Post* to conclude that, "when upwards of 95 per cent of the persons reporting from one district after another only do so to urge excuses against service, it is manifest that there is an enormous proportion of slackers among them."[78]

That wasn't quite fair. Many of the men claiming exemption in the Sydney and New Glasgow areas were miners and steelworkers, whose employment was considered essential to the war effort. In fact, the government had appealed to the miners in April not to enlist because "every ton of coal you help to raise is helping to shorten the war, and save thousands of lives."[79] Curiously, however, the government had not granted a general exemption for miners, so the companies now applied for one and some 2,500 men were exempted without having to apply individually.[80]

Many other men, as the *Daily Post* observed with tongue firmly planted in cheek, appeared to be victims of "an epidemic of rheumatism which settles in the back." As well, "quite a number" of aliens applied for exemption "on various grounds. They try to explain, with much waving of hands, that they 'don't want to fight,'" prompting the *Daily Post*'s editor to observe that they were not averse to "unlawfully shedding blood—on pay nights."[81] When 287 men applied for exemption in Antigonish, the *Casket* concluded more moderately that "all [men] of military age in Category A who could at all be spared, [had] enlisted previously."[82]

The exemption tribunals, on which the *Daily Post* relied to sort things out, granted exemptions liberally, but those who had their claims rejected could appeal right up to Justice Lyman Duff of the Supreme Court, who had been appointed the ultimate arbiter. Some 42,000 men from all across Canada did appeal their cases to him, and he exempted most farmers and their sons because the government had promised during the election campaign to do so. He also exempted Catholic novices in holy orders but not Protestant divinity students. Conscientious objectors such as Mennonites and Doukhobors were exempted, while members of other groups such as Jehovah's Witnesses, to whom pacifism was not a core belief, were not. In January 1918 the government amended the legislation to exempt First Nations men, although at least one Mi'kmaw man, Austin Labrador of Shelburne, was conscripted in June 1918.

Many men failed even to register and were therefore classified as defaulters. Figures released after the war revealed that the percentage of men who failed to register ranged from a low of 4.6% in London, Ontario, to a high of 25.8% in Montreal. Halifax was in the middle range at 15.0%, in good company with Toronto at 13.8% and Vancouver at 15.8% per cent.[83]

Defaulters were pursued and, if caught, arrested. This understandably created problems, and not just in Quebec. In June 1918 military police, some of them allegedly "under the influence of intoxicants and in no way fit to attend to their duties,"[84] arrived in the town of Lunenburg looking for defaulters. Whether this was motivated by the fact that the community had a high default rate, or because most people there were of German ancestry, or because they had elected an anti-conscription Member of Parliament in the recent election, is unknown.

In any event, on Saturday, the fifteenth, they arrested Austin Knickle, a father of twelve children. Then they took Allan Weaver, a fisherman, from his vessel in Lunenburg Harbour and demanded to see his marriage certificate, which entailed a 6.5-kilometre walk to his home in Blue Rocks. Greville Knickle was "taken off his truck and ordered, at the point of a revolver, to produce his papers." As Agnes McGuire, the editor of the *Progress Enterprise* pointed out, "A question to any bystander would establish the identity of any of these men, but that would be acting like a rational being." On Monday, an American was arrested on Smith's Wharf despite the fact that he had a certificate from the US consul in Liverpool, and another man "who was doing absolutely nothing" was also arrested. On Tuesday a man was ordered to present his papers, and when he said they were on his vessel and started to go for them, the police officer "drew his revolver" and took him to jail. "After much trouble the captain had him liberated." Later that afternoon they arrested another man, and when J. B. Young, a well-known shipowner, asked why, "one of the policemen immediately drew a revolver and threatened to shoot Mr. Young" but only arrested him. He also warned the crowd that had gathered that "if any one interfered he would shoot him dead."[85]

Meanwhile, the government finally made the logical but politically difficult decision to break up the 5th Division, which had been sitting in England for months, making 21,000 officers and men immediately available to reinforce the Canadian Corps. As Currie well knew, Canada could not sustain five divisions in the field, and he strongly opposed the British policy of reducing the number of battalions in divisions to make the army seem larger than it actually was. Perley agreed with him and eventually Borden did too, so in February 1918 the 5th was finally dissolved. For Nova Scotia, this meant that the 185th Battalion, which had survived the breakup of the Highland Brigade because it had been attached to the 5th Division, was finally disbanded. As the division's historian has said, "Political expediency [had] led to its formation, the appointment of its commander, its continued survival in the face of Canadian manpower shortages, and finally to its eventual disbandment."[86]

It wasn't enough. When Germany launched Operation Michael, its last major offensive, in March 1918 and broke through the Allied lines, the need for reinforcements became more urgent even than it had seemed and the government cancelled the exemption for farmers' sons. Outrage spread throughout rural Canada, making it clear that any farmers who had supported conscription had actually voted to conscript other people's sons, not their own. Farmers from all across the country organized rallies, signed petitions, and lobbied the politicians. Trainloads of them converged on Ottawa and rallied in front of Parliament, where they pounded on the locked doors, demanding that Borden come out and face them. He did meet with them but didn't back down.

Since the government had just won a comfortable majority in the 1917 election, there was nothing the farmers could do except to express their outrage. But having concluded that they could no longer trust any politicians because the Union government was a coalition of Liberals and Conservatives, they began to organize with a view to electing farmers to represent rural Canada outside of the party system. The result over the next three years was a political revolution that saw provincial governments toppled by informal coalitions of farmers and urban workers that in some cases didn't even have a leader.

In Nova Scotia, the Murray government survived the 1920 provincial election, losing only two seats, but the farmer-labour candidates won eleven seats, reducing the discredited Conservatives to only three seats. When the next federal election came in 1921, the Liberals returned to power but with only a plurality of seats, while the new Progressive Party, representing farmers and organized labour, came second. The Conservatives came a pathetic third. More significantly, the two-party system had come to an end and a new era had dawned in Canadian politics.

In view of the profound political, religious, and ethnic divisions that had been aroused in the country, and the fact that for the first time in its history a Canadian government had actually forced men to fight in an overseas war, what had been achieved? The government had succeeded in raising 100,000 men with conscription—well, 99,561 to be precise—but only 47,509 of them went overseas and only half of them—24,132—joined battalions in France. That suggests that conscription had not been necessary, but to be fair, political leaders like Lloyd George and Borden were assuming in 1917 that the war would continue into 1919 if not beyond. Even if it had, however, would another 100,000 Canadians really have made a difference, given that the United States had entered the war and would soon provide literally millions of troops?

Chapter 7

THE HOME FRONT

Two weeks ago this land was happy in its feeling of happiness, summer brooded over the land, and everything was peace. But how different now.[1]

On the afternoon of August 13, 1914, Mrs. H. H. Lane hosted a "delightful afternoon tea" at her home in New Glasgow. This in itself was not unusual, but what "gave especial pleasure to her guests" was that each of the dishes of ice cream served displayed a tiny British flag. "The pretty compliment took the members by surprise and each member wore her flag home as a souvenir of a particularly happy occasion."[2]

It was a trivial if charming little event, of no real significance except that it suggests the innocence of the age. Many people, in Nova Scotia and elsewhere in Canada, assumed that the war was going to be like earlier imperial wars: far-off affairs to which Canadians would contribute, but of no great significance in the lives of most people. They soon learned that this war was different, in both magnitude and ferocity. It was, in fact, the first modern war that impacted those at home almost as much as those who served overseas.

As we have seen, the first concern was coastal defence. The second was economic. Would the war stimulate the sluggish economy of 1914 or depress it further, creating more unemployment? The initial impact was not encouraging. Banks raised their lending rates and commodity prices immediately rose, a reflection in both cases of the uncertainty about the war's impact on the financial markets and international trade.

W. H. Schwartz & Sons, the Halifax spice merchants, announced on August 6 that they would have to "advance our prices to a war basis" because "it will be impossible to get supplies, only at risk of capture and greatly advanced cost, freight and insurance." But they assured their customers that their products would maintain the same high quality as usual, if that was any consolation.[3] Hugh Mackenzie, the Halifax coal merchant, waited a couple of weeks before raising his prices "owing to the advance in Freights and extra Marine Insurance."[4]

A month later, however, twenty Halifax merchants—including Mackenzie—published a notice promising that they would try "to carry on our business with the least margin of profit possible," because any merchant "who attempts to defraud the public at a crisis such as this is as much a traitor to his flag as the man who sells the plans of a fortress."[5]

Merchant's Department Store in Sydney took a different approach. It ran a large tongue-in-cheek ad on August 7 proclaiming:

GOD SAVE THE KING
WAR DECLARED
On Prices at Merchant's Store

General Clearance With an Army of Well
Trained Clerks Attacks The Enemy,
Original Price, Resulting in
Awful Bloodshed.
Reinforcements are Arriving Every Hour.
Come and Join the Ranks of Patriotic
Bargain Hunters in Our
Store. Bombard Original
Prices with Dollar Bills.
Make Them Prisoners of War and March
Away Happy and Victorious.
Britons Never Shall Be Slaves![6]

Clever as it was, this ad reflected the naïve innocence of August 1914. Within a few months it would likely have been regarded as tasteless.

Others sought to profit from the situation too, but not so innocently. Political patronage was a big part of life at this time and many politicians, following the example set by Sam Hughes, carried on as usual. H. E. LeVatte, the warden of Cape Breton County, asked Major A. E. Carpenter, who commanded the Royal Canadian Regiment troops in Cape Breton in August 1914 "if supplies, etc., required for Militia purposes in Cape Breton can be purchased from the public at large, or if it [*sic*] can only be purchased on the advice of certain people in each community." Carpenter, somewhat surprisingly, albeit honestly, responded that "supplies are supposed to be purchased from friends of the political party in power, so long as their prices do not exceed current market rates."[7]

This was actually a reasonable interpretation of patronage policy in 1914, but it soon became clear that the sudden flood of government money for war supplies was creating too much temptation. The biggest scandal, at least in Nova Scotia, involved the purchase of horses for the First Contingent. Approximately 8,000 horses were needed and about 600 of them were purchased in Nova Scotia. Unfortunately, some were too old or infirm to be of any use.

The explanation for this was not hard to find. Instead of sending qualified men to buy the horses, Arthur Foster, the Conservative MP for Kings County and a teacher by profession, was authorized to handle the purchases on the mainland, while Lieutenant Colonel Harvey MacLeod and Major Walter Crowe were in charge in Cape Breton. Foster purchased 428 horses, many of which were among the aged or ill ones. When the scandal broke in the House of Commons, Borden insisted that no one in the government knew of or had approved Foster's appointment.[8] This was probably technically true because the government had appointed Sir Adam Beck, a prominent Ontario Conservative politician, to purchase the horses in eastern Canada.

Borden eventually appointed a royal commission to investigate the situation. It concluded—but not until 1917—that there had indeed been corruption in the purchasing of horses but that it was not Foster's fault because he had not personally purchased them. He was guilty only of being "weak in administration and grievously so in financial supervision and methods."[9] By this time he had already resigned his seat in Parliament and been appointed superintendent of the Canadian National Railway's Colonization Department.

The scandals related to military supplies were not confined to horses. Others involved the purchase of cheaply made army boots that fell apart when they got wet and the purchase of unsuitable wagons. The *Eastern Chronicle* charged in April 1915 that "not a dollar...is being paid out without some one getting a rake off" in the "shameless carnival of graft...in Canada since the war broke out."[10] Adding insult to injury, at least in Amherst, was the fact that the Amherst Boot & Shoe Company had donated "good, solid and serviceable" boots to the Cumberland County volunteers, which the 17th Battalion's Major Daniel Murray claimed "were...as near waterproof as could be expected of leather."[11]

These were, perhaps, the relatively minor hiccups that might be expected of a government and society still thinking in terms of pre-war values and practices. When it became evident that this was going to be a long war that would be won or lost as much by ability of nations to produce vast quantities of steel, coal, armaments, and munitions as by battles fought by armies, Nova Scotian businessmen wasted no time in seeking contracts.

Indeed, the war was a godsend to the province's industrialists. Nova Scotia Steel, Dominion Steel, and the Rhodes Curry Company, all major national enterprises, were struggling in the summer of 1914 because the economy was in recession. Scotia shut down its steel mill in Sydney Mines, Dominion laid off hundreds of workers, and Rhodes Curry shut down its railway car factory. This resulted in layoffs in the coal mines. Then, when the war broke out, Scotia also stopped work at its iron mines at Wabana because much of that ore was sold to Germany, and that market was obviously gone. As it happened, more than 7,000 tons of ore that had already been sold did reach Germany after the outbreak of war, but that wasn't Scotia's fault.[12]

One small Nova Scotian manufacturer was doing quite well in 1914, however. The Canada Tool and Specialty Company in Pictou County had the exclusive contract (because it owned the patent) to manufacture sights for the Ross rifle, the weapon used by the Canadian militia. The company was owned by a group of local investors headed by R. H. MacKay, a New Glasgow businessman and politician. Scotia, Dominion, and Rhodes Curry did not immediately benefit from the war but Canada Tool did, and by April 1915 it was producing 800 sights a day.[13] This proved to be a short-term bonanza, however, because the Ross, while an excellent rifle for target shooting, hunting, or casual militia use, was entirely unsuitable for use in wartime, especially in the muddy conditions of the Western Front. When it was replaced in 1916 by the British Lee-Enfield rifle, Canada Tool lost its major customer.[14]

The first Nova Scotian companies—aside from Canada Tool—to receive government contracts were the textile mills for plain cotton, canvas, and military clothing. The province had a significant textile industry at this time that included the Nova Scotia Cotton Manufacturing Company, one of Halifax's largest employers, the Clayton and Sons factory, described in 1906 as "the leading wholesale clothing house of Eastern Canada,"[15] the Nova Scotia Knitting Company, the Stanfield textile factory, and the Cosmos Cotton Company.

Clayton and Sons received a large contract for greatcoats; the Nova Scotia Knitting Company in Eureka and the Stanfield mill in Truro both received contracts for underwear; and the Cosmos Cotton Company in Yarmouth received a large contract for canvas. When the Eureka mill burned down in October 1914, the company moved its operations into the former Windsor Cotton Company building, which had been vacant since 1912, enticed by the town's offer of a grant, free water, and a ten-year exemption from taxes.[16] In 1917 the Amherst Woollen Mills, the former Hewson mill owned by Stanfield since 1911, was contracted to provide 40,000 blankets for the US Army. "Some difficulty was experienced in securing the consent of the Canadian government to permit the shipment of the woolen goods from Canada," the *Eastern Chronicle* reported, "but a delegation to Ottawa effected the removal of the regulation."[17]

Meanwhile, the Acadia Sugar Refining Company, the largest private-sector employer in Halifax, received an order from the British government for 10,000 barrels of refined sugar, which were shipped in November 1914. This was, as the *Yarmouth Herald* observed, the first time that refined sugar had been exported from Halifax to Britain and was "an instance of the war helping Halifax industry."[18] The Amherst Boot and Shoe Company received an order for 2,000 pairs of boots in August 1914 and other "large contracts" in December 1914.[19]

Things got much more serious when the War Office asked Hughes about Canada's ability to produce artillery shells. He promptly called a meeting of the leading steel producers who assured him that, given a few weeks to retool their mills, they could produce 4,000 shells a week. In view of the fact that none of them had any relevant experience, this appeared to be somewhat cavalier, because shells had to be machined to a very precise standard.

The question was whether Canadian open-hearth steel could be machined to the level of precision achieved by the American-produced acid steel used by the Dominion Arsenal, at this point the only manufacturer of artillery shells in Canada. Hughes turned to Thomas Cantley, the general manager of Nova Scotia Steel, to find out, and Cantley immediately had his plant produce sample ingots to War Office specifications. These were made into shells at the Dominion Arsenal, and tests "established beyond doubt" that the quality of Canadian steel was equal to that of US acid steel.[20]

The delighted Hughes passed this information on to the War Office, which agreed to accept shells made from open-hearth steel, whereupon Hughes established the Shell Committee, a small group of four men representing the major steel mills, to determine capacity and needs and then to assign the contracts. Cantley was one of those men. There was no tendering so, not surprisingly, the four companies represented on the committee got most of the initial contracts.

Scotia Steel's first contract was for 200,000 shrapnel shells, a huge order, but Cantley was an ambitious man. He now demonstrated that his company could also produce basic steel suitable for high-explosive shells, opening up an even larger market. It also meant that acid steel would not have to be imported from the United States, and Canadian mills could enter the high-explosive shell industry. Cantley readily shared the required technical information with other steel companies, with the result that steel mills and foundries throughout Canada were able to produce steel for munitions or shell casings in the war.

The significance of this for Scotia, Pictou County, and Nova Scotia can hardly be exaggerated. Scotia largely abandoned its other lines and focused on shell production in New Glasgow, while its Sydney Mines plant and Dominion Steel produced ingots for shells. Scotia operated at full capacity until 1917 and also issued subcontracts to other local companies, such as the Eastern Steel Company (a Scotia subsidiary) in Trenton, the McNeil Machine and Motor Company in New Glasgow, the J. W. Cumming Manufacturing Company, and the Albion Machine Company, while MacDonald's box factory produced between 400 and 500 boxes daily in which to ship shells. Scotia also subcontracted companies such as International Engineering Works in Amherst and the Burrell-Johnson Iron Foundry in Yarmouth to finish shell casings. Amherst's Canadian Car and Foundry Company received a contract to manufacture the boxes in which shells were shipped.

Contracts came from foreign governments as well. Canadian Car received an $80 million order from the Russian government for shrapnel shells, reportedly "the largest single order for war materials on record,"[21] and the Eastern Car Company, a Scotia subsidiary, received an order for 2,000 rail cars from the Russian government.[22] The cars were built in Trenton and shipped to Russia from Pictou on steamships belonging to Scotia Steel. The French government ordered more than 4,000 rail cars in April 1916 as well.[23]

Unemployment was a thing of the past by the spring of 1915, when the *Eastern Chronicle* reported that the mills were working at full capacity and would have trouble keeping up with demand.[24] Among those who benefited from the economic boom in Pictou County were 400 of its black citizens, who worked in the plants alongside their white neighbours.[25] Not surprisingly, workers flooded into the New Glasgow area, placing a strain on housing, and some people converted their homes into boarding houses. According to James Cameron, health authorities found sixteen boarders sharing eight beds in one "small dwelling." Nightshift men occupied the beds by day, and dayshift men by night.[26] It was the same in Sydney and Sydney Mines.

But all was not as rosy as it might have seemed. A political crisis had arisen in Britain over the shortage of shells, poor quality control, and alleged profiteering. Both British and Canadian companies were significantly behind in their deliveries, and in Canada the operations of the Shell Committee were coming under attack by businessmen—and opposition politicians—who complained of the cozy way in which contracts were allocated. The shell crisis arrived in Canada when the newly appointed British minister of munitions, David Lloyd George, refused to deal with the Shell Committee

Fig. 7.1: This rare photo shows members of the Shell Committee inspecting Nova Scotia Steel's facilities, July 1915. Thomas Cantley is on the far left. Next to him is David Carnegie, the committee's technical advisor, and on the far right is Alexander Bertram, who chaired the committee.

because he thought Canadian prices were too high. The inevitable royal commission was appointed, with the result that the Shell Committee was replaced by the Imperial Munitions Board, which managed all British war contracts in Canada for the duration of the war. Sir Joseph Flavelle, a highly respected Toronto industrialist, was appointed its chairman.

The way in which the Shell Committee operated undoubtedly appeared corrupt, and Hughes has been much criticized over the years because of it. Historian Michael Bliss, who has investigated the matter, concluded, however, that the members of the committee "were personally honest." They had taken on an enormous and complex job with no precedents, no guidelines, and no idea of how difficult it would become, and while it was true that they "had distributed the first orders at extremely high prices," the manufacturers had "very heavy start-up costs" in converting their mills. Besides, all the contracts had been approved by the War Office.[27]

The benefits to the Canadian economy, never mind the war effort, were enormous, and that included Nova Scotia. By the middle of 1916, Scotia alone was producing 120,000 shells a month in New Glasgow and 10,000 tons of ingots at Sydney Mines, and Dominion Steel was producing more than 30,000 tons of ingots a month.[28] But it was not to last. In the spring of 1917 the British government began cutting back on Canadian shell orders, partly because production in Britain had improved substantially but also because shipping insurance rates had risen so high that the government wanted to focus on food imports.

This inevitably led to reduced production and layoffs in Canada. The Borden government sought to offset the job losses by ordering 1,000 rail cars each from Eastern Car and Canadian Car, and promising to order another 5,000 within a year.[29] But almost 1,000 men were laid off and as if on cue, Eastern Car's plant in Trenton was destroyed by fire in September. By March 1918, the production of shells in Nova Scotia had "practically ceased."[30] Inevitably, Flavelle was accused of discriminating against Nova Scotia in favour of companies in Ontario. It was true that he favoured Ontario companies, but Bliss argues that was because Nova Scotia Steel had proven to be an unreliable supplier.

Despite the impressive figures cited above, Bliss claims that by the end of September 1916 Nova Scotia Steel had shipped fewer than 20,000 of the 250,000 4.5" forgings it had promised to deliver that summer.[31] It's unclear why this was the case, but we do know that it was struggling financially, despite its size and apparent success. That year Hayden Stone, a New York investment company, made a significant investment in the company and sacked Robert Harris, who had been president since 1904. Cantley was promoted to president but when production problems continued the Americans got control of the company in 1917 and sacked him too.

It seems remarkable that, while Thomas Cantley and Nova Scotia Steel led the development of the shell industry in Canada, J. H. Plummer and Dominion Steel led the development of the explosives industry. The War Office had asked in December 1914 if Canada could make the explosives as well as the shells for high-explosive shells. The key ingredient was trinitrotoluol (TNT), which was produced from the waste gases of coke ovens. There were only two steel mills in Canada with by-product coke ovens: Dominion and Algoma Steel in Sault Ste. Marie, Ontario. Because Algoma imported its coal, Plummer immediately saw an opportunity because he knew that Cape Breton coal was ideal for the process because it was rich in hydrocarbons.

A recovery plant was required, however, and he contacted Thomas Edison, who was then installing one at a steel mill in Pennsylvania.[32] Edison visited Sydney and the plant—the first toluol plant in Canada—was completed within sixty days. The government promptly awarded Dominion Steel a contract in February 1915 and production began in April. The toluol was shipped to the Canadian Explosives Company at Beloeil, Quebec, where it was converted into TNT. By the end of the war Dominion had produced 708,743 imperial gallons, which were converted into 41.8 million pounds of TNT.[33]

The shipbuilding industry also thrived during the war. At least thirty-eight vessels were built in 1917 and the builders were "making big profits," as were the owners because of high freight rates.[34] This situation partly reflected the booming economy but also the fact that so many merchant vessels were being lost to submarines until the convoy system was adopted. This may explain why Nova Scotian shipbuilders showed little interest when the Imperial Munitions Board sought to buy wooden vessels.[35] Only the Southern Salvage Company of Liverpool responded and it built just one cargo ship, the 2,335-ton *War Halifax*. The other seventeen wooden ships built under this program were built in New Brunswick, Quebec, and Ontario. Alexander Graham Bell built "a number of small boats" in Baddeck for the navy, employing a number of women to do it.[36]

But when the Imperial Munitions Board sought to acquire steel-hulled steam-powered cargo vessels, Thomas Cantley was quick to respond. He promptly built a shipyard at Trenton and secured a contract to build three vessels that were launched in 1917 and 1918.[37] Cantley was displaying his usual prescience. He knew that the Murray government had been trying since 1905 to develop a steel shipbuilding industry, and that the federal government was already redeveloping the port of Halifax by building new terminals in the South End of Halifax.

This huge, complex, and expensive project had begun just before the outbreak of war and continued through the war years. It involved building new piers (the Ocean Terminals) in the South End of the city closer to the harbour entrance, and replacing the existing railway that ran south from Bedford to the Intercolonial Station on North Street with a new connecting line to the new piers that would cut through the South End. The old line had been built through the

North End because most of Halifax's industries had developed in that area, but in terms of servicing the new port, it was on the wrong side of town and too far into the harbour. As the project neared completion, and at the very time that Cantley was building the province's first steel-hulled steamships, the provincial government appointed a shipbuilding commission to advise on what could be done to encourage the development of a steel shipbuilding industry.[38]

Thus, what was really happening here was an extraordinarily ambitious and comprehensive scheme to strengthen the port of Halifax by stimulating a modern shipbuilding and ship repair industry, while providing a larger local market for the province's steel mills and coal mines. The *Eastern Chronicle* did not exaggerate when it described the scheme as "the most courageous plan" since the creation of the Dominion Coal Company in the 1890s. Indeed, it was "epochal" because it actually linked the two events and would, it was hoped, establish Nova Scotia's "supremacy in maritime affairs in this dominion if not on this continent" and "eventually reclaim the heritage that is hers by the gift of nature and the enterprise of her people."[39]

The centrepiece of the scheme was Halifax Shipyards, a shipbuilding and ship repair company. It would replace the Halifax Graving Dock Company, a long-established ship maintenance and repair facility that was actually the "largest...of its kind on North America's east coast"[40] and served both the Royal Navy and the US Navy, as well as merchant vessels, occupying about 762 metres of harbour frontage from the dry dock at Richmond to Pier 6. Halifax Shipyards was owned by a Montreal consortium headed by Roy Wolvin, a Montreal financier prominent in the shipbuilding business on the Great Lakes, and J. W. Norcross and James Carruthers of Canada Steamship Lines. According to Wolvin, C. C. Ballantyne, the minister of marine and fisheries, who was also a wealthy Montreal businessman, "rather insisted that Mr. Norcross and I should undertake the work."[41]

When Samuel Brookfield, who owned the Halifax Graving Dock Company, refused to sell, the government expropriated the business and sold it to Wolvin and his associates. Within a year Wolvin rounded up British investors and took over Dominion Steel, then in 1921 he merged it with Nova Scotia Steel to form the British Empire Steel Corporation. BESCO was the largest industrial enterprise in Canada in the 1920s, controlling all of Nova Scotia's steel and coal production, manufacturing railway cars, rails, plate steel, and other products. BESCO also owned the only major shipyard in eastern Canada, which the government supported by committing to purchase four 10,000-ton steel-hulled ships—the largest ever built in Canada. The government also sweetened the deal by contracting Nova Scotia Steel to build two ships and helping Dominion Steel to build a plate mill—essential for steel shipbuilding—by guaranteeing to purchase 50,000 tons a year for five years.[42] The provincial government had already made its contribution in 1901 when it passed legislation exempting owners or shareholders in steel ships built and registered in Nova Scotia from paying taxes on their investment for twenty years.[43] Halifax City Council did its part by unanimously approving a ten-year exemption from property tax and asking the House of Assembly to extend that exemption to twenty-five years.

If Nova Scotians thought their economic ambitions had not been sufficiently supported by federal governments since Confederation, they certainly could not complain now. The Borden government had invested an enormous amount of financial and political capital in trying to establish Nova Scotia as an even more important industrial centre than it already was, while also strengthening the port of Halifax. And "for the next sixty years, no other single company influenced so significantly the City of Halifax and the Province of Nova Scotia both economically and socially."[44]

Coal mining also thrived during the war. Maintaining and even increasing production to fuel the war industries soon became a problem, however, because of the shortage of miners. Contrary to the popular misconception that miners were not allowed to enlist, they actually did enlist in large numbers until being exempted by the Military Service Act in 1917 and were actively recruited in 1915 when the British Army needed tunnellers. When Nova Scotia Steel was being criticized in 1916 for not meeting its shell production deadlines, Cantley blamed the shortage of coal, which he attributed to "the very large enlistment among our colliery employees."[45]

In fact, coal production peaked in 1915, then declined for the next several years. This resulted in a coal shortage that was described in 1916 as "quite serious," with soft coal rising in price, deliveries slow, and hard coal now a luxury. As the *Kentville Advertiser* suggested, albeit with some exaggeration, "the dusky diamonds are reaching up to the regular diamond in value."[46] In August 1918, R. H. MacKay, who had been appointed fuel administrator for Nova Scotia, rather insensitively declared that people "ought to be satisfied to get any at all." "A war is on," he unnecessarily pointed out, and people should "not demand the impossible."[47]

Meanwhile, the agricultural economy was thriving as well. Commodity prices rose during the war and the *Eastern Chronicle* expected 1916 to be "the greatest year the Nova Scotian farmer has ever experienced."[48] This was obviously good for farmers, but not so good for everyone else because wages were not keeping up with rising prices. By June 1917 the *Casket* thought food prices should be regulated.[49] The typically outspoken *Eastern Chronicle* agreed, warning the government that "sooner or later" it was "going to suffer for the criminal lack of action or interest they have displayed in this regard."[50] The government did create the Canada Food Board and appointed food controllers in the summer of 1917 to encourage production, avoid waste, and manage shortages, but not to fix prices. It licensed and monitored food sales in public establishments and encouraged food or ingredient substitutes for high-demand items. Propaganda posters urged "fuel-less Sundays," "meatless Fridays," and the elimination of wasteful shopping and cooking practices. Newspapers co-operated by publishing not very appetizing war menus.

Dissatisfaction was inevitable as prices rose faster than wages and there were shortages in a province where the farmers were producing more food than ever. The two major groups of industrial workers, the miners and steelworkers, had unions speaking on their behalf and by 1916 they were demanding higher wages. No one spoke for the rest of the population except newspaper editorialists. The *Eastern Chronicle* claimed in May 1916 that the cost of living had risen by nearly 50% and that wages had risen by "at least" 40% in some trades but not for miners.[51] The coal and steel companies did raise wages but not enough to satisfy most men, so yet another royal commission was appointed. It recommended modest wage increases that did not satisfy the workers, and the miners turned from the ineffective Provincial Workmen's Association to the more radical United Mine Workers of America (UMW) to represent them.

Labour unrest had actually declined after the outbreak of war. From thirty-two strikes in the Maritimes in 1912 and again in 1913, there were only seven in 1914 before the outbreak of war, none in 1915, and only three in 1916.[52] But this did not mean that all was well on the industrial front. Quite aside from working conditions and inflation, workers, especially those in the steel industry, were becoming increasingly concerned about the "devaluation of traditional skills" because of the impact of new technology on "older craft patterns of work." When Nova Scotia Steel brought in American managers in 1915, the attempts to increase efficiency caused more than 2,000 workers to stage a major walkout that briefly brought production to a halt.

The provincial government did pass legislation to compensate workers injured on the job. This was certainly an important advance in labour legislation, especially for coal miners, who toiled daily in dangerous conditions. Rockfalls, floods, gas, and even explosions were not uncommon. There had been an explosion in Pictou's Allan Mine in December 1914 and a fire in the Drummond Mine at Westville in 1915.[53] No miners were killed in those events but several hundred found themselves out of work. When a gas explosion occurred in No. 12 colliery at New Waterford on July 25, 1917, however, it was—and remains—the most serious explosion in the history of Cape Breton coal mining, killing sixty-five men and boys.[54]

Not surprisingly, workers at the Eastern Car plant also objected to working alongside enemy aliens. According to the *Truro Daily News*, "the loyal Britishers" refused in December 1917 to work alongside "Aliens" or men who allegedly "were chattering against Britain or her Allies." The Dominion police reportedly were called in and "a number of aliens…left the district."[55]

Some industrial workers, especially in mills and factories, also worried about the implications of hiring of female workers during the war.[56] From our perspective a century later, allowing women to work outside the home is usually regarded as an important advance on the road to full equality in society, but the reality at the time was more complicated. Women were needed because of the growing shortage of manpower, but most of the work in the mills and factories was heavy dirty work. And truth be told, employers welcomed women not just because they needed workers but also because they accepted lower wages than men. In other words, what we see in retrospect as female liberation also constituted exploitation. Many men understandably worried about the implications of this trend, at the same time questioning the physical stamina of women to do the work. It would be a mistake, however, to think that the influx of women into the workforce was caused just by the war. Women had been moving into factory and other jobs since at least the 1880s; the manpower shortage during the war just accelerated the trend.

On the whole, the war was highly beneficial to Nova Scotia economically. The demand for everything it produced—coal, steel, ships, agricultural products, fish, and lumber—skyrocketed. Just how much Nova Scotia benefited is difficult to determine. According to Chris Sharpe, the Imperial Munitions Board issued contracts worth $1.1 billion to 718 companies. About 59% of those companies were in Ontario and 25% were in Quebec, for a total of 84%, or about $764 million. That left 16% to be shared by the Prairies and the Maritimes, and Sharpe says that twenty-nine companies in the Prairies received contracts with a total value of $7 million.[57] That suggests that about $329 million went to the Maritimes. Since Nova Scotia had the steel plants, coal mines, and other related heavy industry, it must have received the bulk of that. It was a huge influx of money in a relatively small place during a four-year period.

As we have seen, the war was good for Halifax because, as Nova Scotian novelist Hugh MacLennan once observed, its harbour faced "one of the most vital stretches of water in the world."[58] The *Times* of London described Halifax in 1917 as the "third most important [port] in the world," handling fifteen million tons of shipping that year.[59] Troopships and hospital ships also used the port; it was the examination port for North American shipping going to Europe,

Fig. 7.2: Women workers, shown here at Nova Scotia Steel in 1917, helped keep mills and factories productive during the war.

it was the Royal Navy's base of operations in the North Atlantic; and it had the largest ship repair and service dockyard on the east coast of North America. The tranquil, pleasant city described by Beckles Willson and Thomas Raddall in 1912 had become a much busier and exciting place and, as Hugh MacLennan observed, "the people in their hearts were not sorry."[60]

Halifax was also a more crowded place because it not only housed the 3,500 garrison troops and militia regiments engaged in local defence, it also had to find space for the literally thousands of troops that passed through the city en route to England. The First Contingent had sailed from Quebec City in October 1914, but from the spring of 1915 most battalions going overseas sailed from Halifax. Neither the armoury nor the Wellington Barracks could accommodate that many men, so tents and later barracks were erected on the North Common. The Provincial Exhibition buildings, then located in the North End between Almon and Young Streets, had to be requisitioned as well. People soon became accustomed to seeing lots of young men in uniform on their streets, and businessmen discovered that there was an upside to war.

Other communities naturally thought they should benefit from the situation and five of them did. Kentville benefited because Camp Aldershot was already there on its outskirts. Sydney became a naval patrol base for both Canadian and American vessels, had coast artillery batteries positioned around its harbour, and was a convoy port, not to mention the vessels transporting coal, iron ore, and steel products. The other three to benefit were Amherst, Windsor, and Digby, all of which, perhaps only coincidentally, had Conservative members of Parliament.

The most successful was Amherst, whose once-thriving economy had been suffering in recent years. Its economy revived dramatically because of war contracts, but the town also benefited from having troops stationed there while preparing to go overseas. The first to arrive was the 22nd Battalion in March 1915, and more than a thousand people gathered at the train station to welcome it. A few days later the 585 officers and men of the 6th Canadian Mounted Rifles Battalion arrived as well, joining 200 local recruits of the 40th Battalion who were already training in the town. The 150th Battalion spent the winter of 1915–16 in Amherst; then the 123rd Battalion was there briefly in August 1916. The 12th Brigade of artillery and the 187th Battalion came in September, followed by the 207th Battalion in January 1917. Amherst had become "military to the last drop," as the *Daily News* put it, and couldn't have been happier.[61]

Amherst also benefited from the internment camp, the largest of several in the country, that housed prisoners of war and enemy aliens who were considered a security risk. The camp contributed significantly to the local economy because it required supplies, and the militiamen guarding it spent money in the town. Even the internees contributed because they were allowed—indeed encouraged because of the growing shortage of manpower—to take paid employment outside the camp. They worked on the Nappan Experimental Farm, built Dickey Park, improved the grounds of Highland View Hospital, did road work in Prince Edward Island and railway work at Edmundston, and worked on construction projects in Campbellton.[62]

There were some who feared that an internment camp posed a risk to the community, but most came to realize that these men were not dangerous. A minor riot did break out in June 1915 over the unsatisfactory living conditions, and shots were fired, killing two detainees and wounding four others.[63] This prompted an official inquiry that resulted in the sacking of Major George Oulton, the local militiaman who served as the camp commander. He was replaced by Colonel Arthur Morris, who had thirty years' experience in the British Army.[64]

The most famous internee was neither a German prisoner of war nor an enemy alien. Leon Trotsky was a prominent Russian revolutionary leader, who had been living in exile with his family in New York. He and some other Russians sailed for home when the revolution broke out in April 1917, but Trotsky and his family were removed from the ship when it stopped in Halifax for examination. His wife and children were allowed to stay in Halifax, but Trotsky was sent to the internment camp at Amherst on the grounds that he was "dangerous to the Allies,"[65] which indeed he was.

He was only there for a month before being allowed to continue his journey, and apparently settled in very well and became very popular with most of the detainees, though not the German officers. Not surprisingly, he spent his time "educating" the detainees and prisoners on capitalism and the war. One of the senior Canadian militia officers stationed there, Major Carmen Wightman, thought that "if he had stayed there any longer... [he] would have made communists of all the German prisoners."[66] That may have been an exaggeration but when he left he was cheered by hundreds of German sailors while the camp orchestra played "The Internationale." Within months he was Russia's foreign minister and helped to take Russia out of the war.

Kentville, already the shire town and commercial centre of Kings County, benefited from having the largest military training camp in eastern Canada on its outskirts. Established in 1904 on Aylesford Plain, or what was more commonly called "the barrens," Camp Aldershot was used before the war for the militia's annual training camps, but during the war it became a significant training camp for battalions preparing to go overseas. At its peak in 1916 there were 7,000 troops there. Most of the men lived in tents, although some temporary buildings were erected during the war. Aldershot became even more important in 1917 when Camp Sussex in New Brunswick was closed, making it the only training camp in the Maritimes.

The proximity of the camp was good for business in Kentville, where the men usually went in the evenings seeking entertainment, because the only thing closer was Ferguson's pool hall at the corner of Aldershot and Lanzie Roads. Of course there were organized sports at the camp, especially baseball, and Garnet White of Amherst who was there with the 85th, jokingly observed in June 1916 that the swimming was fine as well, referring to the almost constant rain that month.[67] The Nicklet Theatre supplemented films with "the very best vaudeville acts," which its manager believed were "the equal" of those performing at Acker's or the Strand in Halifax.[68] John McDougall, an Albertan who was there with the 97th Battalion in 1916, wasn't impressed, however. In his view, Kentville was "a little one horse town" and was "sure dead."[69]

The town fathers fully recognized how important the camp was to its prosperity. When there was an epidemic of measles and pneumonia in February 1916, they provided a building to be used as a hospital.[70] Kentville "society" entertained the officers with a garden party at the Agricultural Research Station in July 1916 and a dance in August attended by some 300 "leading citizens" and officers.[71] J. D. Logan of the 85th Battalion, a former academic and journalist, attempted to encourage closer relations by getting together with some others and publishing *The Highlander*, a weekly newspaper intended to keep locals informed about the Highland Brigade's activities.[72]

Windsor, which badly needed the economic stimulus when the war broke out because it was still struggling to recover from a devastating fire in 1897, hosted troops at Fort Edward. The 112th Battalion mobilized there, the 239th Battalion spent time there in the autumn of 1916, and the Imperial Recruits Depot, which trained British volunteers from the United States, moved there from Halifax in January 1918. The Jewish Legion, which recruited North American Jewish men to serve in three segregated battalions with the British Army in the Middle East, also trained there before going to England. By the end of the war more than 10,000 troops had trained at Fort Edward.[73]

During the summer months the troops were housed in "floorless and cotless" tents that "stretched as far as the eye could see."[74] In winter they were quartered in the local armoury and a converted sawmill that became known as the Mill Barracks. The camp hospital was in a tent in summer but moved into the YMCA in winter. The YMCA also served as a recreational facility. Hosting hundreds of Jews was a new experience for Windsor and, indeed, for military authorities. David Ben-Gurion, later the first prime minister of Israel, quickly displayed his leadership qualities when he negotiated with the camp commander to establish a kosher kitchen.[75] The Jewish Legion recruits were also allowed to carry the blue-and-white Jewish flag along with the flags of Canada, Britain, and Australia when they marched in the Dominion Day parade on July 1. When they celebrated the Jewish New Year with a banquet held in the Windsor Opera House on September 6, 1918, more than one hundred "prominent Canadian and English officers and men," along with municipal officials, joined them. This almost certainly was, as Sarah Beanlands observes, the largest kosher dinner ever held in Nova Scotia to that date.[76]

Even Digby benefited, perhaps because it was directly linked to Saint John, and therefore Camp Sussex, by a ferry. The 209th, 237th, and 4th Pioneer Battalions trained there in the summer of 1916. Thomas Johnson of Swift Current was impressed by how welcoming the people of Digby were to the visiting soldiers. "From the first they did all they could to make us feel at home.... They invited us to their homes—the townspeople as a whole I mean—and we grew to know them as our real friends, & we were very sorry to part with them."[77] The officers were billeted at The Pines hotel, which had been built on The Raquette by H. B. Churchill in 1904, while the other ranks camped in tents. The 237th even picked up a few recruits in Digby.[78]

Pictou did not fare so well, despite its strong military tradition. A company of the 106th Battalion was stationed there during the winter of 1915–16 and was quartered in Brown's Warehouse on Market Wharf. According to James Cameron, Amherst had tried to attract these troops by offering the Militia Department free quarters and water but Pictou's town council "out-wire-pulled" the Cumberland town.[79] One company for a few months wasn't much, but perhaps that was all that could be expected by a county that had a habit of electing Liberals. Similarly, Springhill briefly and apparently unexpectedly hosted 12 officers and 250 men from the Medical Corps in 1917.[80]

The presence of hundreds if not thousands of young men far from home undoubtedly enlivened the communities that accommodated them. But problems could be expected as well, especially if those young men had access to alcohol. Even though sixteen of Nova Scotia's eighteen counties had adopted prohibition, illicit alcohol was readily available, although it was more expensive than it might have been if it were being sold legally.[81] When Fred Cook arrived in Sydney from Ottawa to inspect the North Sydney cable station, he reported that "strapping young fellows in uniform [were] reeling drunk on the streets," and on at least one occasion even the troops guarding the station were all drunk.[82]

Halifax and other communities established clubs and canteens as wholesome alternatives to taverns for the soldiers and sailors. The YMCA erected a large canteen and recreation hall opposite Government House, and there was a Khaki Club on the corner of Granville and Duke Streets, later the site of the Split Crow pub. The IODE had a Union Jack Club on the corner of Hollis and George Streets, and the American Red Cross opened a canteen on the top floor of the Keith Building on Barrington Street in 1917.

Alcohol wasn't the only problem associated with large numbers of young men far from home. The Reverend John McCarthy, the Catholic priest at Holy Family Church in Amherst, soon came to believe that their presence was having "an extremely deleterious effect on the town's morals." He got into the habit of patrolling the streets every evening, and "when he discovered young people...with what he considered bad companions or in suspicious circumstances, he marched them back to their homes" and gave their parents "a vigorous lecture on the proper care of children."[83]

If premarital romance was a problem in Amherst, it must have been a much larger one in Halifax, where thousands of lonely young men (including men from the British, American, and Canadian navies) wandered the streets looking for richer entertainment than canteens offering tea, coffee, newspapers, and card games. No doubt they were encouraged by young women attracted to men in uniform preparing to go to war. We know of only one somewhat humorous incident that occurred in 1915, when a young soldier stationed on McNab's Island accidentally shot a girl on the Grand Parade, apparently while trying to impress her with his pistol.[84]

The Halifax police reportedly tried to be tolerant of soldiers and sailors enjoying a night out but they felt obliged to step in if there was any violence, and they relied on the military and naval police to back them up when necessary. Most incidents were minor, involving drunkenness and fighting on the streets, but occasionally, minor disturbances flared into serious riots. On the Saturday evening of May 25, 1918, "mob rule" prevailed for more than three hours on Barrington Street and the city hall "was bombarded with stones and bricks," many of its windows were smashed, and Molotov cocktails were thrown into the building.[85]

Sydney experienced similar problems, albeit on a smaller scale. After the St. Lawrence Patrol was stationed there to patrol the gulf and escort convoys, Sydney had hundreds of sailors and merchant seamen as well as coastal defence troops in its midst. After the United States came into the war, it also had American sailors and the American seaplane base at North Sydney. The streets were crowded day and night with men in uniform, and business thrived.

As in Halifax these men had to content themselves with the usual tame diversions such as dance halls, sports, and church-sponsored social events. In July 1918 the Navy League established tea rooms in the old St. George's rectory on the Esplanade, where women from the IODE and other volunteers provided hot meals, as well as club rooms with newspapers, writing tables, and a piano. The rectory's "little green gates" were always open, and there was also a garden "where one may sit and smoke and talk."[86] But there were the inevitable incidents associated with large numbers of bored young men away from home and looking for girls and alcohol. Most incidents were minor affairs, as when a drunken sailor tried to get into an automobile and "the owner objected and backed up his objection by giving the sailor a punch on the nose which knocked him flat and caused him to lose considerable blood. While lying down he amused the crowd which gathered by telling them what he thought of a man who owned a car and wouldn't give a poor sailor a ride."[87]

In September 1918, however, there was a riot in Sydney. As usual, it began when a group of sailors—both Canadian and American—tried to prevent a police officer from arresting a sailor on Charlotte Street. The police managed to disperse them but the next night they returned, armed with "improvised clubs and other weapons." Perhaps unwisely, after again trying to disperse them, the police arrested a sailor. This time the crowd followed and gathered outside the jail, making threats, and the police felt compelled to draw their pistols to keep it at bay. According to the *Daily Post*, while "sticks, bottles and stones flew in all directions," women, children, and civilians "followed every move of the crowd and commented, some more emphatically than elegantly, on the different turns of the affair."[88]

Canadian and American naval authorities moved quickly to ensure the incident didn't damage relations either between the services or between the services and the community. The sailors agreed to pay for the property damages and issue an apology, and police chief J. B. McCormack acknowledged that two of his officers had mishandled the situation and disciplined them. There was no more trouble, but from this point the US Navy restricted shore leaves and sent its own police patrols ashore to assist in handling any situations that might develop.

Meanwhile, wounded men were beginning to arrive home on hospital ships and fast liners like the *Olympic* by 1916, adding another dimension to the military population in Halifax and Sydney. Halifax already had the Cogswell Military Hospital, as well as the small naval hospital at the dockyard and a small infirmary at the Wellington Barracks. But now Camp Hill Hospital was built specifically to deal with convalescent soldiers, although its first patients turned out to be people injured in the explosion. There was also the Clayton hospital, at least until it burned down in December 1917. Pine Hill Divinity Hall established a military hospital as well, which was directed for a time in 1918 by Stuart Hunt. In Sydney, two special military hospitals were established, one in Moxham's Castle—a somewhat grandiose Scottish-style mansion built by a former manager of the steel plant—and the other in Jack Ross's mansion on King's Road near the intersection of Alexandra Avenue.

The arrival of wounded men in Halifax proved to be somewhat controversial because at first the military authorities disembarked the badly wounded ones onto small boats before the transports docked at Pier 2. This was done no doubt so that the general public would not notice the more disturbing cases. "Fortunately," as David Mossman has written, "a specific complaint registered by a local official, to the effect that even a sick cat shouldn't be treated like that, led to all future landings of wounded men being made after the ship docked."[89]

Many of these men were not bedridden, and it wasn't long before civic organizations began organizing garden parties, outings in automobiles, and even harbour cruises. The YMCA and YWCA joined to form the Patriotic Service Battalion, whose mission was to provide "social entertainment for the soldier and sailor boys." By June

1918 there were four such "battalions" in operation in the city. They even had a uniform: "the popular white middy...with the YWCA blue triangle on the sleeve."[90]

We have already seen how the war began to change the role of women in society by encouraging, indeed requiring, them to manage the family farm on their own or to enter the paid workforce in factories. Equally and perhaps even more important was the fact that women's organizations contributed significantly to providing support services for returned soldiers, sailors, and merchant seamen as has been described above.

Women also enormously expanded their traditional role of organizing their communities to address problems of various kinds and raising the money to make it possible. Provincially, it began with Agnes Dennis, May Sexton, and Edith Archibald, leading members of the Halifax Local Council of Women, an umbrella organization formed to link local women's groups with each other and with the National Council of Women. When the war broke out, they promptly formed the Nova Scotia Provincial Red Cross Society to coordinate the production and collection of medical supplies, financial support for hospitals, and other aspects of the province's war effort. Because these women were well connected in Halifax's business, political, and educational communities, they were able to achieve a great deal.

Wartime fundraising began when the Red Cross led the campaign to raise money to provide aid to the civilian population of Belgium. The campaign kicked off with a patriotic concert attended by an estimated 20,000 people in downtown Halifax. There was a large choir plus the band of the 63rd Regiment and, rather remarkably, 220 Russian immigrants who sang their national anthem and traditional hymns. Patriotic songs were sung and, according to the *Morning Chronicle*, "the very cradle of liberty in this Dominion was...rocked by a wave of patriotism such as this Province and Canada have never witnessed before."[91]

Nova Scotians responded generously, no doubt partly because there was a substantial Belgian community in the industrial communities around New Glasgow and Sydney Mines, which had been brought in by Nova Scotia Steel in the 1880s, and the Acadia Coal Company was owned by a Belgian company. All kinds of fundraising activities took place throughout the province,[92] and the first Belgian relief ship, the *Tremorvah*, sailed from Halifax on October 29. When it arrived in Rotterdam it was met by John Howard, Nova Scotia's agent general from London. This reflected the belief in Nova Scotia that, while all Canadians contributed, the project was "conceived and nurtured" in Nova Scotia, which contributed more than any other province. Whether or not this was true, by the end of the war, Nova Scotians had contributed the extraordinary amount of $1.6 million in cash and $1.5 million in supplies.[93]

This was just the beginning of what proved to be a four-year-long appeal by various organizations such as the IODE and the Women's Institutes for financial and other donations to worthy war-related causes. These included sending "comforts" to soldiers in the field or in hospitals and prisoners of war, and sending supplies to Canadian military hospitals. By the end of the war, the Nova Scotia Red Cross had raised an estimated $1 million.[94] Women's groups throughout the province got involved, making socks, mittens, and bandages, as well as raising funds to buy cigarettes, candy, and magazines for the soldiers. Charles Smith undoubtedly spoke for all overseas soldiers when he thanked the community for his Christmas parcel. "I know you would feel repaid for all your trouble (as well as amused), if you could see us boys when we get parcels from home. After all, I think we are only grown-up children, for we are like kiddies opening the stockings on Christmas morning."[95]

When the IODE raised funds to equip a hospital ship, Nova Scotians contributed $10,000, twice the quota assigned to the province. And the Women's Institutes had no difficulty raising the money needed to pay for a field ambulance.[96] Nova Scotians also responded enthusiastically to the machine-gun campaign in 1915–16, which began when the press reported that the Canadian troops overseas did not have enough machine guns. A number of millionaires promptly made large donations to a fund to purchase more, and the idea caught the popular imagination. Cities and organizations virtually competed, with the result that Halifax paid for twenty machine guns, Cape Breton paid for thirty, Stellarton and Truro each contributed two, and even little Milford (Shubenacadie) paid for one. By September, when $1.5 million had been raised, Sam Hughes decided that this was not an appropriate way to fund military equipment and most of the funds were returned to their donors.[97]

This did not discourage the Halifax branch of the Over-Seas Club—later the Royal Overseas League—from raising enough money to contribute an airplane to the Royal Flying Corps. A year later Drummond Matheson of New Glasgow, who was a pilot in 25 Squadron, wrote to his father that the plane purchased was an FE2b (Farman Experimental), a two-seater equipped with two Lewis machine guns. "I have not had a flight in her yet...but I will fly her soon though unless something happens to her in a hurry."[98] He did fly it on October 22, when he shot down his first German aircraft.

The biggest fundraising campaigns were for the Canadian Patriotic Fund and Victory Bonds. The fund was established to encourage recruitment by providing financial support to families. Headed by Sir Herbert Ames, a wealthy Montreal businessman with a social conscience, it urged Canadians "to fight or pay." When Nova Scotia exceeded its quota in 1915, the fund doubled its 1916 quota to $500,000, an amount that proved to be more difficult to raise. Despite a personal appeal from Ames, Nova Scotia, for whatever reason, did not support the Patriotic Fund to the extent that other provinces did. By the end of the war, Nova Scotians had contributed $1.8 million, about $3.50 per capita, compared to the national average of about $6.33.[99]

The explanation may have been that by 1916 there were too many worthy causes appealing for money. The editor of the *Amherst Daily News* complained in March 1916 that his staff could not spend all their time "taking down free notices with regard to public meetings, entertainments and the various work carried on by the different societies of the town." The *Bridgewater Bulletin* suggested in April 1917 that "there is such a thing as overdoing patriotic endeavor....Give the people a chance to lay up their contributions for such time as they are urgently needed and do not 'ride a willing horse to his death.'"[100]

Unquestionably, the largest financial campaign during the war was the sale of Victory Bonds. The Canadian government had never attempted to borrow money from its own citizens because it had never thought they had it. But Sir Thomas White, the minister of finance, tried it in 1916 and was flabbergasted when he raised $100 million. The Nova Scotia Steel and Coal Company led the way in its home province by subscribing $500,000,[101] setting an example that the *Eastern Chronicle* suggested "other munitions manufacturers would do well to emulate."[102]

White very sensibly followed up with annual Victory Bond campaigns, offering long-term bonds with excellent interest rates. Each issue was launched with an intense sales campaign that linked purchases to the war effort, so that lending money to the government became an act of patriotism. By the end of the war, $2 billion had been raised and Nova Scotia more than met its quota every year. This, of course, was an investment, not a donation.

A less welcome innovation was the introduction, also in 1916, of a tax on business profits, then a "temporary" tax on personal incomes in 1917. This was not actually a very controversial initiative because the provincial government had already introduced a property tax based on assessments, which supplemented the regular municipal property tax, justifying it on the ground that the war had "been the cause of a considerable reduction in the ordinary revenues."[103] In June 1917 it began charging a five-cent tax on all long-distance telephone calls as well.[104] As well, by 1917 many people, especially Liberals and representatives of organized labour, were condemning the large profits being made by businessmen while workers were being pressured to enlist for overseas service. The federal tax rates were extremely low and only affected people with substantial incomes, so most people paid no tax and those who did paid very little. The introduction of income taxes, however, marked a significant change in how governments raised revenue.

IN DECEMBER 1917 HALIFAX EARNED THE UNENVIABLE DISTINCTION of being the only city in Canada to experience first-hand the dangers of modern warfare. The morning of December 6, 1917, began innocently enough. It was sunny but cool and no snow had yet fallen. At 9:05 AM, when many men were already at work in the dockyards, factories, and foundries and others were on their way to work or school, two ships collided in the Narrows. The *Imo*, a four-masted Norwegian tramp steamer under charter as a Belgian relief ship, was moving from Bedford Basin to the harbour en route to New York, guided by harbour pilot William Hayes. Meanwhile, the *Mont-Blanc*, a French-owned freighter, was entering the harbour to join a convoy forming up in Bedford Basin prior to sailing to Bordeaux. It was being guided by harbour pilot Francis Mackey.

The story of the Halifax explosion has been told many times, so it seems unnecessary to tell it again here. It is worth pointing out, however, that this was not the first collision in Halifax Harbour during the war. There had been two others just months earlier. On the morning of June 14 HMCS *Deliverance*, a Canadian naval patrol vessel, collided with the incoming Norwegian barque *Regin* off Chebucto Head. It was the Liverpool-built *Deliverance* that had dragged HMCS *Niobe* off the rocks at Cape Sable on its maiden voyage in 1912. The damage to the *Deliverance* in this collision was so severe that Captain Horatio Brannen headed for shore at full speed, but the vessel sank 550 metres off Herring Cove. Brannen and his crew survived.[105] Just six weeks later there was another collision when the *Letitia*, a passenger liner sailing regularly as a hospital ship between Liverpool, England, and Halifax, ran aground while being guided into the harbour in thick fog in the same area. Naval vessels quickly came to the rescue and safely rescued the 74 hospital staff and 546 patients.

One might have thought that two collisions within six weeks would have suggested that the harbour pilotage system was not working well. Nothing had been done to improve it, however, so the collision between the *Imo* and the *Mont-Blanc* a few months later should not have come as a complete surprise. But it was a surprise to Terrence Freeman, the port examining officer, to discover that the *Mont-Blanc* was carrying explosives and he had no special instructions for dealing with ships carrying dangerous cargoes. Nor did the federal government's Public Traffic Regulations contain any guidance for munitions ships, despite the fact that the country had been at war for three years.

There very nearly was a second explosion in the harbour on December 6. The British freighter *Picton* had earlier run aground, damaging its rudder, and was moored at the Acadia Sugar wharf that morning. Its cargo of foodstuffs and 1,500 fused shells was being removed by longshoremen in preparation for repair work when the *Mont-Blanc* exploded only about thirty metres away. Sixty-nine of the longshoremen were killed and the *Picton* was set on fire. *Picton*'s captain, James W. Harrison, recognized that his vessel might explode as well so, after extinguishing the fire, he commandeered three tugboats to drag it into the stream, where it was secured with an anchor. Two days later, he was ordered to beach it in Eastern Passage, but when he did it burst into flames again. Nearby residents understandably fled while men from the 63rd Regiment extinguished the flames. The *Picton* was then towed further out into the stream, where it remained until January 29, when a box of ammunition caught fire as it was being unloaded at the Ocean Terminal pier. This caused another panic but the small blaze was speedily extinguished and the ammunition was unloaded without further incident.

More than 2,000 men, women, and children in the North End of Halifax were killed and another 6,000 were injured in the greatest man-made explosion before atomic bombs were dropped on Japan in 1945. Among them were almost 400 dockworkers, sailors on the *Niobe* and other vessels, students at the Royal Naval College, and soldiers and their families at the Wellington Barracks. The damage to military buildings such as the Wellington Barracks, the naval dockyard, hospital, and the Royal Naval College was extensive, but the harbour fortifications remained largely intact, except for the wooden buildings on the north shore of George's Island that were seriously damaged by flying debris. None of the troops at the harbour fortifications were hurt, however. Thus, Charles Durkee of Beaver River was killed at the Wellington Barracks, while his son Forrester, serving at McNab's Island, was unhurt.[106]

Colonel W. E. Thompson, the adjutant general of Military District 6, immediately called in all available troops from their various posts and sent them out into the streets to look for injured people, help them get to places where they could receive medical treatment, help recover bodies, and try to find people who might still be alive in the rubble of their homes. Among the first to be deployed were 150 American men from the Imperial Recruits Depot, who were on parade in the armoury at the time. They worked all day on the waterfront even though some of them had been injured in the explosion. Other troops from the armoury and the huts on the Common were ordered out immediately and by one o'clock every man who could be spared from the 63rd and 66th Regiments and from the artillery manning the forts had joined them, rescuing people from the ruins of buildings, extinguishing fires, clearing streets, and patrolling the streets and furnishing guards where necessary.

It was not just the soldiers who pitched in to help the stricken city. As it happened, virtually the whole Royal Canadian Navy fleet was in port at the time, including the St. Lawrence Patrol, which had just moved to Halifax for the winter. There were also three British and two American ships in port, and they were quickly joined by two American troop transports returning from Europe that had changed course for Halifax when they spotted the huge black cloud on the horizon. On arrival the *Tacoma* transferred its medical officers and staff to the *Old Colony*, while equipment was transferred from the *Morrill* to set up operating rooms. The *Tacoma* also provided 250 men to help patrol the streets.

Dr. Frederick McKelvey Bell, the assistant director of medical services for MD 6, quickly took charge of medical operations and provided extraordinary leadership. He had served overseas for more than two years before being posted to Halifax, so he had extensive first-hand experience with battlefield wounds and conditions, experience that was now unexpectedly relevant on the home front. He later told a newspaper reporter that he "had never seen anything on the battlefront equal to the scenes of destruction that he witnessed in Halifax today."[107]

He faced a daunting situation: the Rockhead Hospital and the Pier 2 Casualty Depot had both been destroyed, and the Cogswell Military Hospital had been badly damaged. There were, of course, the Victoria General Hospital, the Halifax Infirmary and, luckily, the just completed Camp Hill Hospital. Intended for the wounded soldiers arriving home from Europe, it was soon "jammed with badly hurt civilians...with patients lying on the beds, under the beds, even in the halls. The hard-driven doctors and nurses could only patch up those who were able to walk and send them home."[108] Meanwhile, other buildings such as the Oxford School on North Street and the Waegwoltic Club were converted into emergency hospitals.

Dartmouth tends to be ignored in accounts of the explosion, but its North End was also devastated, including the Mi'kmaw village at

Turtle Grove. An agreement had just been concluded in November to establish a new reserve at Albro Lake, but unfortunately, the community had not yet moved. Important industries such as the ropeworks on Wyse Road, Starr Manufacturing's rolling mill, and the Halifax Breweries building were destroyed. Harry Chapman summed it up succinctly: "North Dartmouth was in shambles."[109]

But as in Halifax, the damage was not confined to the North End. The downtown core was "awash in a sea of broken glass, rubble and debris."[110] Soldiers and voluntary firemen were called out to help fight fires, to rescue people trapped in the rubble, and to urge everyone to vacate their homes at least temporarily. Many people gathered in public spaces like Victoria Park, Notting Park, the Dartmouth Common, and Silver's Hill, where they waited hopefully for their wounds to be treated or to be transported to hospital. The dead were loaded onto carts or trucks and taken to the town's two undertakers. Dr. Daniel Parker turned his home on Pleasant Street into a makeshift hospital, as did Henry Rosenberg on Crichton Avenue. Greenvale School became a medical aid station and the Nova Scotia Hospital at Woodside, although damaged, was able to take in 150 patients. Remarkably, the Dartmouth ferries were still functional—there were no bridges yet—and they worked all night transporting victims to hospitals in Halifax and taking rescue workers, equipment, and supplies to Dartmouth.[111]

Prime Minister Borden was en route from Charlottetown to Pictou in the final days of the 1917 election campaign when he heard about the disaster. He cancelled his meetings and went directly to Halifax, arriving "in the midst of one of the most terrible blizzards I ever experienced."[112] He immediately authorized $500,000 for immediate aid and next day met with Abraham Ratshesky, the Boston businessman and state senator sent by Massachusetts Governor Samuel McCall to provide "every assistance you may be in need of."[113] As is well known, Massachusetts sent doctors and nurses, relief supplies, and money in an extraordinary demonstration of sympathy and practical support, to the appreciative astonishment of Haligonians. Other states, especially but not exclusively in New England, also sent medical personnel, supplies, and money.

Cities and towns throughout Nova Scotia also helped, sending doctors, nurses, undertakers, and supplies. They also accepted patients for treatment in their hospitals and improvised hospitals set up in churches, schools, and other facilities. One unexpected casualty of the explosion was Dr. Nathan Shacknove of Whitney Pier. He returned home after helping out in Halifax and committed suicide, reportedly after having "brooded over the disaster for several days."[114]

It didn't take long for news of the disaster to reach the troops in Europe, some of whom—especially those in the 25th and 85th Battalions and the Royal Canadian Regiment—were from Halifax. We can only imagine the alarm caused by the news, which was

Fig. 7.3: American volunteers in front of Bellevue House on Spring Garden Road, where they established a temporary hospital after the explosion.

limited by the fact that communications with Halifax were cut off for days. The army made every effort to obtain reliable information for them and most men remained on duty. Some, of course, eventually learned that their families were safe but others had family and close relatives killed or badly injured. A few men were allowed to return home on compassionate leave, after which they were either discharged or reassigned as instructors at Camp Aldershot.

Massachusetts's generosity did not end in 1918. Upon their return home, many of the people involved in the relief effort formed the Halifax-Massachusetts Relief Associates, a group that worked with Halifax and the provincial government for the next five years to improve the lives of survivors and general health conditions in the city. This involved an expenditure of $50,000 a year, which was matched by $15,000 from the Canadian government and $10,000 from the Nova Scotia government. In total, the Associates raised $716,000, a huge sum at the time, all of it donated by the people of Massachusetts.

When the Spanish influenza epidemic swept North America in 1918, Nova Scotia demonstrated its appreciation, albeit on a smaller scale, by sending doctors to Massachusetts to help out, and in December of that year the province sent Boston the first giant Christmas tree as a special thank-offering. The gesture was not immediately repeated, but it was revived in 1971 and continues to this day. How significant this annual gift is to the people of Boston and Massachusetts generally is difficult to assess, but the process of selecting the tree, cutting and shipping it off to Boston continues to be very significant in Nova Scotia and particularly Halifax. It reminds people not only of the terrible disaster that took place in December 1917 but also of the profound generosity of the people of Boston and the Commonwealth of Massachusetts and constitutes a unique bond of kinship between the two communities.

Chapter 8

THE WAR AT SEA

Stirring times bring stirring opportunities
and these be great days for Halifax.[1]

FOR MOST CANADIANS THE WAR WAS BEING FOUGHT IN Europe, which seemed a long way away. Nova Scotians, however, knew that the war might very well come much closer because they lived on a peninsula jutting into the Atlantic Ocean, vulnerable to enemy naval action and coastal raids as it had been throughout its history.

There was certainly cause for concern in August 1914 because at least two German cruisers were known to be operating in the Western Atlantic when the war broke out. Just where the *Dresden* and *Karlsruhe* were was not known. They had last been seen off the coast of Mexico, but some believed they had moved north into

Newfoundland waters. If so, they were in an ideal position to attack ships sailing from Canadian and American ports. The British consul in St. Pierre and Miquelon believed they were in the area, and another report claimed that they had actually been sighted off St. Pierre. The French cruiser *Friant* was also in the area, so "a naval fight seems imminent in these waters."[2]

The superintendent of the Western Union cable station at Heart's Content, Newfoundland, thought the German warships were preparing to attack the station, and on August 4 the Marconi Company officially requested "immediate protection" for its wireless station at Glace Bay, claiming that "several Austrian steamships" were "meditating an attack" on it.[3] As improbable as that was, the War Office appealed to the Canadian government to do something, although it is difficult to know what it had in mind since Canada had only two naval ships on the east coast.

Meanwhile, commercial vessels and liners hastened to reach nearby ports. Six Canadian steamships arrived safely on the fifth: three were colliers carrying Cape Breton coal and two others were Norwegian vessels chartered by the Black Diamond Line, a subsidiary of the Dominion Coal Company.[4] Captain J. E. Roop of Bear River and his crew were not as lucky. Their steamer, the *Frankdale*, was at Hamburg, preparing to sail for Florida when the war broke out and both vessel and crew were detained.[5]

The German luxury liner *Kronprinzessin Cecilie*, which had just left New York for Bremerhaven carrying 1,000 passengers and about $11 million in gold and silver bullion, immediately turned about and raced for Bar Harbor, Maine. A local yachtsman guided the ship into the harbour, where it remained until November. "So began the love fest of Bar Harbor and its German guests," as John Malcolm Brinnin relates. Captain Charles Polack and his officers "became part of the summer's social whirl that saw them kissing the hands of hostesses at lawn parties, dancing at balls, [and] going out on fishing and lobstering expeditions and sailing parties." When the ship's band gave concerts on the village green, "a huge crowd assembled" and there were cheers when it played "America." When it played "Watch on the Rhine," the patriotic anthem, "the crowd demanded an encore."[6] Nova Scotians might be forgiven if they felt that this was taking American neutrality too far.[7]

Even though it was unlikely that either the *Dresden* or *Karlsruhe* would be diverted into Canadian waters, Sir Christopher Cradock, who commanded the 4th Cruiser (soon redesignated the North America and West Indies) Squadron, sent HMS *Essex* and HMS *Lancaster* north while he followed with HMS *Suffolk*, his flagship, and HMS *Bristol*. When the *Suffolk* arrived at Halifax, the men of the 63rd Regiment volunteered to refuel it, giving the sailors a break from the heavy, dirty task of physically carrying hundreds of sacks of coal onto the ship. They "worked all afternoon, some of them insisting that it was a pleasant change from being cooped up in Wellington Barracks." That evening, after a front-page appeal by the *Morning Chronicle*, fifty civilians took over the task. When they finished, "the boys were as proud of their black hands and faces as the old warriors are of their battle scars." The next day forty volunteers from the Starr Manufacturing Company took a turn, followed by 200 men from the City Works Department, who gave up half a day's pay to do so.[8]

The arrival of the *Lancaster* actually increased fears because its captain had requested that his ship's presence not be reported publicly. Not surprisingly, therefore, its appearance off St. Paul Island on August 10 aroused fears that it was one of the German raiders, prompting Canadian Naval Service Headquarters to hold in port all ships due to sail out of St. Lawrence ports. Nor was confidence inspired when the *Morning Chronicle* reported the very next day that the *Essex* had "sighted one of the German cruisers about 200 miles [322 kilometres] off Halifax."[9]

All these rumours naturally led to alarmist reports by people claiming they had actually heard gunfire off the coast. The most dramatic of them came from Mayor McKay of New Waterford, who claimed that "he and others" had actually seen

> *three ships in action about five miles [eight kilometres] from shore, and to the east. The puffs of smoke from their guns were plainly visible. The action had lasted about half an hour when the nearest ship made for New Waterford and it was thought that the captain was going to beach her. Suddenly she sheered off towards the Low Point lighthouse. Her decks were cleared for action and it is thought she flew the French flag.*

Regrettably, we cannot know what McKay and the others saw that day, but it was not a naval battle. Charles Peters, the keeper of the Low Point lighthouse, "ridiculed" McKay's story, pointing out that "anything in the nature of an encounter within sight of New Waterford could hardly have escaped his attention," and all he had seen that day was the arrival of "two ordinary merchant ships, the *Portia* and the *Brooksby*,...one about 1:30 and the other at four o'clock."[10]

As silly as these reports seem in retrospect, the fear of attack from German sea raiders was real. William Hayes, the RCR soldier stationed at Glace Bay, recalled that when he fell ill and was taken to St. Joseph's Hospital "the matron feared that because a soldier was in the hospital, the enemy had every right to shell the building." When he told her, perhaps with tongue in cheek, that "should occasion arise, the Red Cross Flag at the mast would give all the protection necessary...she seemed much relieved."[11]

It was a good thing she didn't subscribe to the *Toronto News*, which actually reported "the bombardment of Glace Bay by German cruisers" seeking "to destroy the wireless station and the collieries."[12] Where the *News* got this information is not known but it clearly didn't bother to confirm it with anyone before rushing into print. Even so, when rail cars being shunted at the ferry wharf in

North Sydney jumped the tracks three weeks later and crashed into the post office building, the postmaster and his assistant "naturally thought that they had been struck by a shell from a German ship."[13]

As late as September 10 both Halifax Harbour and Sydney Harbour were briefly closed to navigation because the elusive German cruisers were still thought to be in the area.[14] Captain Stewart and the crew of the *Beatrice*, a collier returning to Sydney from Bay Roberts, Newfoundland, feared that they had encountered them when their vessel was "brought to a sudden standstill by the boom of two cannons, fired from a grey battle-colored sea warrior" about ninety-six kilometres off North Sydney. This time the warship was HMCS *Niobe*, and after running up the Union Jack the *Beatrice* was allowed to continue on its way. Stewart was reported to be "not overjoyed by the experience."[15]

The Canadian Navy was not in a position to contribute much to the war in 1914. Four years after its creation, there was only the bare nucleus of anything that might actually be described as a navy. A naval college, housed in the old naval hospital building at Halifax's naval dockyard, had been established to train officer cadets and two cruisers had been acquired from Britain. One of them, the 11,000-ton *Niobe*, was stationed at Halifax. The government had also transferred ten small patrol vessels from the Fisheries Protection Service and the Canadian Coast Guard into the navy. Although only lightly armed, they could at least carry out coastal patrols. But the navy's total personnel in 1914 consisted of only 350 officers and men, the majority of them on loan from the Royal Navy. There was also the Royal Naval Canadian Volunteer Reserve (RNCVR), a militia-type organization, but it had only recruited 250 of its planned complement of 3,600 men, most of whom were also former British sailors now living in Canada.[16]

The *Niobe* had not been a great success as the flagship of the Canadian Navy. On its first cruise, to Yarmouth in July 1911, it ran aground off Cape Sable. The resulting inquiry ruled that the navigating officer was negligent because he was not on the bridge when the ship was operating in dangerous coastal waters, and that the captain, the Canadian-born William Balfour Macdonald who had come to Canada with the *Niobe*, was negligent for not ensuring that his officers were performing their duties properly.[17] More importantly, the repairs took six months and left the ship with a permanently reduced maximum speed. When repairs were completed in 1912, the *Niobe* was tied up at the dockyard and its crew was sent to Esquimalt.

When the war broke out, therefore, the *Niobe* was "exceedingly deficient in trained personnel, her engines suffering from disuse, [and] the ship in general very far from being in condition to go to sea."[18] It was immediately reactivated but needed a month in dry dock to make it seaworthy. It also needed a crew, which was acquired by drafting all the engineers of the Fishery Protection Service, personnel from two British sloops at Esquimalt, and by scraping up all the naval reservists the navy could find. Even then, the *Niobe*'s first voyage was to St. John's to pick up 107 men from the Newfoundland Royal Navy Reserve. When the Royal Canadian Navy went to war, only 390 of the 707 crew of its one major warship were Canadians.[19]

The *Niobe* did perform well in its brief participation in the war, however. It escorted the *Canada* when it carried the Royal Canadian Regiment to Bermuda and according to W. H. Hayes, "She left us behind many a time, only to return and play around us like a cat watching her kittens. She was marvellous and a credit to the Officers and ship's company who manned her."[20] After bringing the British troops back to Halifax on its return voyage, the *Niobe* briefly patrolled the Gulf of St. Lawrence before joining the 4th Cruiser Squadron in its blockade of New York.

This involved boarding and searching vessels leaving port and checking their cargoes and manifests to ensure that only permitted goods were getting through to Germany. It also included removing

German reservists returning home and taking them to Nova Scotia where they were interned. It was, as its executive officer, Lieutenant Commander Charles Edward Aglionby, recalled many years later, "very monotonous work, especially after the first few weeks when, owing to reports of possible submarine attacks, we had to keep steaming up and down, zig-zagging the whole time." When the American press complained that they were operating too close to the harbour entrance, they had to move further out to sea, but "the American Navy were very friendly to us, and when their ships passed us they used to cheer [the] ship and play British tunes."[21]

It was the *Niobe* that seized the first German vessel, the *Brindilla*, on October 14. It handed the ship over to the *Caronia*, a former Cunard liner now serving as an armed merchant cruiser, which brought it into Halifax. The three Germans among the crew were sent to the Citadel as prisoners of war, making them the first enemy prisoners to be detained in Canada. Not a single enemy ship sailed from New York during the nine months that the *Niobe* participated in the blockade, and despite its limitations, it proved to be "a valuable addition" to the squadron.[22]

The *Niobe* never participated in a naval battle but it came close when it was ordered down to Newport News, Virginia, in an effort to catch the *Prinz Eitel Friedrich*, a German armed raider heading for that neutral port. Unfortunately, the *Niobe* got delayed by a ninety-nine-mile-an-hour gale and by the time it arrived the *Prinz Eitel Friedrich* had reached port. The ship was given twenty-four hours to put to sea again but opted instead to stay and be interned.[23]

When the *Niobe* returned to Halifax a few months later, badly in need of reconditioning, its operational career was over. The old ship was worn out and the cost of refitting it would have been too high in view of its obsolescence, so it was tied up at the naval dockyard and continued to play an important role in the war at sea as the depot ship, the personnel and administrative base for the coastal patrols.[24]

It was not replaced because the Admiralty was already warning that the approaching danger from German submarines in Canadian waters meant that Canada needed a fleet of real warships. Borden agreed to build one but asked the Admiralty to lend Canada destroyers and submarines in the meantime. That was unrealistic in wartime, so the navy purchased or chartered ten vessels, mostly private yachts, and refitted them for coastal patrol work. One was the *Tarantula*, which J. K. L. "Jack" Ross of Montreal and Sydney purchased in the United States and donated to the navy. An enthusiastic yachtsman, he also got himself commissioned and commanded the vessel, renamed the *Tuna*. Thus, the Canadian Navy grew within months to twenty-two vessels, including the *Rainbow* and two largely useless submarines on the west coast.

Developing a modest fleet to focus on patrolling Canadian waters made sense because the war at sea, like the war in Europe, was not the war that British naval leaders had expected. Instead of the great fleets fighting set-piece battles as in previous wars,

Fig. 8:1: Jack Ross, left, donated the *Grilse* to the navy and commanded it in 1915–16.

this naval war was largely about enforcing the economic blockades that each side imposed on the other. The Royal Navy inspected all vessels going to Europe to prevent war matériel from reaching Germany, while the German Navy relied on its submarine fleet to prevent similar supplies from reaching Britain.

Germany's blockade of Britain was remarkably effective because its submarines laid mines in the approaches to Britain and intercepted vessels on the high seas, sinking hundreds if not thousands of them. This had a direct impact on Nova Scotia because the province had so many vessels and seafarers engaged in global trade. Samuel Purdy was probably the first Nova Scotian sea captain to have his vessel attacked by a submarine. The *Condor* was sailing from New York to Valparaiso in October 1914 when it was intercepted by the *Karlsruhe.* Purdy and his crew were taken aboard one of the warship's scout vessels that already had on board the crews of twelve other vessels. All were dropped off at Tenerife in the Canary Islands, then taken to Germany and interned.[25] Captain D. W. Mahoney of Parrsboro had a narrow escape just days later. He was loading guano at a port in Peru when his vessel, the *Tamar*, was boarded by officers from a nearby German warship that was loading coal. He managed to persuade them that they could not sink his ship because they were in neutral waters.[26]

Several Nova Scotian vessels were sunk during 1915 but not by torpedoes. Submarines operated mostly on the surface in this war, submerging for only short periods because that was all their batteries would allow. Thus, most ships were sunk by striking mines or after being stopped by a submarine. If ships struck mines, the result was usually disastrous but if they were intercepted by a submarine their crews were either taken aboard before the vessel was sunk by means of an explosive device or they were allowed to take to their lifeboats. If they were taken aboard the German submarine or raider, they were taken to Germany for detention or dropped off at a neutral port.

The steamer *Sharon*, for example, carrying steel products to Wales from Sydney, struck a mine off the north coast of Ireland in January and all thirty crew members, many of them from North Sydney, died.[27] In June the steamer *Strathcona*, captained by Charles Owen Allen of Kentville, was sunk by *U-40* west of the Orkney Islands while carrying supplies to France. Allen and his crew spent eight days on the submarine, then two years as prisoners in Germany.[28] The crew of the steamer *Wacousta* was allowed to disembark before their ship was sunk by *U-35* in the Mediterranean in November, while carrying 175 railway cars manufactured by the Nova Scotia Steel Company to Vladivostok.[29]

These events were taking place in distant waters, but Nova Scotians were also reminded that the war was not far off when three ships sailing from American ports sought refuge in Halifax between July and November after catching fire in the Atlantic, apparently the result of explosions caused by bombs planted by enemy saboteurs. A fourth raced for Halifax but had to be abandoned before it could get there.[30]

In June 1915 the Admiralty again warned Canada that Germany was building larger vessels capable of travelling longer distances and recommended that the Royal Canadian Navy increase its patrols, especially in the Gulf of St. Lawrence. Two more yachts acquired in the United States were refitted as HMCS *Stadacona* and HMCS *Hochelaga* and became part of the St. Lawrence Patrol, Canada's first wartime fleet. Commanded by Captain Fred Pasco, a retired Royal Navy officer, its seven vessels operated out of Sydney in the summer months and Halifax during the winter.[31]

The fateful day came in July 1916, when the *Deutschland*, one of the new larger submarines, arrived in Baltimore, demonstrating that submarines were now capable of operating in the Western Atlantic. That was confirmed in October when *U-53*, a combat submarine, visited Newport, Rhode Island. After enjoying an effusive welcome, it returned to sea—without refuelling—and proceeded to sink five Allied merchant ships off Nantucket Island, prompting the *New York Times* to acknowledge, somewhat incredibly, that "no one had thought of the long gray visitor as a destroyer of shipping and perhaps of lives."[32] That perhaps explained why the multimillionaire Andrew Carnegie felt comfortable cruising the coastal waters from Bar Harbor to Nova Scotia that summer.[33]

U-53 then disappeared and was thought to be moving north into Canadian waters. This naturally made coastal communities nervous and caused an alarming if comical reaction near Canso. After a vessel "suspiciously resembling" U-53 was reportedly seen "from various points" near the Hazel Hill cable office, the sentries guarding the station fired "several volleys…into the heavy wood below the office" because "some" of them thought they had seen a shot fired from there. Cecil Boyd, a local resident, later described the event:

> *Reports of strange men in peculiar uniforms being seen jumping in the lake and performing marvelous feats were also current, but there were no captures or casualties reported until the following night, when one of Mr. McIsaac's horses, perhaps mistaking the barracks for a barn in the dark, tried to approach. Not being as familiar with military language as he might have been, he disregarded the halt of the sentry and next morning, as the writer passed, he lay heels in the air, a gory corpse. As we went our way we soliloquized thusly "perchance his dying words were these, 'Ah! Woe is me! Had I but known that Halt meant whoa and that not to halt meant greater woe, I might have worn the halter for many a year to come.'"*[34]

A month later Captain W. G. Tudor, captain of the Dominion Coal Company's vessel, the *Hochelaga*, reported "persistent rumors" that U-53 had been sunk off Sydney by HMCS *Stanley*, one of the St. Lawrence Patrol's vessels. The rumour was not officially confirmed and one of Tudor's crew observed that "it was impossible to secure information" from the naval authorities.[35] In fact, there was nothing to confirm. *U-53* had returned home after attacking the ships off Nantucket and it spent the rest of the war operating in European waters.

More serious, because it was very nearly true, was the report in December 1916 that the *Grilse* had gone down in a gale off Port Mouton, taking with it forty-four officers and men. It had sent out an SOS signal and when search vessels could find no trace of it,

Fig. 8.2: RCN antisubmarine Canadian trawlers in the North West Arm, Halifax.

the ship was assumed to have sunk. It was, the *Kentville Advertiser* thought, "the worst tragedy that has occurred on the Nova Scotian coast for many years."[36] A week later, much to everyone's surprise, the *Grilse* arrived in Shelburne, "battered and disabled...but with her engines still working." Six men had died and two others were severely injured but "like true British sailors," the crew had "stuck to their posts and by heroic endurance and seamanship of the highest skill brought their [ship] to port."[37]

Because of the alarm caused by *U-53* in 1916, the Admiralty again urged Canada to expand its coastal antisubmarine patrols. Ottawa responded by ordering the construction of twelve small antisubmarine trawlers, rounding up a few more local vessels, and also putting the *Acadia*, a fisheries research ship, into service. For its part, the Admiralty ordered 160 small antisubmarine vessels from Canadian—but not Nova Scotian—shipyards, promising that some of them would be allocated to the Canadian Navy if needed.

The situation dramatically worsened in January 1917, when Germany declared that it would now carry out "unrestricted submarine warfare" on all shipping going to Allied destinations. This meant that it would attack American ships as well and that U-boats would attack without warning and not necessarily give crews the opportunity to disembark first. This was the critical point of the war at sea. Shipping losses mounted drastically, to the point that German submarines were sinking as much as 25% of the merchant shipping crossing the Atlantic, creating serious shortages of war matériel and food supplies. By the end of April, naval authorities in London believed that Britain was within weeks of defeat.

Among the many ships sunk in the first half of 1917 were several Nova Scotian vessels, among them the *Harry W. Adams* in January, the *Tritonia* and *Bessie A. Crooks* in February, the *James Burton Cook* and the *Norma Pratt* in March, the *Dykland, Pontiac,* and *Storstad* in May, and *The Scottish Hero* in June. The number of sinkings did not seem to discourage people from travelling, perhaps because they took place well away from Canadian coastal waters. Clarence Mackinnon and his wife travelled to Trinidad in December 1916, and Helen Creighton, her mother, and a number of other friends enjoyed an extended cruise in the Caribbean in the spring of 1917. Mackinnon later recalled that "as yet we suffered no sense of fear" because "we had an imperial confidence that Britannia ruled the waves."[38]

The situation was desperate, however, but two things turned it around. The first was that David Lloyd George, who had become prime minister of Britain in December 1916, finally succeeded in persuading the Admiralty to organize merchant shipping in defended convoys. Long resisted because the naval "experts" thought convoys just provided a larger target; this decision was in fact the key to victory. Within three months shipping losses fell to less than 1%, because the U-boats had great difficulty in finding the convoys. The second major development was that the United States entered the war in April. Its vast financial, industrial, and manpower resources virtually guaranteed victory in the war, although it would take some time for the country to mobilize.

Initially, the Canadian convoy assembly points were Halifax and—for the summer traffic—Sydney. Convoys were then divided according to speed, the faster ones sailing from Halifax and the slower ones from Sydney. Rear Admiral Bertram Chambers was appointed port convoy officer at Sydney, and Captain Walter Hose was appointed commodore of patrols.

Sydney Harbour was not, however, a defended port like Halifax, aside from the almost useless field guns that had been mounted in 1914. This quickly changed when it was placed under naval control in August 1917 and an antisubmarine net was installed, extending from South Bar to Stubbert's Point. The gate was opened by the *Una*, a demasted schooner, while the *Lansdowne*, a former government steamer now part of the navy, kept guard with its one six-pounder Hotchkiss gun. Harbour defences were also strengthened by moving the battery at Sydney Mines to Cranberry Head and building new ones at Fort Petrie, across the harbour from the battery at Chapel Point, and at Low Point. These batteries had 4.7" quick-fire guns on coastal defence mounts "that were a great improvement" over the earlier field artillery guns.[39]

The coastal patrol service continued to grow, although its vessels were small, slow, and weakly armed. In the summer of 1917, the St. Lawrence Patrol had fifty new drifters and trawlers and six government steamers and converted yachts, but many of the newly built drifters and trawlers had defects or were not yet fully equipped.[40] In May 1918 the US Navy lent the Canadian Navy six 110-foot-long submarine chasers. Three were stationed at Halifax and three went to Sydney.

The war at sea reached its climax in March 1918 when Germany launched a submarine offensive to coincide with its last massive attempt to shatter the Allied forces on the Western Front. For Nova Scotians, the most dramatic—and horrifying—incident was the sinking of the *Llandovery Castle* off the coast of Ireland on June 27. The *Llandovery Castle* was a Canadian hospital ship that brought wounded soldiers to Halifax for convalescent care. Attacking hospital ships violated international law, of course, and was even against the standing orders of the German Navy. The German government initially insisted that the ship had struck a mine, but when survivors reported the facts, it shifted ground and claimed that the ship had been thought to be transporting American troops even though it was marked with a large red cross.

This was bad enough, but what made it even worse was that *U-86* surfaced and machine-gunned some of the survivors in their lifeboats. The result was that of the 258 crew and medical personnel on board, only twenty-four survived, making this the worst Canadian naval disaster of the war. It could have been even worse. If the *Llandovery Castle* had been sailing from England instead of to it, it would have been carrying more than 600 wounded soldiers.

Among the dead were Lieutenant Colonel Thomas MacDonald, the Port Hawkesbury physician who commanded the hospital unit, and most shockingly, all fourteen of the Canadian nurses on board. The Allied press claimed that the nurses were among those shot by *U-86*'s crew but this was not true. They died when their lifeboat was sucked into the vortex caused by the sinking ship. Two of them were Nova Scotians. Pearl Fraser, the ship's nursing matron, was the daughter of Duncan Cameron Fraser, a Pictou County lawyer and former lieutenant governor of Nova Scotia, and his wife Bessie. Their son, Laurier, had just been killed in action in March.[41] Minnie Follette, who had survived the sinking of the hospital ship *Letitia* in August 1917, was the daughter of Oscar and Lydia Follette of Ward's Brook, Cumberland County. Two hospital staff from Nova Scotia also died: John Purcell of Portuguese Cove and John Spittal of Coldbrook.

The ruthless—and pointless—attack on the *Llandovery Castle* had a profound impact on public opinion in Nova Scotia. The *Yarmouth Telegram* wrote that the "hellish crime" was "so heinous that the Devils in Hell must have felt a shock of horror at the atrocity of the Kaiser's tools."[42] Those seeking scapegoats jumped to the conclusion that German sympathizers or agents in Halifax had somehow facilitated the atrocity by passing information on to the German submarine.[43] The *Bridgewater Bulletin* thundered that "the Hun is here"—a not very subtle reminder that most Lunenburgers were of German descent and had elected an anti-conscription Liberal in 1917.[44]

But the 1918 U-boat offensive focused on the Western Atlantic, i.e., the waters off the coast of the northern American states, Nova Scotia, and the Gulf of St. Lawrence. It began when *U-151* sank the *Dwinsk*, an American troop transport, off the coast of New England, and its crew was brought into Shelburne by a Gloucester fishing schooner after nine days at sea. The women of the local Red Cross Society provided clothing and other comforts, "probably the first [time] in Canada where a Red Cross has had the pleasure and privilege of ministering at first hand to victims of the Hun subs."[45]

That was followed a month later when the crew of the Norwegian *Marosa* arrived on Cranberry Island, near Canso, ten days after its vessel was sunk at sea. Two weeks later the schooner *Judge Boyce*, captained by Archibald Publicover, brought into LaHave the eighty-seven-man crew of the *Tokuyama Maru*, a Japanese freighter. The *Kentville Advertiser* did not exaggerate when it declared that "the war has come to Nova Scotia," and those who thought it "was far away and we were safe now have their eyes opened."[46]

For the most part, however, the U-boats focused on destroying fishing boats. *U-156* sank twenty-one in the Gulf of Maine in August. Most of them were American but many of their captains and/or crew members were Nova Scotians. A case in point was the *Muriel*, whose captain, Eldridge Nickerson, was born at Shag Harbour but lived for many years in Everett, Massachusetts, and fished out of Gloucester. He and his men spent the night rowing to Yarmouth after the *Muriel* was sunk on August 3. *U-156* also sank a freighter, the *Dornfontein*, off Brier Island and the *Luz Blanca*, a tanker that had just left Halifax for Tampico, on the eighteenth.[47]

Despite the German policy since 1917 of sinking ships on sight, the attacks on fishing vessels in Nova Scotian waters continued to be very gentlemanly affairs. Their procedure was to surface and come alongside the fishing vessel and allow their crew to depart in their dories, sometimes after giving them a tour of the submarine and even lunch, before sinking the vessel with an explosive device.[48] An American sailor whose vessel was captured by *U-151* reported that he and his fellow crewmen "carried their phonograph with them and traded records with the Germans who were willing to play anything except 'My Country Tis of Thee.'"[49]

The U-boat captains made a point of assuring their victims that they did not want to harm them, only to sink their vessels. The crews still had to make their way into the nearest port, however, and because fishing boats did not have wireless radios, the first news anyone had of their fate came when their crews arrived in their lifeboats, whereupon they regaled the local press with accounts of their adventure.

Then Richard Feldt, U-*156*'s captain, became creative. After stopping the Halifax-based steam trawler *Triumph* near Canso and allowing its crew to take to a lifeboat, he placed a German crew on board with two light guns, wireless equipment, and a supply of bombs. Because it was a local trawler, it was able to approach other vessels without causing any alarm. This enabled it to sink five schooners that day and three more the next. They included the *Lucille M. Schnare, Uda A. Saunders, C. M. Walters, E. B. Walters, Marion Adams, Verna D. Adams, Clayton W. Walters,* and the *Gloaming*, all of Lunenburg. The *Bianca*, built in Liverpool in 1917, and the *Pasadena* of Mahone Bay were also sunk, along with two American vessels, the *J. .J. Flaherty* and the *Erik*. By now the *Triumph* had run out of fuel, so it was scuttled and U-*156* headed for home, only to strike a British mine in the North Sea, making it the only German transatlantic raider that failed to return safely from North American waters.

Before heading home, however, U-*156* was involved in an incident that understandably caused considerable embarrassment to the Royal Canadian Navy. When HMCS *Hochelaga* spotted the surfaced submarine just south of St. Pierre while participating in a four-ship patrol, it turned back to the flotilla leader, "urging caution and suggesting that they await reinforcements" instead of immediately attacking it.[50] By the time HMCS *Cartier* got there, U-*156* had submerged and disappeared. Thus, in the only direct confrontation between a Canadian naval vessel and a German U-boat during the war, the Canadian naval officer in charge failed to do his duty.

This was obviously hugely embarrassing to the navy and *Hochelaga*'s captain, Lieutenant Robert Legate, was promptly court-martialled and dismissed from the service. In his defence, the

Hochelaga was only a converted yacht with very light armament, but at the same time a surfaced submarine was highly vulnerable and only lightly armed as well. More significant probably was the fact that Legate was not a professional naval officer. Before the war he had served as fourth officer on a ship that serviced the undersea telegraph cable, and he had joined the navy in April 1917.[51] As Marc Milner points out, the leniency of the court martial suggests that he was treated "with some consideration" because his superiors understood the limits of their personnel, "both in quantity and quality."[52] Still, as Sydney's *Daily Post* commented, Legate had been given an opportunity "that is given to very few men more than once in a life time. It was within his grasp to bring honor not only to himself but to other members of the service" but "he hesitated and—he lost."[53]

The submarine offensive had the effect of making Sydney Harbour, which Kingsmill had written off in 1914 as being of no real significance, "the most important military port in Canada."[54] The Halifax convoys were shifted to Sydney, partly because—as local promoters had been pointing out since the 1860s—it was the closest North American port on the short great circle route to Europe. This meant that ships sailing from American ports could save days of backtracking to join convoys by making for Sydney. But it was also because the waters off Halifax are more shallow, which meant that there was much greater risk of mines being be laid there.

Ships sailing from Montreal and Quebec also joined convoys in Sydney and rendezvoused with the ships from American convoys on the Grand Banks. Some Quebec convoys sailed through the Strait of Belle Isle, the shortest and fastest passage to the great circle route. Because the Strait of Belle Isle was a difficult passage, however, the majority of convoys continued to sail through the gulf south of Newfoundland and had to be escorted by the St. Lawrence Patrol. This meant that the naval staff at Sydney not only had to organize and dispatch two convoys every eight days, but they also had to provide escorts for the convoys sailing from Halifax to Sydney and those sailing between Sydney and Newfoundland ports, which included the vessels that brought iron ore from Bell Island to the two steel plants. The St. Lawrence Patrol also patrolled the Gulf of St. Lawrence and escorted the Newfoundland ferry. This could only be done if more naval ships were provided, and several were transferred from Halifax. The US Navy, which had accepted responsibility for coastal patrols and antisubmarine operations as far north as Lockeport, also lent the USS *Yorktown* to patrol the Grand Banks as well as two torpedo boats and six submarine chasers.[55]

Although there were only three submarines involved in the coastal offensive, they certainly made Nova Scotians understand that the war was being fought just off their shores, and made them nervous. Blackout regulations had been imposed in September 1916 requiring "all seaport towns in Nova Scotia" to show no lights after dark, but this was later modified to exclude lights not visible from the sea. They were enforced in Halifax but not in Sydney until 1918 because the steel plant's lights could not be extinguished at night, and the glare from the slag heap could be observed from up to fifty kilometres at sea.[56] Lights were extinguished in 1918, nonetheless.

Halifax city council now established a Committee on Public Safety to prepare an action plan in case the city should be attacked. It included sirens and identified buildings that could be used as shelters, and advocated the establishment of emergency nursing stations throughout the city.[57] The committee even contacted authorities in England regarding air raid precautions.[58] Eventually the *Morning Chronicle* pointed out that there had not been a submarine attack in four years and that protecting Halifax from enemy submarines was the function of the Royal Navy, which seemed to be managing the situation quite well.[59]

Just to calm public fears, however, naval authorities staged a mock raid to see if small vessels could sneak into the harbour at night. Not surprisingly, they were spotted by the garrison artillery, which fired upon them, using blanks. The *Morning Chronicle* assured its readers that "the results of the evening's practice is [*sic*] exceedingly gratifying to the military authorities and should serve to calm whatever members of the public have been disturbed."[60]

Even so, some remained convinced that enemy aliens in Halifax and elsewhere were aiding the enemy. The *Halifax Herald* offered a cash reward for information leading to the arrest of enemy agents that it believed infested Halifax, and claimed that "mysterious signalling by lights" had been observed "from points in and about Chester to islands and to points out at sea." Specifically, it charged that on the night of August 19/20,

> *when a U-boat was known to be off Chester, there was great activity in signalling. A visitor who had some experience in codation, engaged a motor boat and went out to sea to confirm his suspicions. He found that signals were being flashed from Chester to a point on or near Tancook Island, and also from this point the signals were reflashed to a motor boat some distance at sea, from which, in turn, the messages were relayed to some point on the Nova Scotia coast.*[61]

Claiming that "we know there are people of foreign birth summering at points where they could be useful to the enemies of the country," the *Herald* demanded to know why "the many isolated coves" were not being patrolled, and why a man known to be of German origin "who occupies an advantageous point on the eastern side of St. Margaret's Bay" was allowed to remain there during a war. Was he, the *Herald* wanted to know, "a link in the chain?"[62]

This allegedly dangerous German turned out to be James Lietchi, a retired Dalhousie professor, admittedly a German immigrant many years earlier, who had retired to Lunenburg in 1906. Neighbours had reported seeing lights on his farm late one night, which made them suspect that he was "signalling Germans from his home on the Cossman farm." Military authorities investigated and were soon satisfied that the light was just a lantern used by a hired man working after dark. Major General Lessard, the commanding officer of Military District 6, also assured people that "suspicious characters" in Nova Scotia were being kept "under close surveillance." To its credit, the *Bridgewater Bulletin*, which had displayed a disturbing level of prejudice in recent months, came to Lietchi's defence, pointing out that he was "an old man, a gentleman, a scholar, and, we believe, true to the country of his adoption." The "imputation cast on him by hasty and ill-principled people"—which the *Bulletin* had published—was "a shame and a disgrace."[63]

The underlying question that stimulated much of the fear that someone was aiding the U-boats was how they were able to operate so effectively in Nova Scotia's shallow coastal waters, which were often treacherous. Lessard provided the explanation, which was that "the majority" of the U-boat captains or senior officers were seamen who had lived in the region.[64] This may have been an exaggeration but it was certainly true of *U-156*, and a sailor on *U-151* told a captured American sailor that men for the submarine offensive had been "drafted from among sailors formerly in the merchant marine with American ports."[65]

This was certainly true of *U-156*, the most successful of the submarines. Richard Feldt, its captain, told the captain of the *Gladys M. Hollett* that he had commanded a Gloucester fishing vessel before the war and "had made the acquaintance of many Lunenburg captains." In fact, "he had...a complete record of all vessels" in the Lunenburg fleet, including "the names of skippers and number of men in the crews, tonnage, destinations, etc."[66] *U-156*'s first officer had also lived in the United States for many years and still owned a summer home on the Maine coast.[67] Some sailors from American schooners that were sunk said they recognized him because he had formerly served in the US Fisheries Service.[68] Another officer on *U-156* told Cyrus Walters, captain of the *E. B. Walters*, that "he had a brother sailing out of Lunenburg," and Walters "said he believed he knew who the Hun referred to."[69]

Meanwhile, the government announced the formation of a Royal Canadian Naval Air Service to support the coastal patrols and the escort of convoys. The British, American, and Canadian naval leaders who met in Washington just after the US declaration of war to draw up a collaborative plan for coastal defence had all agreed it should include the use of aircraft, but it took a year to persuade the government to embrace the idea.

When the government, in anticipation of the impending U-boat campaign, decided to form the RCNAS in April 1918, the Admiralty sent over a senior officer to organize it. That took until September 5, but recruiting began in August. More than 600 men applied and eighty recruits were almost immediately sent to Boston for seaplane training and another eighteen to England for airship instruction.

The only way anything effective could be done was if the US Navy took charge because the RCNAS was starting from scratch and the RAF could not spare officers or machines. The US Navy had included Nova Scotia in its plans for the Atlantic coastal defence even before the war, so it was able to move quickly. It began with two seaplane bases, at Baker's Point in Eastern Passage and at Kelly's Beach at North Sydney, and additional bases were planned for Cape Sable, Canso, Cape North, and the Magdalen Islands, but were never built. Inevitably, Bate McMahon got the contract for the construction work.

The bases were American in every respect. They were commanded by Lieutenant Richard E. Byrd, whose official designation was Officer-in-Charge, US Naval Air Force in Canada, but he worked from the Baker's Point facility while Lieutenant Robert Donoghue commanded the North Sydney base, reporting to him. All the aircrew and support personnel were American and the bases were even allowed to fly the American flag. Their aircraft were Curtiss HS2 seaplanes, or flying boats as they were described; plans called for dirigibles and kite balloons but they did not arrive before the war ended. The task of the four, then six, aircraft at each base, was to escort all Halifax and Sydney convoys, both inward and outward. Working in relays, the planes could escort convoys as far as about 100 kilometres out to sea. They also did as much coastal patrolling as possible.

Two aircraft made their first flights over Halifax early in September, not only surprising the city's residents but also causing some consternation to the local coastal defence commander, who had not been informed that aircraft had been added to the defence system. "This I would be glad to get," he commented dryly, "as the fortress is equipped with anti-aircraft defences."[70]

Aircraft were still rare in Nova Scotia, so their appearances aroused considerable interest. When one of them caught fire and made an emergency landing in Halifax Harbour on August 30, there naturally were "many rumors, which in time became

Fig. 8.3: This US Naval Air Service base in North Sydney was part of the war effort.

greatly exaggerated,...that there had been [an] aerial battle above McNab's Island."[71] At the beginning of November two aircraft visited Chester, Lunenburg, Bridgewater, Liverpool, Shelburne, and Yarmouth to promote the 1918 Victory Loan campaign and attracted great crowds everywhere. As they flew along the coast from Halifax, "they attracted throngs of the fisher-folk in the little villages from their cottages. It was a miraculous sight to all of them." Inevitably, "some of those who had not seen the announcement of the flight in the press had visions of a German invasion, but in every case curiosity conquered alarm."[72]

In Lunenburg "the wharves were crowded with people, the harbour was packed with numerous boats of all kinds anxious to view what is considered the greatest phenomenon of the age."[73] At Bridgewater, where the planes landed on the LaHave River near the Acadia Gas Engines factory, "hundreds of people lined the riverbanks gazing at a spectacle few had expected to see in their lifetimes."[74] At Liverpool, "an immense body of persons gathered at

Fig. 8.4: When this US Naval Air Service plane landed at Bridgewater in November 1918, it was undoubtedly the first to do so.

Fort Point" and along the waterfront.[75] Similar flights took place in Cape Breton by aircraft from the North Sydney base.

The RCNAS never really got off the ground, so to speak, before the war ended on November 11. The men training in Britain and the United States were brought home, the service was disbanded on December 5, and the Americans were gone before Christmas. All air patrols had been carried out by American pilots, but there had been no contacts with enemy ships or submarines. There were three fatalities, however: John Crilly, William Shaffert, and Robert Johnson died in the Spanish influenza epidemic.[76]

In all, 110,000 tons of shipping were sunk between Cape Hatteras and Newfoundland from May to October 1918. This sounds like a lot but in terms of the war effort it was not significant because the vessels lost were fishing boats and coastal freighters. This involved a cost and even a risk to fishermen and some chose not to go to sea that summer. But sinking these vessels could not contribute to a German victory in Europe. In fact, the German Army was in retreat by the end of August and the end of the war was in sight. The last Nova Scotian vessel to be sunk was the *Industrial*, which was torpedoed on October 15 en route from the Turks and Caicos Islands to LaHave with a cargo of salt.[77]

Had Canada's new navy contributed to winning the war and protecting coastal communities? It had certainly played a much larger role in escorting merchant shipping and patrolling coastal waters in 1917–18 than anyone had thought possible in 1914. Indeed, it had grown from ten ships into a fleet of more than one hundred by 1918 and was handling much of the coastal patrolling in the Gulf of St. Lawrence and along the Atlantic coastline.

It didn't sink any German warships or submarines but, as the US Navy later concluded in its postwar assessment, the U-boat offensive failed because "every transport and cargo vessel" sailed on schedule and after July 1917 almost all of them got through. This success was attributable to the convoy system, to be sure, but it also reflected the work of the small and lightly armed patrol vessels of the Canadian and American navies.[78] The Royal Navy never had to divert one major antisubmarine warship from the critical battle in the Eastern Atlantic to protect the coastal waters of Canada and Newfoundland.[79] And as Marc Milner points out, it was the Canadian naval staff in Halifax and Sydney who "organized shipping, developed defended ports and secure anchorages, regulated patrols, monitored wireless communications, and provided support for British cruisers that secured adjacent waters."[80] And it was not insignificant that Nova Scotians were the only Canadians who experienced the war at home.

Chapter 9

THE END AT LAST

How much longer will this war last? Aren't you nearly discouraged? There seems [sic] *no signs of an ending, but I suppose we must carry on.*[1]

As NOVA SCOTIA ENTERED 1918, THE ATTENTION OF Haligonians was focused on two issues: determining who was responsible for the Halifax explosion, and rebuilding the shattered city. Public opinion, fanned by the press, had already moved beyond shock to outrage as officials, both civilian and military, ducked for cover while seeking a scapegoat to take the blame. The situation was complicated by the fact that, while the navy controlled the port, the pilots who guided ships in and out of the harbour were civilians who came under the jurisdiction of the

Halifax Pilotage Commission, and the port's senior naval officers had been told to interfere with it as little as possible.

It seems unnecessary to go into the unsavoury details of the investigation, which have been fully described elsewhere. Because the *Mont-Blanc*'s captain and pilot, who had caused the collision, were dead, their actions were not questioned in a botched inquiry that placed all the blame on Frederick Wyatt, the port's chief examining officer, Aimé Le Médec, the *Imo*'s captain, and Francis Mackey, its pilot. All were charged with manslaughter and negligence but Nova Scotia's Supreme Court declared that it lacked jurisdiction so no one was ever found responsible for the disaster. Wyatt and Le Médec went on to pursue their careers elsewhere and the senior naval officers at the port were posted elsewhere, leaving Mackey—the least influential person involved—as the scapegoat. He lost his pilot's licence and was unemployed until a new federal government reviewed the case and reinstated him.[2]

Meanwhile, the federal government, by now well aware of the mismanagement of the Halifax Pilotage Commission, appointed a royal commission to investigate its administration and practices. Its scathing report cleared the way for the government to use its powers under the War Measures Act to seize control of the port for the duration of the war. It also established the Halifax Relief Commission to manage all aspects of relief and reconstruction. It was chaired by Tecumseh Sherman Rogers, a judge of the Nova Scotia Supreme Court, and included W. B. Wallace, a Halifax County Court judge, and F. W. Fowke, a merchant from Oshawa, Ontario. Ralph Pickard Bell was appointed secretary and the ubiquitous George Cutten was appointed the commission's director of rehabilitation.[3]

Temporary housing had to be built for the 8,000 homeless and, not surprisingly, the contract went to Bate McMahon, which was already erecting two of the new buildings at the Ocean Terminal and a long stretch of new track for the Intercolonial Railway. Bate

McMahon built tenement-style apartment houses as temporary residences while existing housing was repaired and restored if possible and the devastated areas were cleared for new construction. Tenement housing was not ideal, of course, but it was intended to be only temporary and could be built quickly. Building equipment, supplies, horses, and 2,200 workers were brought in and housed at the exhibition grounds. Local construction companies that received contracts brought in 1,500 more men.

Within thirty days Robert Low had succeeded in building accommodations for 1,000 people on the South Common in forty two-storey buildings housing 320 apartments. Four sixteen-unit apartment buildings and temporary stables were built as well, and the "Governor McCall" apartments—named after the governor of Massachusetts—provided shelter to an additional 2,200 people when completed in March. These structures, although simple and rough, did provide shelter from the winter weather with water, electricity, and a sewage system.[4]

At the same time, Bate McMahon had 200 workers camped in tents at Fort Needham, clearing and excavating an area in the North End which the *Morning Chronicle* claimed had been "for years a challenge to civic or private enterprise." The result was the 320 hydrostone houses built in the Hennessey Field area, while another 100 wooden houses were built nearby. Thus, what had been "an unsightly swampy waste" with "irregular haphazard buildings on… rough, rugged, ugly roads" was transformed into "broad, well-graded courts and walks, pleasant 'parked' spaces…with dwelling houses which will be a credit to the North End and to the City." No one, the *Morning Chronicle* thought, "can fail to recognize how great is the opportunity which a great catastrophe has opened, and to be glad that at last the North End seems to be coming into its own."[5]

Meanwhile, the war took a nasty and alarming turn in March when the German Army launched Operation Michael, its last desperate offensive on the Western Front. It was a massive affair, intended to shatter the British Army and force the French to seek peace terms. Even though the Allies had been expecting it, Operation Michael was initially very successful because of its scale and ferocity. The Germans came so close to St. Omer, the British Army headquarters, that the hospitals there were threatened. Among them were the two Nova Scotian hospitals: No. 7 (Dalhousie), now commanded by Dr. Edward Hogan of Weymouth, and No. 9 (St. Francis Xavier), now commanded by Dr. Henry Kendall of Sydney.

They were evacuated north to Etaples, which proved to be no safer than St. Omer because they were attacked by sixty German aircraft on May 18. To be fair, the Germans were probably trying to destroy the train station and railyards but they also hit several of the hospitals. Both Nova Scotian hospitals suffered casualties. No. 7's Dr. Hogan was wounded and Fred Laidlaw of Wittenburg, Colchester County, was killed. No. 9 had three men killed, including Dr. William Fielding McIsaac of Antigonish and Horace MacMillan of Isaac's Harbour, and twelve wounded. At the same time, Nursing Sister Lottie Urquhart of New Glasgow, who was serving with No. 6 Canadian General Hospital, was one of six nurses awarded the Military Medal because she set "an inspiring example," continuing to attend her patients when four bombs fell on her wards.[6] Another raid on the twenty-ninth at Doullens, where No. 3 Canadian Stationary Hospital was located, resulted in the deaths of Dr. Ethelbert Meek of Five Islands and two nurses.

The spring offensive ran out of steam by summer because, despite their dramatic advances, the Germans had suffered 800,000 casualties and had no more reserves. The Allies had nearly as many casualties, but American troops were now arriving in large numbers to replace them. By August there were one million US troops in France and 300,000 more were arriving each month. The implications were obvious. That was when the Allies attacked Amiens, which marked the beginning of the end of the war, because the Allies remained on the offensive right up to November 11 when Germany surrendered.

Those three months became known as "Canada's Hundred Days" because the Canadian Corps played "a disproportionate role" in it, a dubious distinction that reflected the reputation it had earned since 1916 as an effective fighting force.[7]

It paid a high price for the honour: 45,835 casualties, 45% of the Corps's strength on August 8 and 20% of all Canadian casualties suffered during the war.[8] It is worth noting that most of the reinforcements received during this period—24,132—were conscripts,[9] and by all reports they fought as well as the volunteers. Some of them died, including Ernest Amirault of Middle East Pubnico, who was killed on October 8, and Anthony Doucette of Tusket, who was killed two days later.

The attack on Amiens caught the Germans by surprise because, as Ernest Miller of Noel explained, "for four days before we reached the front we did all our marching by night, and lay hidden in the woods and villages by day." Then the 900-gun artillery barrage was delayed until the troops were actually leaving their trenches. That was when "Hell broke loose, as the war writers say. In other words the barrage opened with a crash and we were off."[10] Lewis Peebles of Mulgrave, a lieutenant in the Canadian artillery, described the barrage as "the awfullest [*sic*] thing ever heard on this earth," with "great red tongues of vivid fire...flashing and leaping from deep throated and murderous guns."[11]

Some 420 tanks participated in the attack, making this the first battle in which they played a major role. John Ronald MacLellan of Belle Cote noticed that the way the war was being fought had changed. "The roar of the guns, the bursting of shells, the fast flying aeroplanes overhead and the slow moving tanks beneath them, the dash of the cavalry and the rush of the infantry, all contribute to make the recent battles different from any others in this or ancient wars."[12] He was right.

Even so, the hard work was done, as usual, by the infantry. It started well, Miller commenting that "for the first few miles the advance was easy....more like a promenade than a fight."[13] There was an explanation for this. When "Billy" Adams of Canaan captured thirteen Germans "in a cold cellar," he observed that "they were glad to go, they were dam [*sic*] well fed up." As a bonus, Adams also liberated "four parcels" of their recently received packages from home, "and you talk of cake, well I had it that day, a lot fresher than what we get from Canada, then I took 150 cigars."[14] But the fighting got harder as the day went on. Arthur Johns, a farmer from Woodville, described it as "the hottest place I have been in....I never expected to get out of it, and I remember that through it all I was saying to-morrow is Amy's birthday."[15]

After three days of hard fighting, the city was taken, at a cost of 40,000 casualties, including nearly 12,000 Canadians. Among those killed was Lieutenant Colonel Thomas Raddall, known to his men as "Old Tom" because he was forty years old in 1918. The Germans lost almost twice as many men as the Allies but, more significantly, 15,000 surrendered and 400 German guns were captured. Arthur Johns told his wife that "the Canadian boys did not spoil their reputation but rather put more lustre upon it."[16] The *Times* of London agreed, declaring that the Canadian assault was "the biggest thing Canada has done in the War," an assessment that Julian Byng fully endorsed, as have military historians.[17]

Ten Canadians were awarded Victoria Crosses at Amiens, among them John Bernard Croak, a twenty-six-year-old coal miner from New Aberdeen. Born at Little Bay in Newfoundland, he had moved with his parents to Cape Breton seeking work. Croak was awarded the Victoria Cross not only for capturing a machine gun and its crew but also for leading his platoon, despite being wounded, in the capture of three more machine guns and an entire garrison. He died of his wounds later that day.

According to Robert Clements, the capture of Amiens was significant for the Canadians because the men now "sensed the kill. The whole Canadian Army was eager to get on with it and clean up the whole bloody mess once and for all."[18] The Reverend A. J. MacDonald, the Presbyterian chaplain with the 25th Battalion, sensed this as well, saying that the men "went into the fray confident of victory."[19] General Erich Ludendorff agreed with them; he called August 8 the blackest day of the war and sensibly told the kaiser that the war must be ended.

Fig. 9.1: John Bernard Croak, a coal miner from New Aberdeen, was awarded the Victoria Cross for his heroic actions at Amiens, France.

Amiens was followed by an assault on the Hindenburg Line, which Currie described as "without doubt one of the strongest defences on the Western Front."[20] It was taken after a week's fighting and the Germans withdrew across the Canal du Nord, the defensive barrier protecting Cambrai. Because the Germans were entrenched on the other side, Currie was reluctant to launch a frontal assault across the canal. Instead, he moved two divisions to the south and attacked across a dry section of the uncompleted canal to seize a narrow bridgehead, then expanded outward and got behind the German defences while the other two divisions attacked in the north.

The attack began on September 27 behind a heavy artillery barrage that included 17,000 gas shells. Most Canadians are probably unaware of the fact that the Canadian Corps had become by now "the major user" of gas shells on the Western Front.[21] After the most savage and sustained battle in the history of the Corps, the canal was secured on October 1 in what has been described as "the single greatest achievement of the Canadian Corps" because "an all but impregnable position had been taken."[22]

As usual, fatal casualties were heavy—2,089 men, including Lieutenant Colonel Charles Stewart, who had been commanding the Princess Patricia's Canadian Light Infantry since March. A member of a prominent Amherst family, Stewart had been expelled from the Royal Military College, then served briefly in the Royal North West Mounted Police before disappearing in the Yukon, emerging in August 1914 to join the PPCLI. He was a hard-drinking, free-spirited, and courageous man whose men would follow him anywhere. He was also the last officer of the "Old Originals" to command the PPCLI in the war.

Cambrai, the main German rail centre in northern France, was taken a week later in a battle that included an attack by the Canadian Cavalry Brigade southeast of the city at Le Cateau. Lieutenant General Charles Kavanagh, commander of the British

Cavalry Corps, described the work of the cavalry as "the best action carried out by any cavalry unit on any front during the war."[23] It was also the last cavalry charge of the war and, although many may not have realized it at the time, the end of cavalry as a meaningful component of modern armies. James Cann, a farmer from Hebron, who had enlisted in the 10th Canadian Mounted Rifles in May 1915, was one of the many Canadian cavalrymen who participated in but did not survive this historic event.

Liberating French towns and villages was an emotional experience for the Canadians. Many had been totally destroyed and abandoned, while others were still inhabited but had suffered under the long German occupation. Charles Murray of New Glasgow, serving in the 85th Battalion, reported that some people were "jubilant with laughter and clap their hands and shout, while others give way to weeping." When the 85th entered one town, led by its band playing "La Marseillaise," "you never saw such a demonstration. Poor Mr. Mooney had the girls clinging around his neck and lovely bunches of flowers were given him."[24]

The Germans now withdrew to their last defensive line, the Hermann-Stellung Line, which stretched from the Dutch border through Valenciennes to the Oise River. When the Canadians captured Valenciennes, the last major French city still in enemy hands, on November 1, the war was effectively over. Germany, Austria-Hungary, and the Ottoman Empire were discussing peace terms with the Allies, the German Army was in disarray, and the US Army had forty-two divisions in the field and more on the way. Still, tragically for the soldiers on both sides, there was no surrender.

The Canadian Corps entered Belgium on the seventh, with the 25th Battalion driving the Germans out of Elouges, a town only eighteen kilometres from Mons where the first shots of the war had been fired in 1914. Angus L. Macdonald—who later became a much-loved premier of Nova Scotia—was shot by a sniper that day and "was a prisoner in the enemy lines until the next morning," when he was found "lying on the floor of an old building."[25] Two days later the Canadians were on the outskirts of Mons. George Chapman, who had enlisted in the 185th in Sydney Mines, told his sister that day that "old Fritz...will sign the peace terms now and the general opinion is that we have seen the last of the fighting."[26]

He was both right and wrong. Germany was ready to surrender, although still haggling over terms, and the Allies had no intention of holding back until it capitulated. They especially wanted to capture Mons because that was the point from which the British had begun their retreat in November 1914. As the Canadians approached and encircled the town, they sustained 645 unnecessary and pointless casualties. Four Nova Scotians, all serving in the Royal Canadian Regiment, died at Mons on the tenth and eleventh: Frank McLean of Pictou and Donald Shields of Brooklyn on the tenth; Clarence Sholds of Shelburne was wounded that evening and died at 5:30

Fig. 9:2: Arthur Currie takes the salute in Mons, November 11, 1918.

the next morning; and Archibald McLellan of Egypt (Inverness County) was killed early on the eleventh.

An hour later, at 6:30, Currie received official word that the armistice had been signed and would take effect at 11:00 AM. At this point the pipe band of the 42nd Battalion—Will Bird's unit—was marching through the town announcing its liberation even though there were still pockets of resistance to the east of the town. That meant more casualties.

The last Canadian soldier killed in the war was twenty-five-year-old George Price, a native of Falmouth who was serving in the 28th (Saskatchewan) Battalion because he was living in Moose Jaw when he was conscripted in December 1917.[27] When Price was shot by a sniper just minutes before 11:00 am at Ville-sur-Haine, a village about fifteen kilometres east of Mons, he was not just the last Nova Scotian to be killed in the war; he was also the last Canadian and the last soldier from the British Empire to be killed in the war.[28] In a curious coincidence, the last RAF pilot to be killed in the war was also a Nova Scotian. Twenty-four-year-old Second Lieutenant Alexander "Billy" McHardy of McLellan's Mountain, Pictou County, died in an air battle over nearby Charleroi on November 10.[29]

The reaction of the soldiers in the field to the armistice was generally muted. George Chapman said they showed "no excitement,"[30] and Robert Clements thought "the general mood was one of relief and quiet thanks....The truth was that these men were dreadfully tired, almost beyond human endurance."[31] It was different back home. The news of the armistice sparked spontaneous celebrations and parades all across the country, not unlike those that had cheered the declaration of war in August 1914. In fact, the celebrations began in North Sydney, Sydney, and Truro on November 4 when it was announced that Austria-Hungary had signed an armistice with Italy, coming just days after Bulgaria and the Ottoman Empire signed peace agreements.

The first people in Nova Scotia to get the news were, of course, the telegraph operators at the Western Union cable station in North Sydney. Despite their commitment to confidentiality, word quickly got out into the community and "practically everyone went to Commercial Street and waved flags in frenzied excitement as more than twenty American servicemen marched down the street singing and beating every pot, pan, and noise-maker they had

Fig. 9.3: George Price was the last Canadian and Nova Scotian to be killed in action. He was shot by a sniper.

been able to lay hands on."[32] In Sydney, the fire station's alarm was sounded, whistles began blowing, and "the vessels in the harbor then took up full cry." Later, "dozens of leaders took charge of dozens of parades, but there being no chief, it was a disorganized army of celebrants." Within minutes hundreds of people were on Charlotte Street waving flags and "every automobile in the street was commandeered and was a moving piece of bunting."[33]

The news especially thrilled the area's large Italian community, 800 of whom flooded into Sydney from the surrounding area, some courtesy of the Dominion Coal Company, which provided a special train from New Waterford. There they "paraded through crowded streets" with "gaily decorated horses, carriages, [and] automobiles" in "a moving panorama of flying flags" led by police sergeant Rannie MacDonald and the Sydney Mines YMCA band. The parade ended at the Lyceum Theatre where a packed house listened to patriotic speeches, including one by William Carroll, the former MP, who reminded the audience that John Cabot—popularly thought to be the first European to visit Cape Breton—was an Italian.

Truro's response to the news was similar, if understandably smaller in scale. More than 2,000 people lined the streets of the town, "all in a merry mood over the joyful news," to watch a parade of thirty automobiles, "many decorated with flags and bunting," led by the town band and the fire brigade.[34]

The good folks of North Sydney, Sydney, and Truro were premature in their celebrations, of course, but only by a few days. The correct announcement that Germany had signed an armistice agreement arrived at 4:00 AM on November 11. The *Morning Chronicle* immediately sent telegrams to other newspapers throughout the region and notified "prominent citizens of each community" by telephone, so that before 4:30 "every section of the Maritime Provinces knew that the world was at last free from the scourge of war."[35]

It was not entirely unexpected. Halifax's blackout regulations had been cancelled on October 26 and on the evening of the twenty-seventh "the central portion of the city was a blaze of brightness which dazzled the eyes of those long accustomed to shadow." The shops on Barrington Street stayed open "and there were great crowds along the sidewalks.... Halifax seemed a different city."[36]

On the morning of the eleventh, crowds poured into the streets and "horns blared, bells rang, whistles tooted, and over all rose the shouts of human voices.... Every vehicle carried some sort of decoration, flags and bunting being the most popular." Most shops and restaurants closed at six o'clock, however, fearing that the evening would bring rioting. Happily, that didn't happen and

> *it was merely a repetition of the scenes during the day, perhaps a little more fortissimo with all the brightness of myriad lights, and the brilliancy of rockets and vari-colored Grecian fires. The crowd never seemed to tire of watching the informal procession of crowded automobiles, of jostling along the packed sidewalks, and shrieking its lungs out. It was rough, but it was not ill-natured.*[37]

In Sydney, the news of Germany's surrender was announced at 7:00 A.M. "with the blowing of whistles and ringing of bells." Within five minutes "the first joyful men, women and children had reached Charlotte Street after having hastily thrown on a few garments, and it was not long after until the whole street was packed." Compared with the boisterous celebrations of the seventh, however, people on the morning of the eleventh were quieter, being "content to discuss between themselves the good news and what it means." An ecumenical service of thanks in Wentworth Park attracted 600 people. At its conclusion, Captain Pasco called on the crowd to cheer the king, the Allies, the navy, and the army, "and at the conclusion three cheers were given for him" as well.[38]

The real celebration in Sydney took place on the twelfth, which Mayor William Fitzgerald had proclaimed a public holiday. The streets were thronged with people, "all laughing and care free, although some of them look[ed] at times very near to tears." There was "scarcely a house" in the city that didn't display a flag and some mounted "elaborate decorations of flags and bunting." Stores like Merchant's and Woolworth's naturally set up stands out front to sell flags to anyone who somehow didn't already have one and sales were so brisk "as almost to tax the capacity of the clerks."[39]

Police chief J. B. McCormack led the victory parade on horseback, followed by civic officials, sailors and soldiers. At least 8,000 people marched in it, including representatives of the Jewish community, who sought to show "not only…that they were grateful" for the liberation of Palestine "but also to show their loyalty to the land of their adoption."[40] Music was provided by the Sydney Mines band, a pipe band, the citizens' band, the band of the 94th Regiment "and the colored band."[41] The parade concluded with a large public meeting at Wentworth Park, where Mayor Fitzgerald and Major James Maddin spoke. Sydney's Lebanese community celebrated the liberation of Syria with its own parade on the seventeenth.[42] As the *Daily Post* put it, they were "celebrating the realization of their object for 575 years, freedom from the unspeakable Turk."[43]

The city's elite gathered at the Sydney Hotel, the city's finest, on the evening of the twelfth for a banquet and "speeches, humorous and patriotic." Then they "formed up in line" and with a piper at their head "gaily marched through the hotel dining room, up stairs and down again. Then they sang some songs, had the piper play some more and then it was all over but the shouting. This was so vociferous that the rafters rattled, but it was for peace and victory and 'everybody's doing it.'"[44]

The American sailors in port gave a dance at Hillcoate's Dancing Academy on Charlotte Street that the *Daily Post* thought would "long be remembered by those who were fortunate enough to attend it." In addition to dancing, there was entertainment. Seaman Jones "sang the American 'Rag' songs in an inimitable manner and was compelled to respond to each solo several times. It was a new thing to most of the people there and they enjoyed it immensely." The dance music was provided by a jazz band and, in the words of the *Daily Post*, "they certainly did put some 'pep' into it."[45]

Similar if smaller celebrations took place throughout the province. All seemed to involve whistles, sirens, the ringing of church bells, parades, church services, burning the kaiser in effigy, and a public holiday. A few inevitably involved some brawling on the part of exuberant soldiers and sailors.[46] The *Digby Courier* reported that the town had "never heard such a racket and never will again."[47] West Jeddore had a special treat because four minesweepers and two drifters were in port and they put on a fireworks show in the evening.[48] The residents of Wolfville and Bridgewater also enjoyed fireworks displays, the *Bulletin* somewhat smugly observing that "Bill Hohenzollern did not size-up the people he went up against."[49]

Antigonish more soberly marked the occasion with a solemn thanksgiving service at St. Ninian's Cathedral presided over by Bishop James Morrison assisted by thirty priests and altar boys, while the *Casket* appealed to people not to tarnish the occasion "by the indulgence of passion under pretext of rejoicing or celebration" and to remember that "millions of mothers are weeping for their sons."[50]

It had a point. Amid all the celebrations on the eleventh, people were still receiving the feared telegram announcing that their husband or son had been killed. The families of Harry Smith of Necum Teuch and Lloyd Marshall of Bear River, for example, only learned after the armistice of the death of their sons back in September. No explanation was offered for why it had taken so long to inform them. Harry Smith's brother, Guy, had been killed back in July 1916.[51]

Unfortunately, the celebrations in Truro ended badly when a mob trashed and looted five stores owned by "Syrians." What provoked this appalling behaviour cannot be determined but it seems likely that some people, perhaps under the influence of alcohol, assumed that Syrian immigrants were Turkish Muslims, i.e., immigrants from one of the enemy countries. In fact, virtually all of the

"Syrians" in Nova Scotia were actually Christians from Lebanon, who rejoiced in the victory that liberated their homeland from the Ottomans. William Massey, for example, had come to Canada when only fourteen years of age. "I have been and am loyal to Canada," he said.[52] This may not really have mattered, because rabid patriotism had caused some people to fear foreigners even if their families had been in Nova Scotia for generations.

Naval operations at Halifax and Sydney ceased almost immediately. Captain James Turnbull, the acting port convoy officer, officially closed the Sydney convoy office on November 26, and by the end of December most of the St. Lawrence Patrol vessels had moved to Halifax. Most of the US naval personnel quickly returned home, although a few remained until the spring of 1919. By the middle of December the harbour fortifications were shut down and the garrisons had been removed, leaving only small caretaking detachments.

THE WAR MAY HAVE BEEN OVER BUT THAT DID NOT MEAN THE troops could come home. Currie had agreed to contribute two divisions to the Allied army that would occupy Germany over the next few months, and he conferred the unappreciated honour on the 1st and 2nd Divisions because they had been the first in the field. This meant that the 85th could remain in Belgium while the 25th had to march 400 kilometres in full gear at a time of year when the persistent rain and mud were at their worst. If that weren't bad enough, billets along the way were poor or non-existent and food supplies did not always keep up with the troops. The untimely arrival of the Spanish influenza epidemic worsened a miserable situation.

The 25th Battalion began marching on November 18 and didn't reach Germany until December 4. As it approached the frontier, its pipe band played "The Highland Soldier," then switched into "Blue Bonnets Over the Border" as it crossed the border. It was led on this historic occasion by its mascot, a goat named Robert the Bruce, with Lieutenant Gordon MacNeil of Iona, the 25th's only original officer, carrying the colours. According to Robert Clements, the men were very tired and really didn't want to be there but "for a brief few minutes heads went up, shoulders were squared and sore feet were forgotten" because they "meant every German in sight... to recognize what it meant to them that day to be Canadians."[53]

THE WAR WOULD NOT REALLY BE OVER UNTIL THE TROOPS CAME home and returned to civilian life. Wounded and ill men had been returning since 1916 and their numbers had grown in 1917 and 1918. But there were still more than 267,000 soldiers and an estimated 54,000 dependents to be brought home, a huge organizational task further complicated by the shortage of available shipping. An exceptionally harsh winter, coal shortages, and strikes by British

Fig. 9.4: The 85th Battalion didn't get to occupy Germany but its band led the Canadian Corps troops in the victory parade in London on May 3, 1919.

dock workers and railway workers didn't help. The British government had planned for up to 50,000 Canadian departures per month but because it was winter, the transports had to use Halifax and Saint John, the only large ice-free ports. Meanwhile, the Canadian railways thought they could only handle 25,000 men per month.

Another complicating factor was how to prioritize the soldiers' return. The Militia Department proposed a "first over, first back" policy, so that those who had been away the longest would be the first to return. That seemed logical but Currie objected, arguing that the troops should not return individually but with their units partly because this would be more efficient but also because it would better maintain morale and discipline. It would also ensure that units disembarking in Canada could be properly welcomed by their communities. As usual, and rightly so, the Militia Department accepted Currie's advice.

In practical terms, however, this meant that many men didn't come home until the spring of 1919, months after the end of the war. The delay naturally led to considerable frustration, which was intensified when in some cases men who had never seen combat were sent home before those who had. The result was unrest in the demobilization camps. The most notorious incident took place at Kinmel Park, situated near Rhyl in Wales, in March 1919.[54] About 17,400 men were there, including many Nova Scotians. Among them were the doctors and nurses of No. 9 Stationary Hospital, who had arrived in December 1918 to provide medical services, and men from No. 2 Construction Company.

One might have thought that Rhyl was an ideal location for a camp because it was a popular seaside resort. But it was a summer resort and the Canadians arrived in the winter. James Johnson recalled that "the huts were cold, the rations were small and bad, [and] the weather was rainy and cold." The huts were also so overcrowded that men had to take turns sleeping on the floor. The weather couldn't be helped and the huts were cold because of a shortage of coal caused by miners' strikes. But the army foolishly had the men on half rations and half pay and made them engage in pointless daily training and route marches. Conditions were no better in the hospital. When it was treating 600 cases of influenza in early February, the building was so cold that its water pipes were bursting.[55] Kinmel Park was a classic case of callous mismanagement.

It should not have surprised anyone, therefore, when "hundreds went on a wild rampage" on March 4, "looting everything in sight."[56] The situation quickly got out of hand and before it ended five men were dead and another twenty-three were wounded. Three of the men killed were rioters but two were among those who had been armed and ordered to help restore order. David Gillan was one of them. A miner from Florence, he had enlisted at the age of sixteen and was only eighteen when he died. For the Gillan family, having their son killed in a preventable riot four months after the war ended must have been devastating, but even worse was the fact that they learned of his death through a report in their local newspaper.[57]

However regrettable, the violence did achieve its goal. The transport problem was immediately addressed and within weeks Kinmel Park Camp had been cleared out. Gillan and the three of the four other men killed in the riot never came home, of course, nor did the 204 men who died there from the Spanish influenza during that terrible winter.[58] Among them were Melville Caudle of Truro and Nursing Sister Rebecca MacIntosh of Pleasant Bay, Cape Breton. These three Nova Scotians rest together in St. Margaret's churchyard in the nearby village of Bodelwyddan, where the villagers subsequently erected a modest monument that says, simply, "Someday, sometime we'll understand."

Those who died of influenza at Kinmel Park were only a small number among the literally millions—estimates range from twenty to one hundred million, including 50,000 in Canada—who died in the worst epidemic in human history. It appears to have spread to Canada from the United States and first arrived in Nova Scotia at Sydney in September 1918 when an American troopship, the *Nestor*, arrived with 150 infected men aboard.[59] Within two days the number of sick Americans had risen to 500. All were put ashore for treatment, creating a serious health crisis. Makeshift hospitals were set up in the curling club, the hockey rink, and five church halls. The home on St. Peters Road of R. F. Randolph, superintendent of the steel plant, was requisitioned as well. Major William Tefft, a US Army medical officer, soon arrived with three nurses and two ambulances to assist the *Nestor*'s two doctors and the local physicians.[60] Although the epidemic did not hit the naval establishments and naval vessels severely enough to interfere with operations, it quickly spread to the general population, and public places—schools, churches, restaurants, and theatres—were closed, although the YMCA remained open. Because of the shortage of nurses, women who had taken first-aid courses, probably never really thinking they would be called upon, volunteered their services. In fact, there was little that could be done for patients aside from trying to make them comfortable.

By early October the epidemic had spread throughout the province, and struck both military personnel and the general population. The Fort Massey cemetery in Halifax includes the graves of thirty-four soldiers who died in Halifax between October 15, 1918, and September 6, 1920, the period when the influenza was active. Two cemeteries in Windsor contain seven men from the Imperial Recruits Depot and two in Dartmouth contain one each. At least two of the Jewish volunteers at Windsor died of pneumonia, which was associated with the influenza.[61] Men who had survived the fighting in Europe and been sent home because of their wounds sometimes succumbed as well.

Particularly poignant was the death of Elisha Mills of Truro. He had enlisted in 1915 and served overseas until the Third Battle of

Ypres, when he was reportedly wounded twenty-eight times. He was sent home in 1917, married, and was appointed collector of customs at Pugwash, only to die of the flu at the age of twenty-one.[62] Even more tragic was the death of Minnie Nowe of Riverport in the second wave of the epidemic in March 1920. Her husband, William Nowe, had been killed while serving with the 25th Battalion on October 12, 1918, the day their only child, Georgina, was born.[63]

On October 14 the *Morning Chronicle* reported that there were 500 cases among Halifax's civilian population and "many more among soldiers and sailors," and "as many men as possible" were being treated at Lawlor's Island.[64] Halifax also adapted the reconstruction camp on the corner of Windsor and Almon Streets to serve as an emergency isolation hospital. Two weeks later this figure had doubled to one thousand.[65] The "good" news was that there had only been fifty-three deaths, but this figure was updated a few days later to ninety-eight, seventy-five of them civilians.[66] Lockeport claimed in mid-October that with 300 cases it was the hardest hit community in the province and issued an appeal for nurses or anyone willing to help.[67] By early November, however, the epidemic had done its worst and closures and restrictions were being lifted throughout the province. It was a crisis that Nova Scotia did not need in the closing stage of a major war and after the destruction and loss of life caused by the Halifax explosion.

WE CAN ONLY IMAGINE THE FEELINGS OF THE RETURNING SOLDIERS when they caught their first glimpse of Nova Scotia. "How bright the skies seemed," Clarence Mackinnon recalled, "how clear and crisp the air and how welcome the low dark line that marked the Nova Scotian coast!"[68] Will Bird found himself unable to sleep, knowing that he was nearly home, so he went up on deck at four o'clock in the morning and discovered to his amazement that others were already there. "We stood, hunched together, gazing ahead into the darkness" until "all at once the watchers stirred, tensed, craned forward. It was the moment for which we had lived, which we had envisioned a thousand times, that held us so full of feeling we could not find utterance. Far ahead, but growing brighter, we had glimpsed the first lights of home!"[69]

When the transports sailed up the harbour, their reception was "simply indescribable," according to Bertram Hayes, the captain of the *Olympic*, which brought so many soldiers home to Halifax. Every ship "was decked with flags, and every one of them kept their whistles blowing all the time we were in sight of them. The ends of the piers we passed on our way up town were crowded with people who added to the noise by their shouts of welcome." He was especially touched that "our ship was not forgotten in the general welcome to the troops. 'Welcome to the Old Reliable' was prominently displayed" among the banners of welcome stretched along the sheds.[70]

The *Olympic* was more than just reliable. A sister ship to the *Titanic*, it was a huge vessel that could travel so fast that it did not need to sail in convoys. It carried many thousands of troops, including Americans, back and forth across the Atlantic. On one memorable occasion, while en route from New York to Cherbourg, it rammed and sank a German submarine, then proceeded on its way. An American destroyer, the USS *Davis*, later picked up thirty-one survivors.[71] It was the first time in the history of naval warfare that a submarine had been sunk by a passenger liner.

Knowing that most of the returning troops would arrive at Halifax, Military District 6 had established No. 6 District Depot to process them. Commanded by Lieutenant Colonel D. A. MacRae, formerly of the 25th Battalion, with headquarters in the Wellington Barracks, the depot set up two dispersal stations, in Halifax and Charlottetown. The Halifax station was commanded by Major J. G. Johnstone, an accountant who had joined the 85th Battalion in 1915 but, being fifty-two years of age, had not gone overseas. Second in command was Captain Stuart Hunt, who also commanded the

Leave and Furlough Section. A native of Greenfield, Hunt had served overseas in the 5th Battalion until being invalided home in July 1916 after being wounded at Mount Sorrel. He is remembered today as the author/compiler of *Nova Scotia's Part in the Great War*, published in 1920.

The efficiency of No. 6 Depot was astonishing, partly because pre-arrival documentation was handled in England and aboard the transports. Thus, upon arrival in Halifax, the men turned in their arms and equipment (but kept their uniform and steel helmet), had their medical history sheet signed, and received their war badge, cheque, and discharge certificate—all at the rate of about six per minute![72] Hunt proudly declared that "the fact that over a quarter of a million men were thus entrained, ticketed, berthed and fed en route without a single mishap or complaint serves to illustrate the almost perfect system that prevailed."[73]

The Royal Canadian Regiment was the first predominantly Nova Scotian battalion to arrive, on March 19, 1919. The *Adriatic* was escorted into the harbour by a tugboat "whistling joyously and bearing members of the city's reception committee" because the regiment, "which Halifax regarded as peculiarly its own, was to receive every honour that the proud old city could pay." After the ship docked, the regiment passed through "a number of fine arches" amid "continuous" cheering as it marched to the Common, where it paraded for the last time.[74] Its commanding officer, Lieutenant Colonel C. H. Hill, was a native of Halifax who had spent his whole career in the regiment, becoming its commanding officer in April 1916. He was awarded the Distinguished Service Order for bravery at the battle of Mount Sorrel in June 1916.

Two weeks later the *Caronia* and *Northland* arrived with 5,000 troops, including more than 800 Nova Scotians. The garrison band was on hand to greet them, along with thousands of citizens. They disembarked, deposited their gear in the clearing depot shed, met their loved ones, and were given cigarettes, candy, "and other good things" by the reception committee, before marching to the armoury. "All had happy faces and were glad to set foot on Canadian soil once more," and among them were many "well-known Halifax boys."[75]

Among them were the personnel of No. 1 Casualty Clearing Station, Liverpool's pride and joy. When its townsmen reached home, the train station was crowded with their families and friends. "The town was gay with the red, white and blue of British flags. Hearts were light. 'The War to End War' was over."[76] On June 5, Lieutenant Colonel Ford gave a dinner to members of his old unit that had treated almost 81,000 casualties during the war.[77]

Also among them were the men of No. 2 Construction Company. We don't know what kind of reception they received, but we do know that their hope that contributing to the war effort would reduce racial prejudice and discrimination was promptly crushed. There were actually race riots in Halifax in February 1919 and in New Glasgow in October 1919, and schools and movie theatres remained segregated for another generation.[78] Nor did the Mi'kmaq benefit. In fact they were worse off because men who had served in the army lost their treaty status without gaining the settlement packages and pensions awarded to other veterans.

Another two weeks brought home the 6th Battery—originally Sydney's 17th Field Battery—among 5,500 troops on the *Olympic*. "Few of the original members who left Sydney in 1914 returned with the Battery," the *Morning Chronicle* reported, but it "brought back a long list of honors and decorations won on the field and a record of distinguished service of which all Nova Scotia may be proud."[79]

No. 7 Stationary Hospital arrived on April 23. Its members did not receive as large a welcome at the docks because its transport arrived two days earlier than expected, but they were honoured with a banquet at the popular Green Lantern restaurant that evening, presided over by Dr. A. S. MacKenzie, the president of Dalhousie University. Speeches were made, of course, and Lieutenant Governor MacCallum Grant made a point of praising the work of the nurses, "those dear girls who went overseas to care for our boys."[80] No. 9 Canadian Stationary Hospital, the St. Francis Xavier University medical unit, didn't arrive home until July 8 because it was the last hospital to receive patients in France, the second last to leave for England, and the last Nova Scotian unit to return home.

The arrival of the 15th Battalion on May 7 was of special interest even though it was a Toronto unit, because its lieutenant colonel was Charles Bent of Paradise. He had gone overseas in 1914 as a captain in the 17th Battalion and was among the more than 400 men transferred into the 15th after it suffered huge casualties at the Second Battle of Ypres in the spring of 1915. He became commanding officer in May and except for short absences—to command the 3rd Brigade, for leave in 1917, and after being wounded in 1918—remained in that position until demobilization, leading the 15th into Germany after the armistice.

Bent brought a couple of friends home with him: Fritz and Bruno. Fritz, his horse, had gone to war with the Russian Army, but had been captured by the Germans. Then the Canadians captured him in September 1918 and Bent "inherited" him. Bruno was a Belgian sheepdog that the battalion had adopted as its mascot. Fritz and Bruno enjoyed a happy retirement on Bent's farm and are buried there. They are also honoured on the Forgotten Heroes monument at Bass River, which recognizes the horses and dogs that served in the war.[81]

Fittingly, the greatest celebration was reserved for the 25th Battalion, which arrived on the *Olympic* on May 16. It was greeted with whistles and horns from vessels in the harbour, while thousands of people gathered on "wharves, roof tops and other vantage spots, the Citadel being the favourite...to welcome the boys."[82] After disembarking and being processed, the battalion marched to the Mewburn Barracks on the North Common. Two men carried on their shoulders Major Guy Matheson, "the idol of the entire regiment," as far as the Majestic Theatre on Barrington Street. "Hatless, his fair hair blowing into the wind, with a flushed boyish face, he was carried along as the crowds cheered him. Matheson is one of the warrior sons of Nova Scotia whose names will be immortal."[83]

The triumphal parade passed through arches of greenery on Spring Garden Road, passing Bellevue House where the Duchess of Devonshire (wife of the governor general), MacCallum Grant, Colonel Thompson, and the mayor took the salute. That evening the duchess presided over a banquet in the mess halls of the Mewburn and Elliott Barracks—one was not large enough—and that was followed by "a smoker and musicale" in the evening at the armoury, attended by thousands of their relatives and friends. The guest of honour, at least unofficially, was Robert the Bruce, who was "inclined to be fairly affable to anyone whom he considers his equal, especially if their clothes seem edible."[84]

Fig. 9.5: This wonderful photo shows the 25th Battalion marching on Barrington Street in Halifax on May 16, 1919. In the lower right corner, the men can be seen carrying Guy Matheson on their shoulders.

The 85th Battalion did not arrive home until June 8. Its transport, the *Adriatic*, sailed up the harbour "to the wild discordant sound of tugs and other whistles, bells and guns and horns. In fact everything that could make a noise."[85] Thousands of people were at the docks to greet "the returning warriors"[86] and Joseph Hayes, the battalion's historian, claimed that "such a tumultuous enthusiastic reception was never before seen in old Halifax. It gave a new meaning to the word Home which can never be defined in Dictionaries."[87] The explanation for that was that the railways had offered discounted rates and 20,000 people from throughout the province had descended on Halifax to share in the festivities.

Like the 25th, the 85th paraded through the downtown area, past Bellevue House where the lieutenant governor, the premier, and the mayor took the salute in the presence of "the parents and immediate relatives of those who had not returned."[88] On the fifteenth, led by its popular Lieutenant Colonel J. L. Ralston of Amherst—who had been wounded four times—the battalion marched from Grafton Park (later the site of Halifax's memorial public library) to Government House, led by the band of the Royal Canadian Regiment. There Ralston deposited the 85th's colours. Government House also received the colours of the 25th Battalion but both were subsequently placed in the lobby of the provincial archives building. In 2016 they were returned to Government House, where they are now on display for all to see.

The excitement of arriving back in Halifax to a rapturous reception undoubtedly pleased the men but sweeter still must have been the smaller, more intimate and more personal receptions they received when they arrived home at last in their own towns and villages. Barrington Passage celebrated the return of its five boys in the packed Oddfellows' Hall on May 16. There was music and recitations and even "an act entitled 'Red Riding Hood,' in which about a dozen little tots, dressed in white, took part as fairies."[89] What the veterans thought of the affair can only be imagined, but no doubt they appreciated the good intentions of their friends and neighbours.

In Liverpool, "flag-trimmed teams and automobiles" met every westbound train, "ready to convey the [returning] men to their friends." A banquet in April for forty returned soldiers took place at the Mersey Hotel, after which they had to endure speeches from Mayor George McClearn, Dr. J. W. Smith, the local member of the House of Assembly, and others.[90] The ladies of the Methodist Church in New Germany organized a reception for four local boys on their return that included "a good patriotic programme...and stirring addresses." Near the conclusion, "the whole audience passed by in file giving hearty handshakes and words of welcome to these four splendid specimens of Canadian manhood."[91] The community of Brooklyn (Yarmouth County), gathered on May 28 to plant twenty-four maple trees "on the main road leading west from Henry Pitman's corner to Morrell's corner" in honour of the men who served overseas and Nursing Sister Sara Corning.[92] Some men, however, like Jack Lombard, didn't receive a community welcome when they arrived home because their families didn't know they were coming. Lombard was from Annapolis, but he had been living in Lethbridge when he enlisted and his family had not seen him for seven years.[93]

Aside from a warm welcome, what did the men and women come home to? The world of 1919 was radically different from the world of 1914, not just because of the destruction and slaughter but also because values had changed. No doubt they would have changed over time anyway but the war dramatically accelerated the process. Many hoped that things could go back to "normal," meaning the way they were in the summer of 1914, but that was impossible. Was it even desirable? Despite the amber haze through which we tend to view the world before 1914, pre-war Nova Scotia was not a golden age for the vast majority of people. It was in many ways a good place in which to live, however, and it certainly was a more innocent age in some respects. But the war had changed everything. And many believed, or at least hoped, that the new era would be a better place, because it was too awful to think that sacrifice on such a scale could have no meaning.

AFTERWORD

Self-sacrifice in a just cause is at once a duty and a blessing, and this lesson has both inspired and ennobled the men and women of Canada.[1]

NOVA SCOTIA MADE AN ENORMOUS CONTRIBUTION TO THE First World War. The number of men and women who served in the armed forces—not just Canadian but also British, American, and a few others—was impressive, but so too was the province's remarkable economic contribution. Indeed, the contribution of Nova Scotia's two steel companies through the leadership of Thomas Cantley and J. H. Plummer is one of the great untold stories of Canada's participation in the war. Nova Scotia's contribution to the war at sea was unique also because so many of its men served in the merchant marine and it was the only part of Canada directly affected by enemy action.[2]

Of the more than 619,000 men and women who joined the Canadian Armed Forces during the war, about 425,000 went overseas and more than 61,000 of them did not come home. We don't know exactly how many of them were Nova Scotians. The Militia Department estimated at the beginning of the war that Nova Scotia could contribute 29,500 men, roughly 31% of the eligible male population of military age (95,760 in 1911).[3] In fact, Nova Scotia contributed 35,723 men or 37%, according to Militia Department's records.[4] This figure was based on place of enlistment, however, so it included men who enlisted in the province but were not Nova Scotians and excluded Nova Scotians who enlisted in other provinces. Nor did it include men who served in the navy or in the British or American Armed Forces, so we must accept it as being only approximately true.

How many Nova Scotian men (and women) died in service or very shortly after the war? Almost a century later we still don't know. The Department of Veterans Affairs reported shortly after the war that about 15% of the 425,000 men who went overseas died during the war or shortly afterward. Applying this percentage to Nova Scotia suggests that about 4,500 Nova Scotians may have died in the war, a figure that seems compatible with what we know of the casualty rates of the 25th and 85th Battalions and the Royal Canadian Regiment.

It may not seem like a lot, but it represents four battalions of soldiers or, put another way, 4.7% of the men of military age who lived in Nova Scotia in 1914. When distributed among the small towns and villages of the province, the impact is more apparent. New Glasgow, for example, lost 85 men, Liverpool 84, and Springhill 82. Kentville lost 39, Lunenburg 36, Wolfville 31, Canso and Hazel Hill 29. Judique lost 23, Shubenacadie 19, Tatamagouche 15, Dominion 13, Canning 11, Bear River 8, Havre Boucher 7, Port Mouton 6, Arcadia 5, and Mill Cove 3. Cheticamp, an Acadian community, lost 14 and Hantsport, whose entire population in 1914 was 730 people, reportedly contributed 120 men and lost 21 of them.[5]

It requires little imagination to appreciate the profound impact of such losses, both short and long term, on a population that had never experienced tragedy on such a scale. These men—and women—were mourned by their shattered families and missed in their communities and are remembered even a century later. And there were also those who did return home with physical or psychological wounds.

If this were not tragic enough, families continued to receive telegrams reporting the death of husbands and sons after the armistice. Harold Carleton Davis of Oxford, for example, who had enlisted in the 85th Battalion but later transferred into the Royal Air Force, died on December 5, 1918, during flight training in England. Wilfred Nickerson, a fisherman from Canso who was conscripted in April 1918, was working with the Canadian War Graves Detachment when he was killed accidentally near Vimy Ridge on June 4, 1919. He and two colleagues had gone for a walk after work, when he rather unwisely attempted to dismantle the nose cap of a shell and it exploded. Others, in hospital from wounds received before the armistice, succumbed to them months later. Lyman Robbie of North River, Colchester County, for example, died in a British hospital on March 4, 1919. He was only seventeen years old because he lied about his age and was only fourteen when he enlisted in March 1916, so he was probably the youngest soldier to die after the killing stopped.

Others made it home, only to die in convalescent hospitals in Nova Scotia. Some were struck down by the influenza epidemic, either overseas or after returning home. Others were much later returning home because they were convalescing in British hospitals. Percy Willmot of Sydney, for example, didn't get home until August 1919 and died in December 1919. The Department of Veterans Affairs recognized the complexity of the situation by including in its mortality calculations men who died up to the spring of 1922. But even a casual glance at newspapers and genealogical records shows that many veterans died prematurely in the 1920s and 1930s for a variety of reasons. Others just struggled with physical or psychological problems in a society that tried to be sympathetic but couldn't possibly understand.

Many hoped that the veterans would just be glad to be home and would settle back into civilian life, putting the war behind them. Many indeed were determined to return to what American President Warren Harding called "normalcy," meaning the *status quo ante*, the way things were before this horrific event disrupted everything. But when the American singer and comedian Eddie Cantor sang a popular song in the early 1920s asking "How Ya Gonna Keep 'em Down on the Farm (After They've Seen Paree?)," he was actually addressing an important issue. How could young men who had experienced mass slaughter, living in filthy and often wet trenches, and seeing friends maimed or literally obliterated be expected to come home to the family farm or a job as a bank clerk and not see the world through different eyes? This would be a major problem in the 1920s and, truth be told, for the rest of their lives for many men and their families.

It wasn't long before communities sought to honour their soldiers and nurses, especially those who did not return. New Ross must have been the first in Canada because it erected its monument in early November 1918, even before the war was over. It recorded the names of the fifteen men from the area who had died in the war.[6] Communities throughout the province followed suit, ranging from the cenotaph on the Grand Parade in Halifax to memorials of all kinds, large and small.

Windsor's war memorial honouring the 164 men from Hants County who had died in the war, and its dedication service, were typical. The lieutenant governor attended along with veterans and relatives of the fallen and a large crowd that included choirs from several churches and many schoolchildren. "If one were to judge from the tone of the ceremonies," Angus wrote, "the war had been a kind of religious event," because the president of the Nova Scotia branch of the GWVA offered a prayer to "God, Eternal Warrior against wrong," and prayerful gratitude was expressed for those who had given their lives, "following in the footsteps of the Eternal Son."[7]

This became the standard theme in the 1920s, portraying the war as "a Christian endeavour, a call to Serve the Empire and the Christian civilization for which many felt it proudly stood." Thus, those who gave their lives were martyrs serving an empire that was "a vehicle for righteousness."[8] When Acadia University built a memorial gymnasium to honour the sixty Acadia students who had died in the war, its plaque included the disturbing declaration that they had died for "the Greater Glory of God." It is hard to believe that those who had gone to war felt that way, although they may have agreed with the plaque's other declaration that those who died "loved Honour more than they feared death."[9]

Those who returned home soon discovered that the government that called them heroes didn't have very ambitious plans to assist their reintegration into civilian society. In fact, the government was taking a distinctly stingy approach to the question of pensions. Even before most of the men got home, the Great War Veterans' Association had been founded and by the spring of 1919 it had 65,000 members, 6,000 of them in the Maritimes.[10] Its purpose was to represent the veterans in the fight for pensions and benefits, including a $2,000 gratuity for every man who had served in France. It also tried to make the government understand that its major resettlement program, offering free land grants, had little appeal because "only a very small percentage of the returned men have any desire to become farmers."[11] It was the beginning of what was going to be another long campaign.

Veterans returning to Nova Scotia faced another serious problem. The coal and steel industries had benefited enormously from war contracts, but the war was over. The federal government's commitment to developing a steel shipbuilding industry was very encouraging, as was its heavy investment in the redevelopment of the port of Halifax. But that same government had also nationalized the railways (other than the CPR) and the new Crown corporation, Canadian National Railways, had standardized freight rates, i.e., terminated the long-established subsidy on Maritime goods going to the Central Canadian market. This raised freight rates by 40%, which was almost instantly catastrophic to the region's economy.[12] The collapse of Nova Scotia's economy was signalled by two newspaper reports separated by only two months: in November 1918 the press reported that Nova Scotia Steel had a three-year backlog of orders and the future looked bright, and in January 1919 it reported the company's "temporary cessation of operations."[13]

When the Union government collapsed in the 1921 election, to be replaced by a Liberal government based in Quebec but also dependent on the Progressive Party based in Ontario and the West, the situation worsened. The new government was focused on cutting expenditures and reducing the national debt and showed little interest in the problems of Nova Scotia and the other Maritime provinces. The result was the formation of the Maritime Rights Movement led by the region's business leaders. One of those leaders, F. B. McCurdy, went so far in the early 1920s as to advocate a form of sovereignty association for Nova Scotia. H. W. Corning, the Conservative leader in the House of Assembly, went even further, calling for Nova Scotia to withdraw from Confederation.[14] In the next provincial election, held in 1925, the long entrenched Liberals were defeated by the Conservatives.

The federal government responded with the inevitable royal commission, which recommended a readjustment of railway freight rates. The government did make minor changes and subsidized coking plants using Canadian coal, but this amounted to tinkering because the pre-war trend towards a national industrial economy in which Nova Scotia occupied only a peripheral place continued. This had become clear to all but the blind when the Montreal interests that already controlled Dominion Steel and Coal were handed control of Halifax Shipyards, then also took over Nova Scotia Steel, giving them a monopoly over coal, steel, and steel shipbuilding in the province.

Unfortunately for the new conglomerate, the British Empire Steel Corporation, it could not compete in the Canadian market with the new freight rate policy, and the new federal government did not share its predecessor's interest in Halifax-based shipbuilding. Meanwhile, postwar prices for agricultural products, fish, and lumber all declined, unemployment rose, and wages fell at the very time when thousands of veterans were trying to settle back into civilian society. The situation was so serious that when the Great Depression struck in 1930 many people in Nova Scotia claimed that they didn't notice any difference.

If all this were not bad enough, a man couldn't even get a drink because Nova Scotia like other provinces (except Quebec) had brought in prohibition during the war. This did not prevent people from getting alcohol if they really wanted it, of course, and it did stimulate two new industries: the production of illicit alcohol and the offshore liquor trade, which certainly benefited many coastal communities and offset low fish prices.

Stephen Leacock, the popular humorist who happened also to be a professor of economics at McGill University, recognized that the role of government and the meaning of citizenship were changing because of the experience of fighting a major war. Democracy must be based on a new social contract. "If every [male] citizen owes it to society that he must fight for it in case of need," he argued in 1920, "then society owes to every citizen the opportunity of a livelihood. 'Unemployment,' in the case of the willing and able becomes henceforth a social crime."[15] This remarkably progressive thought, coming from the usually conservative Leacock, showed that he—like many others—was adapting to the changing circumstances of an industrializing economy and the evolving role of government. Unfortunately, Prime Minister W. L. Mackenzie King, who ruled Canada for most of the 1920s, had spent most of the war years in the United States and was not as advanced in his thinking.

Nova Scotians, therefore, did what they had always done: they moved west or down to New England, and for the first time in the province's history its population actually declined in the 1920s.

Those who stayed home elected eleven farmer-labour candidates in the 1920 provincial election and a full slate of Liberals in the 1921 federal election. That didn't improve things, so in 1925 they elected a Conservative provincial government and in the 1925 and 1926 federal elections, elected a majority of Conservatives. That didn't help either because the rest of Canada re-elected King.

The economic crisis that began in 1920 had a profound impact on social conditions in Nova Scotia. There were fifty-eight work stoppages in the industrial economy between 1920 and 1925,[16] culminating in a confrontation between company police and miners near New Waterford in June 1925 when William Davis was killed and several other miners were wounded. Company stores were burned down and the army was called in to restore order. The fishery, agriculture, and forestry were all in trouble, continuing the trends that had already started before the war.

In short, Nova Scotia in the 1920s was a very different place from the province of the pre-war years. The war had briefly stimulated the economy but that was artificial and could not last. The war actually accelerated the trend towards the integration of the regional economy into the national economy. That in itself was not a bad thing; it was, in fact, what local political and business leaders had sought to achieve since Confederation. But they had felt confident that Nova Scotia would be a valued and equal partner in the transcontinental industrial enterprise that underlay Confederation. By 1920 they realized—as Joseph Howe had predicted—that they had actually surrendered control over their affairs to a larger, much more powerful and distant political and economic region. It was not the brave new world that Nova Scotians had envisaged or for which they had sacrificed so much.

Still, they had proven their hardiness and resilience over more than two centuries, and it is unlikely that most people had really taken very seriously the glib wartime promises of politicians and clergymen that victory would result in a new more progressive and equitable society. Nova Scotians would continue to struggle in a national political and economic system that now regarded their beloved province as peripheral and of marginal significance, but perhaps they were sustained by their shared ancestral roots, their rich history, and their treasured culture, confident that, as Leon Dubinsky promised, they would rise again.[17]

NOTES

Preface

1 Robert N. Clements, *Merry Hell: The Story of the 25th (Nova Scotia) Battalion* (Toronto: University of Toronto Press, 2013); Joseph Hayes, *The Eighty-Fifth in France and Flanders* (Halifax: Royal Print & Litho, 1920); Ralph Lewis, *Over the Top with the 25th: Chronicle of Events at Vimy Ridge and Courcellette* [*sic*] (Halifax: H. H. Marshall, 1918); Francis MacGregor, *Days That I Remember: Stories with a Scottish Twist* (Windsor: Lancelot Press, 1976); F. B. MacDonald and John J. Gardiner, *The Twenty-Fifth Battalion Canadian Expeditionary Force: Nova Scotia's Famous Regiment in World War One* (Sydney: J.A. Chadwick, 1983); Will R. Bird, *And We Go On* (1930; repr. Montreal/Kingston: McGill-Queen's University Press, 2014), *Ghosts Have Warm Hands: A Memoir of the First World War* (Toronto: Clarke Irwin, 1968), and *The Communication Trench* (Amherst: privately published, 1933). Jack Munroe of Upper Kempt Head and Dominion wrote *Mopping Up! Through the Eyes of Bobbie Burns, Regimental Mascot* (New York: H. K. Fly, 1918), a colourful memoir of his experiences in Princess Patricia's Canadian Light Infantry, and the diary of Clare Gass, a nurse from Shubenacadie, has been published as *The War Diary of Clare Gass* (Montreal/Kingston: McGill-Queen's University Press, 2000). For memoirs written by Canadian soldiers and nurses generally, see Brian Douglas Tennyson, *The Canadian Experience of the Great War: A Guide to Memoirs* (Lanham: Scarecrow Press, 2013).

2 Dale McClare, ed., *The Letters of a Young Canadian Soldier during World War I: P. Winthrop McClare of Mount Uniacke,* NS (Kentville: Brook House Press, 2000); Brian Douglas Tennyson, *Percy Willmot: A Cape Bretoner at War* (Sydney: UCCB Press, 2007); and David Mossman, *Going Over: A Nova Scotian Soldier in World War I* (Halifax: Nimbus, 2014). A small collection compiled

by Ross Hebb entitled *Letters Home: Maritimers and the Great War 1914–1918* (Halifax: Nimbus, 2014) includes some letters from Nova Scotians.

Chapter 1

1 *Halifax Herald*, May 10, 1910, quoted in William March, *Red Line: The Chronicle-Herald and The Mail-Star 1875–1954* (Halifax: Chebucto Agencies, 1986), 90.

2 Beckles Willson, *Nova Scotia: The Province that Time Has Passed By* (London: Constable, 1912), 39, 53.

3 Thomas H. Raddall, *In My Time: A Memoir* (Toronto: McClelland and Stewart, 1976), 22.

4 Quoted in March, *Red Line*, 90.

5 Willson, *Nova Scotia: The Province that Time Has Passed By*, 45.

6 Ibid. Armstrong says that even during the war the RCN "were still viewed as interlopers in the former imperial port." John Griffith Armstrong, *The Halifax Explosion and the Royal Canadian Navy: Inquiry and Intrigue* (Vancouver: UBC Press, 2002), 23.

7 Hugh MacLennan, *Barometer Rising* (1941; repr., Toronto: McClelland & Stewart, 2007), 181–82.

8 Nova Scotia produced one third of Canada's fish by value and employed about 22,000 men and boys in 1914. David MacKenzie, "Eastern Approaches: Maritime Canada and Newfoundland," in *Canada and the First World War: Essays in Honour of Robert Craig Brown*, ed. David MacKenzie (Toronto: University of Toronto Press, 2005), 351.

9 For more on this, see Brian Douglas Tennyson, "Economic Nationalism and Confederation: A Case Study in Cape Breton," *Acadiensis 11, no. 1 (Autumn1972): 39–53.*

10 On industrial development in Nova Scotia, see Larry McCann, "The 1890s: Fragmentation and the New Social Order," in *The Atlantic Provinces in Confederation*, ed. E. R. Forbes and D. A. Muise (Toronto/Fredericton: University of Toronto Press/Acadiensis Press, 1993), 124, 125.

11 *Souvenir of the 150th Anniversary of the Settlement of Yarmouth Nova Scotia* (Yarmouth: Town of Yarmouth, 1911), 19.

12 MacKenzie, "Eastern Approaches: Maritime Canada and Newfoundland," 351.

13 McCann, "The 1890s: Fragmentation and the New Social Order," 126; George O'Reilly, "Londonderry: Nova Scotia's Giant from the Past May Still Have a Future," *Nova Scotia Minerals Update Newsletter* 7, no. 3 (Winter 1996): 3, accessed August 20, 2015, https://www.novascotia.ca/natr/meb/data/pubs/ftmif/mif07.pdf.

14 McCann, "The 1890s: Fragmentation and the New Social Order," 127.

15 David Frank, "The Cape Breton Coal Industry and the Rise and Fall of the British Empire Steel Corporation," *Acadiensis* 7, no. 1 (Autumn 1977): 6; E. R. Forbes, *The Maritime Rights Movement, 1919–1927: A Study in Canadian Regionalism* (Montreal/Kingston: McGill-Queen's University Press, 1979), 3. Another town that became a major industrial centre was Amherst, because of its proximity to the Cumberland County coalfields and its strategic position on the Intercolonial Railway. "Busy Amherst," as it was called, produced railway rolling stock, steam engines and boilers, woollen goods, boots and shoes, enamelware, furnaces, pianos, and furniture. The largest manufacturer in town, the Rhodes Curry Company, employed 2,000 men in construction and building railway cars, while Robb Engineering—known nationally for its engines and boilers—employed another 500 workers. The shoe and woollen factories each had 200 employees. Between 1901 and 1906, the value of Amherst's industrial production jumped dramatically from $1 million to $4.5 million, and the town's population doubled to almost 10,000. Nolan Reilly, "The General Strike in Amherst, Nova Scotia, 1919," *Acadiensis* 9, no. 2 (Spring 1980): 58.

16 The production of salt fish declined from 800,000 quintals in 1885 to 450,000 quintals in 1910. Quintals were equal to a hundredweight (about 50 kilograms) or sometimes 100 kilogramss. McCann, "The 1890s: Fragmentation and the New Social Order," 138. See also Robert MacKinnon, "The Historical Geography of Agriculture in Nova Scotia, 1851–1951" (PhD thesis, University of British Columbia, 1991), 40.

17 Willson, *Nova Scotia: The Province that Time Has Passed By*, 134.

18 McCann, "The 1890s: Fragmentation and the New Social Order," 126, 127; Colin Howell, "The 1900s: Industry, Urbanization, and Reform," in *The Atlantic Provinces in Confederation*, ed. E. R. Forbes and D. A. Muise (Toronto/Fredericton: University of Toronto Press/Acadiensis Press, 1993), 167.

19 Quoted in Howell, "The 1900s: Industry, Urbanization, and Reform," 176.

20 Ian McKay, "Drummond, Robert" *Dictionary of Canadian Biography*, vol. 15 (Toronto/Quebec: University of Toronto/Université Laval, 2003–), accessed May 15, 2015, http://www.biographi.ca/en/bio/drummond_robert_1840_1925_15E.html.

21 Howell, "The 1900s: Industry, Urbanization, and Reform," 168.

22 *Yarmouth Herald*, June 8, 1914.

23 Ibid., June 30, 1914.

24 Ibid., July 28, 1914.

25 *Bridgewater Bulletin*, June 23, 1914.

26 *Yarmouth Herald*, May 26, 1914.

27 James M. Cameron, *Pictonians in Arms: A Military History of Pictou County, Nova Scotia* (New Glasgow: privately published, 1969), 84.

28 Ibid.

29 Quoted in Sandra Gwyn, *Tapestry of War: A Private View of Canadians in the Great War* (Toronto: HarperCollins, 1992), 9.

30 *Morning Chronicle*, June 2, 1914.

31 *Liverpool Advance*, April 8, 1914, and July 8, 1914.

32 Ibid., April 8, 1914.

33 *Bridgewater Bulletin*, June 30, 1914.

Chapter 2

1 *Amherst Daily News*, August 3, 1914.

2 *Wesleyan*, May 6, 1914.

3 *Morning Chronicle*, July 9, 1914.

4 Clarence Mackinnon, *Reminiscences* (Toronto: Ryerson, 1938), 191.

5 *Truro Daily News*, July 28, 1914; and *Acadian Recorder*, reprinted in *Eastern Chronicle*, July 31, 1914; and *Amherst Daily News*, July 31, 1914.

6 *Truro Daily News*, August 4, 1914.

7 *Sydney Daily Post*, August 6, 1914.

8 *Morning Chronicle*, August 4, 1914.

9 *Sydney Daily Post*, August 3, 1914.

10 Ibid., August 4, 1914.

11 Ibid., August 11, 1914.

12 *Morning Chronicle*, August 5, 1914.

13 Ibid.

14 *Sydney Daily Post*, August 5, 1914. In Amherst it was not until the evening of the sixth that "over five hundred young men and boys," many of them members of the militia, and "several of the older citizens" marched through the streets led by the local militia band. "Patriotic songs and cheers were heard all evening" and "the streets were black with people who had heard the band, and had come from their homes to witness the cause of the cheers." *Amherst Daily News*, August 7, 1914.

15 *Morning Chronicle*, August 5, 1914.

16 *Lunenburg Progress Enterprise*, August 12, 1914.

17 *Antigonish Casket*, August 20, 1914.

18 *Bridgewater Bulletin*, August 4, 1914.

19 *Amherst Daily News*, August 7, 1914.

20 *Eastern Chronicle*, August 18, 1914.

21 *Lunenburg Progress Enterprise*, August 12, 1914.

22 *Sydney Daily Post*, August 6, 1914.

23 *Lunenburg Progress Enterprise*, August 12, 1914.

24 *Halifax Herald*, August 3, 1914.

25 *Presbyterian Witness*, August 15, 1914, and September 12, 1914; both quoted in Murray E. Angus, "Living in the 'World of the Tiger': The Methodist and

Presbyterian Churches in Nova Scotia and the Great War, 1914–1918" (MA thesis, Dalhousie University, 1993), 25, 87.

26 *Wesleyan*, November 25, 1914, cited in Angus, "Living in the 'World of the Tiger,'" 25.

27 See the sermon preached by the Reverend E. W. Florence, quoted in the *Sydney Daily Post*, September 14, 1914. Florence was the rector of St. George's parish in Sydney.

28 *Antigonish Casket*, August 13, 1914.

29 Dalhousie *Gazette*, November 4, 1914; *Halifax Herald*, November 10, 1914 and *Acadian Recorder*, November 11, 1914, both quoted in Scott Matheson, "In the Dust You Will Prevail: The Mobilization of Acadia, Dalhousie, Mount Allison, and St. Francis Xavier Universities, 1914–1918" (MA thesis, St. Mary's University, 2010), 12–13.

30 Frank Graham was born in Halifax to American parents and earned his BA and LLB degrees at Dalhousie. He subsequently earned a PhD at Harvard and was for many years professor of International Finance at Princeton University.

31 As a young man he had enlisted in the 66th Regiment, then in 1883 joined the Royal Canadian Artillery when it became part of the permanent force. Over the years, he rose through the ranks until being appointed commanding officer of MD 6 in 1913. Rutherford is often referred to as a major general but it was not until his deteriorating hearing forced him to retire in October 1915 that he was promoted to that rank. He was succeeded by Major General Thomas Benson, another artilleryman, who remained in Halifax until February 1918.

32 The permanent force in 1914 consisted of the Royal Canadian Regiment (infantry), two cavalry regiments (the Royal Canadian Dragoons and Lord Strathcona's Horse), two artillery regiments (the Royal Canadian Horse Artillery and the Royal Canadian Garrison Artillery), the Royal Canadian Engineers, and various service and administrative corps.

33 Quoted in Brian Douglas Tennyson and Roger Sarty, *Guardian of the Gulf: Sydney, Cape Breton, and the Atlantic Wars* (Toronto: University of Toronto Press, 2000), 126. For a detailed study of the coastal defences around Sydney Harbour and its role as a shipping and naval port in the war, see Tennyson and Sarty, *Guardian of the Gulf*, 113–88.

34 Ibid., 109–10.

35 *Morning Chronicle*, August 2, 1914.

36 *Amherst Daily News*, August 3, 1914.

37 *Morning Chronicle*, August 6, 1914.

38 Charles White, senior naval officer, "Entrance to the Port of Halifax," *Morning Chronicle*, August 8, 1914.

39 *Halifax Herald*, reprinted in the *Amherst Daily News*, August 17, 1914.

40 Keith Doucette, "First World War Touched Everyday Lives in Halifax, Atlantic Canada," CBC News Nova Scotia, August 2, 2015, accessed November 15, 2016, http://www.cbc.ca/news/canada/nova-scotia/first-world-war-touched-everyday-lives-in-halifax-atlantic-canada-1.3177160.
41 White, "Entrance to the Port of Halifax."
42 *Morning Chronicle*, August 5, 1914.
43 Bryan Elson, *Canada's Bastions of Empire: Halifax, Victoria and the Royal Navy 1749–1918* (Halifax: Formac, 2014), 147–48.
44 Ibid., 70; and Dianne Marshall, *Georges Island: The Keep of Halifax Harbour* (Halifax: Nimbus, 2014), 72.
45 Marshall, *Georges Island*, 70.
46 Elson, *Canada's Bastions of Empire*, 104.
47 *Morning Chronicle*, August 4, 1914.
48 Ibid., August 6, 1914. The first sworn-in troops to leave the armoury that evening were the sixteen members of the Corps of Guides—a mounted unit whose role was to collect military information in the field—attached to the 63rd. They had not been issued with service revolvers, however, so "each went down [town] and laid out $7 of his money on revolver and ammunition and $1.25 for pouch." *Morning Chronicle*, August 6, 1914.
49 Elson, *Canada's Bastions of Empire*, 139.
50 Ibid., 140.
51 William Johnston, William G. P. Rawling, Richard H. Gimblett, and John MacFarlane, *The Seabound Coast: The Official History of the Royal Canadian Navy, 1867–1939* (Ottawa: Department of National Defence, 2010), 1: 467.
52 Elson, *Canada's Bastions of Empire*, 140–41.
53 *Morning Chronicle*, August 14, 1914.
54 Elson, *Canada's Bastions of Empire*, 144, 145.
55 Tennyson and Sarty, *Guardian of the Gulf*, 120.
56 Elson, *Canada's Bastions of Empire*, 146.
57 Hunt, *Nova Scotia's Part in the Great War*, 259.
58 George Sylvester, letter to George Sylvester (uncle), October 18, 1914, quoted in Des Leddin, *The Headmaster's War: George Sylvester and the Great War for Civilization* (Skibbereen: Redbarn, 2015), 12.
59 When the 40th Battalion was disbanded in England to provide reinforcements for battalions already in the field, Sylvester was transferred into the 14th Battalion, a Montreal unit, and was killed at Courcelette on September 26, 1916.
60 Tennyson and Sarty, *Guardian of the Gulf*, 114.
61 *Sydney Daily Post*, August 1, 1914.
62 *Amherst Daily News*, July 31, 1914.
63 Tennyson and Sarty, *Guardian of the Gulf*, 115.
64 Grant was the son of MacCallum Grant, the Halifax businessman who served as lieutenant governor from 1916 to 1925. John Grant served in the Royal

Navy throughout the war and later became the first commandant of the Royal Canadian Naval College at Esquimalt in the 1930s. His younger brother, Harold Grant, also graduated from the original naval college and served in the Royal Navy during the war and commanded Royal Navy cruisers in the Second World War, rising to the rank of rear admiral.

65 W. H. Hayes, "On to Bermuda," *The Connecting File* 9, no. 1 (January 1931), accessed July 8, 2015, www.regimentalrogue.com.

66 Quoted in Tennyson and Sarty, *Guardian of the Gulf,* 116.

67 His father-in-law, Philip Worgan, was a retired Royal Navy commander who for many years had been superintendent of shipping at the Dominion Coal Company's International Pier in Sydney.

68 *Sydney Daily Post,* August 5, 1914. The Black Diamond ships belonged to the Dominion Coal Company.

69 Lee Windsor and Roger Sarty, "New Brunswick's Artillery Goes to War, 1914–1915," *Canadian Military History* 24, no. 1 (2015): 107.

70 Both quoted in Ibid., 108.

71 Rannie Gillis, "North Sydney Cable Office Busy Place in 1910," *Cape Breton Post,* April 6, 2014.

72 Tennyson and Sarty, *Guardian of the Gulf,* 116.

73 Ibid., 124.

74 Ibid., 125.

75 Ibid., 121.

76 See Ibid., 122–23.

77 *Sydney Daily Post,* September 12, 1914. Marcus Dodd was the son of Edmund Murray Dodd and was active in the militia in the 1870s. His brother Murray Dodd was also a lawyer and judge and served in the House of Commons from 1879 to 1882.

78 Tennyson and Sarty, *Guardian of the Gulf,* 125. A prominent lawyer in Sydney who represented the Dominion Iron and Steel Company and the Dominion Coal Company, Walter Crowe was an officer in the 17th Field Battery, mayor 1897–1903, and one of the founders of the Lingan Golf Club.

79 *Sydney Daily Post,* November 24, 1914.

80 Tennyson and Sarty, *Guardian of the Gulf,* 130.

81 Michael Christie, *The Barrington Passage Wireless Station* (Yarmouth: privately published, 2002), 85. Glidden Campbell was one of six brothers from Weymouth who enlisted during the war. Two were killed and three were so shell-shocked that they spent the rest of their lives in psychiatric hospitals. Only Glidden returned home. See Elissa Barnard, "A Weymouth Family Ripped Apart by the Great War," *Chronicle Herald,* first published in 2014, accessed November 20, 2016, http://thechronicleherald.ca/thegreatwar/1228171-a-weymouth-family-ripped-apart-by-the-great-war#.WDWOFuErJ0.

82 Hunt, *Nova Scotia's Part in the Great War*, 257, 262.

83 On the shooting incident, see Christie, *The Barrington Passage Wireless Station*, 131–33. William Whitehouse married Nettie Mae Nickerson of Woods Harbour on April 22, 1916, and Charles Joudrey married Blanche Belliveau, also of Woods Harbour, on February 22, 1917.

Chapter 3

1 Written by Francis Owen, 17th Battalion, to be sung to the tune "There's a Tavern in the Town." *Eastern Chronicle*, October 5, 1914. Owen, who was from Toronto, was one of the many men transferred into the 17th from other battalions in late September to boost its numbers.

2 Some believed that Hughes also nursed a grudge against the professional soldiers, whether British or Canadian, because he had not been awarded the Victoria Cross for his service in the South African War.

3 Fetherstonhaugh, *The Royal Canadian Regiment*, 193.

4 *Morning Chronicle*, September 15, 1914.

5 On the Bermuda experience, see Jean-Pierre Gagnon, "Canadian Soldiers in Bermuda during World War One," *Social History/Histoire Sociale* 23, no. 45 (May 1990): 9–36.

6 Cameron, *Pictonians in Arms*, 87.

7 *Halifax Herald*, undated, quoted in the *Liverpool Advance*, September 9, 1914.

8 *Morning Chronicle*, August 13, 1914.

9 He was killed near Lens in August 1917 while serving in the 13th Battalion.

10 He served at Gallipoli and in France and was wounded at Gueudecourt in October 1916. He rose to the rank of captain and was awarded the Military Cross in 1918. Following the war he returned to the bank, eventually becoming president in 1956. He was awarded honorary degrees by Memorial University and Acadia University and in 1959 was named an Illustrious Son of Nova Scotia. His son, also called Charles Sydney Frost, attended the Royal Military College and served in the Princess Patricia's Canadian Light Infantry in the Second World War, going on to command the Royal Regiment of Canada from 1959 to 1962.

11 *Shelburne Gazette*, February 25, 1918, reprinted in the *Yarmouth Herald-Times*, February 26, 1918. Cameron had a short war. He arrived in France with the 59th Battalion of the Australian Imperial Force on December 15, 1917, was wounded eight days later, and died on January 24, 1918.

12 *Sydney Record*, May 30, 1914.

13 *Sydney Daily Post*, August 15, 1914.

14 *Morning Chronicle*, August 12, 1914, and August 13, 1914.

15 *Halifax Echo*, reprinted in the *Sydney Daily Post*, August 20, 1914.

16 Hunt, *Nova Scotia's Part in the Great War*, 227.

17 See Mark McGowan, "Harvesting the 'Red Vineyard': Catholic Religious Culture in the Canadian Expeditionary Force, 1914–1919," *Canadian Catholic Historical Association Historical Studies* 64 (1998): 47–70.

18 Quoted in the *Sydney Daily Post*, August 24, 1914.

19 Her correct name was Margaret Marjory Fraser but she used the name "Pearl," so that is how I refer to her.

20 *Amherst Daily News*, August 11, 1914

21 Quoted in the *Amherst Daily News*, August 19, 1914.

22 *Morning Chronicle*, August 20, 1914, quoted in Janet E. Mullins, *Some Liverpool Chronicles* (1941, repr., Hantsport: Lancelot Press for C. D. Hemeon, 1980), 123–24.

23 Mullins, *Some Liverpool Chronicles*, 123.

24 *Morning Chronicle*, quoted in Mullins, *Some Liverpool Chronicles*, 124.

25 Ibid., 124.

26 *Morning Chronicle*, August 21, 1914.

27 Ibid.

28 Ibid.

29 *Amherst Daily News*, August 21, 1914.

30 He was killed while serving as a private in the 85th Battalion in September 1918.

31 *Truro Daily News*, August 27, 1914.

32 *Amherst Daily News*, August 21, 1914. Simpson's claim to be commissioned a lieutenant was denied. He subsequently enlisted in the 25th as a private but did not go overseas with it either. He was conscripted in July 1918 while still living in Amherst and did rise to the rank of lieutenant. Kennedy appears not to have served.

33 *Yarmouth Herald*, August 25, 1914.

34 Ibid.

35 *Sydney Daily Post*, August 28, 1914.

36 Wilfred Doane, letter to his father, September 1, 1914, published in the *Yarmouth Herald*, September 8, 1914.

37 *Sydney Daily Post*, August 28, 1914.

38 Ibid., August 31, 1914.

39 Ibid.

40 Charles Holden, letter to Mr. and Mrs. C. M. Firth, August 29, 1914, published in the *Liverpool Advance*, August 29, 1914.

41 Arthur Hunt Chute, *The Real Front* (New York: Harper & Brothers, 1918), 9, 11–12.

42 Wilfred Doane, letter to his father, September 1, 1914.

43 Ibid., September 9, 1914, published in the *Yarmouth Herald*, September 15, 1914.

44 Ibid.

45 Undated letter from unidentified soldier to the editor, published in *Sydney Daily Post*, September 18, 1914.

46 *Eastern Chronicle*, September 29, 1914.

47 Ibid., September 15, 1914.

48 Peter Moogk, "From Fortress Louisbourg to Fortress Sydney: Artillery and Gunners on Cape Breton, 1743–1964," in *Cape Breton at 200: Historical Essays in Honour of the Island's Bicentennial 1785–1985*, ed. Kenneth Donovan (Sydney: UCCB Press, 1985), 143.

49 Ibid., 146.

50 Doane, letter to his father, September 15, 1914, published in *Yarmouth Herald*, September 22, 1914.

51 Dispatch from Valcartier, August 27, 1914, published in *Liverpool Advance*, September 2, 1914.

52 Wilfrid Hearn, letter to the editor, undated, published in *Sydney Daily Post*, September 16, 1914.

53 For its nominal roll, see *No. 1 Clearing Hospital* (Ottawa: Canadian Expeditionary Force, 1915), http://data2.archives.ca/e/e444/e011087858.pdf. Four of its eight doctors were Nova Scotians: F. S. L. Ford (Liverpool), Morris MacKinnon (Amherst), Harold Dickson (Pictou), and John Stewart (Halifax). Harold Pickup of Granville was a medical student.

54 Dispatch from Valcartier, September 1, 1914, published in *Liverpool Advance*, September 2, 1914.

55 C. A. Andrews et al., letter to Robert Borden, September 13, 1914, published in *Pictou Advocate*, March 27, 1915.

56 Hunt, *Nova Scotia's Part in the Great War*, 67.

57 Stuart Hunt claims that the controversy arose because "excessive advertising of the Unit by a too friendly press in Halifax aroused Provincial jealousies" and "made it appear to outsiders that the Nova Scotian officers were doing a lot of advertising, an opinion that was far from the truth." Hunt, *Nova Scotia's Part in the Great War*, 66.

58 The actual distance was about fifteen miles, or about twenty-four kilometres.

59 Doane, letter to his father, September 23, 1914, published in *Yarmouth Herald*, September 29, 1914.

60 Lester Wile, letter to his mother, November 2, 1914, published in *Bridgewater Bulletin*, November 17, 1914.

61 B. L. Neiley, letter to John Grattan, October 9, 1914, published in *Eastern Chronicle*, November 19, 1914. Struan Robertson described Brown as "a wonder." Robertson, letter to James A. Fraser, November 20, 1914, published in *Eastern Chronicle*, December 22, 1914.

62 Lester Wile, letter to his mother, November 2, 1914.

63 Kenneth Clarke, letter to his mother, October 8, 1914, published in *Bridgewater*

Bulletin, November 10, 1914.

64 F. W. Pickles, letter to his wife, October 5, 1914, published in *Yarmouth Herald*, December 17, 1914.

65 Lester Wile, letter to his mother, November 2, 1914.

66 Russell H. Harlow, letter to Mabelle [Mable] Harlow, undated, published in *Liverpool Advance*, November 11, 1914.

67 Ibid.

68 J. F. C. Fuller, *Memoirs of an Unconventional Soldier* (London: Nicholson & Watson, 1936), 7–8.

69 Bruce Donald, letter to the editor, December 14, 1914, published in *Bridgewater Bulletin*, January 5, 1915.

70 J. F. C. Fuller, *Memoirs of an Unconventional Soldier*, 7–8.

71 Ibid., 8.

72 Chute, *The Real Front*, 16.

73 Harold Suttie, letter to his mother, November 8, 1914, published in *Yarmouth Herald*, December 15, 1914.

74 Chute, *The Real Front*, 18.

75 Keith Rogers, letter to the editor, November 24, 1914, published in *Yarmouth Herald*, December 22, 1914.

76 Thomas Carter, letter to his mother, undated, published in *Pictou Advocate*, December 12, 1914.

77 Chute, *The Real Front*, 19.

78 Bruce Kelley, letter to the editor, December 14, 1914, published in *Bridgewater Bulletin*, January 5, 1915.

79 Dr. Morris Mackinnon, letter to his mother, April 13, 1915, published in *Amherst Daily News*, April 29, 1915.

80 Russell Harlow, letter to Mabelle Harlow, undated, published in *Liverpool Advance*, November 11, 1914. Dannie Burrows also optimistically encouraged his mother to "cheer up, we will be all right. Your Boy will be back again." Daniel Burrows, letter to his mother, November 8, 1914, published in *Truro Daily News*, November 25, 1914. Both men did survive the war.

81 Lester Wile, letter to his mother, November 2, 1914, published in *Bridgewater Bulletin*, November 17, 1914.

82 Kenneth Clarke, letter to his mother, October 18, 1914, published in *Bridgewater Bulletin*, November 10, 1914.

83 The pound was divided into twenty shillings, each worth about twenty-five cents. A half crown was worth two and a half shillings or about sixty-seven cents.

84 Wilfred Doane, letter to his father, January 1, 1915, published in *Yarmouth Herald*, February 23, 1915.

85 Quoted in Tim Cook, *At the Sharp End: Canadians Fighting the Great War, 1914–1916* (Toronto: Viking, 2007), 76.

86 Willard Allen, letter to Biney [unidentified], March 15, 1915, published in *Yarmouth Herald*, April 6, 1915.

87 Quoted in *Wesleyan*, March 24, 1915.

88 Struan Robertson, letter to F. B. McCurdy, February 4, 1915, published in *Pictou Advocate*, March 27, 1915. See also *Amherst Daily News*, March 4, March 11, and March 26, 1915. Alderson said of Robertson that "commanding a battalion was not quite his vocation in life." Quoted in Matthew K. Barrett, "Lieutenant Colonel S. G. Robertson, 17th (Nova Scotia Highlanders) Battalion," *The Partisan*, January 30, 2015, accessed June 15, 2015, https://matthewkbarrett.com/2015/01/30/the-partisan/.

89 14th Battalion War Diary, February 7, 1915, accessed February 22, 2016, http://www.royalmontrealregiment.com/17th-canadian-infantry-battalion. See also Cameron, *Pictonians in Arms*, 89–91.

90 *Amherst Daily News*, March 11, 1915.

91 Cameron, *Pictonians in Arms*, 91.

92 Chute, *The Real Front*, 23.

Chapter 4

1 *Yarmouth Herald*, November 24, 1914.

2 Ten men named next of kin with Nova Scotia addresses but because it is difficult to establish what the connection was with either those people or the province, I am counting only those whose connection is clear. They were Charles Stewart, Richard Tyler, and Leland Anderson of Halifax, William Bryant of Norton, George Marlin of Round Hill, Alexander Viets of Digby, and Jack Tait of Melrose. Stewart came from a prominent Amherst family and was a colourful character. Despite his age (forty-four), he joined the PPCLI as a lieutenant, displayed reckless bravery, and rose to command the battalion in March 1918. He was killed while leading his troops at Cambrai in September 1918. See Jean Pariseau, "Stewart, Charles James Townshend," *Dictionary of Canadian Biography*, vol. 14 (Toronto/Quebec: University of Toronto/Université Laval, 2003–), accessed November 23, 2016, http://www.biographi.ca/en/bio/stewart_charles_james_townshend_14E.html.

3 Harriet Graham letter, undated [December 3, 1914], published in *Eastern Chronicle*, December 24, 1914.

4 Ibid.

5 Ibid.

6 For biographical information on Tate, see Bruce Macdonald, "Jack Tate: First Nova Scotia Soldier Killed on the Western Front," *Halifax Chronicle Herald*, accessed September 15, 2016, http://thechronicleherald.ca/

thegreatwar/1271932-jack-tate-first-nova-scotia-soldier-killed-on-the-western-front#.V9pnzZMrJ0s.

7 *Sydney Daily Post*, October 27, 1914. Born in Lens in 1886, Anatole Descamps served in the 87th Regiment. Lens was a mining community, and there was a Léon Descamps, a miner from Lens, who settled in New Waterford in 1912. They were almost certainly brothers.

8 Wilfred Doane, letter to his father, May 5, 1915, published in *Yarmouth Herald*, May 18, 1915.

9 Norman Rogers, letter to his father, May 7, 1915, published in *Eastern Chronicle*, May 28, 1915.

10 Quoted in Pierre Berton, *Marching as to War: Canada's Turbulent Years 1899–1953* (Toronto: Anchor Books, 2002), 146.

11 W. T. M. MacKinnon, letter to Mrs. T. B. Morse, June 30, 1915; published in *Berwick Register*, June 30, 1915. Reprinted in Audrey and Paul Grescoe, eds., *The Book of War Letters: 100 Years of Private Canadian Correspondence* (Toronto: McClelland and Stewart, 2003), 97.

12 *Amherst Daily News*, April 29, 1915.

13 Ibid., December 12, 1914.

14 *Sydney Daily Post*, November 25, 1914.

15 *Yarmouth Herald*, November 24, 1914.

16 When the 25th returned home in May 1919, the government "honoured" it by finally giving it Highland status and authorizing kilts—a meaningless gesture because the battalion was immediately disbanded—although its legacy lives on in the Nova Scotia Highlanders.

17 Lewis, *Over the Top with the 25th*, 7; and Clements, *Merry Hell*, 31.

18 Clements, *Merry Hell*, 31–32.

19 *Morning Chronicle*, May 16, 1919.

20 Georges Vanier, letter to his mother, May 20, 1915, quoted in *Georges Vanier, Soldier: The Wartime Letters and Diaries, 1915–1919*, ed. Deborah Cowley (Toronto: Dundurn Press, 2000), 34–35.

21 Howard Johnstone, undated letter to the *Sydney Daily Post*, May 28, 1915. The great-grandson of James William Johnstone, who had been premier of Nova Scotia in 1857–60 and 1863–64, Howard Johnstone was a journalist who was also for a time secretary to Thomas Cantley, general manager of the Nova Scotia Steel and Coal Company.

22 D. A. MacKinnon, "The 36th Battery, CFA," in Hunt, *Nova Scotia's Part in the Great War*, 43.

23 Hunt, *Nova Scotia's Part in the Great War*, 43.

24 Other Nova Scotians served in No. 2 Tunnelling Company as well. On Gloade's experience in the war, see "Sam Glode: Travels of a Micmac," *Cape Breton's Magazine* 35 (December 1983): 21–29. This memoir is from an interview conducted by Thomas Raddall in 1944. Today the name is usually

spelled "Gloade." He was awarded the Distinguished Conduct Medal for his services.

25 Quoted in Gordon Reid, ed., *Poor Bloody Murder: Personal Memoirs of the First World War* (Oakville: Mosaic Press, 1980), 9.

26 Quoted in Ibid., 23.

27 Alfred Cook, letter to his sister, Sarah, September 5, 1915, quoted in Ross Hebb, ed., *Letters Home: Maritimers and the Great War, 1914–1918* (Halifax: Nimbus, 2014), 39.

28 Clements, *Merry Hell*, 49–51. The officers made restitution but also insisted on a change of management.

29 Ibid., 44. Lieutenant Karl Weatherbe, a Halifax man who served as a lieutenant in the 6th Battalion Engineers, noted on June 6 that "A. Cozzie's fried fish shop...has been placed out of bounds for all troops." Karl Weatherbe, *From the Rideau to the Rhine and Back* (Toronto: Hunter-Rose, 1928), 25.

30 Quoted in Kenneth Radley, *Get Tough Stay Tough: Shaping the Canadian Corps 1914–1918* (Solihull, UK: Heleon, 2014), 146.

31 Wilfred Doane, letter to his father, August 31, 1915, published in *Yarmouth Herald*, October 19, 1915. The delivery of this letter was delayed because it was in a mailbag that went down when the ship carrying it, the *Hesperian*, was torpedoed on September 4. Divers recovered the bag.

32 Johnson, quoted in Reid, *Poor Bloody Murder*, 28. Ryan returned to Kentville, re-enlisted as a sergeant under an assumed name, and served overseas with the 52nd Battery.

33 *Morning Chronicle*, October 18, 1915.

34 Lewis, *Over the Top with the 25th*, 11.

35 Ibid.

36 Library and Archives Canada (LAC), RG 9, III, A. Series 8, File 8-1-52. Alderson, "Words Spoken to the 25th Battalion, Canadian Infantry, in France, on the 15th October 1915."

37 His father, Henry Gibson Bauld, also served as a Liberal in the House of Assembly from 1916 to 1925.

38 Lewis, *Over the Top with the 25th*, 12.

39 Ibid. See also Francis MacGregor, *Days That I Remember* (Windsor: Lancelot, 1976), 39.

40 MacGregor, *Days That I Remember*, 40.

41 W. S. Mahoney, letter to his aunt, Mrs. Mary MacDonald, December 25, 1916, quoted in *Catholics of the Diocese of Antigonish, Nova Scotia, and the War 1914–1919, with Nominal Enlistment Rolls by Parishes* (Antigonish: St. Francis University Press, n.d.), 220.

42 Edward Greenough, letter to his mother, undated [early January], published in *Kentville Advertiser*, January 28, 1916. He subsequently transferred into the 6th CMR Battalion.

43 Osborne Perry, letter to his mother, December 29, 1915, quoted in Harry Thurston, *A Monument Speaks...and Tells the Story of its Dead* (Yarmouth: privately published, 1989), 270.

44 Quoted in Reid, *Poor Bloody Murder*, 109.

45 Alistair Fraser, letter to his sister, undated, published in *Eastern Chronicle*, October 22, 1915. Fraser had joined the 17th Battalion in 1914 but served in the 15th until being badly wounded at Vimy Ridge in April 1917. He resumed his law practice after the war and served as lieutenant governor of Nova Scotia from 1952 to 1958.

46 "Gitz Rice, Song Writer, Dies," *Montreal Gazette*, October 17, 1947.

47 Lewis, *Over the Top with the 25th*, 21.

48 Clements, *Merry Hell*, 135–36.

49 G. C. McElhenny, "The 25th Battalion," in Hunt, *Nova Scotia's Part in the Great War*, 75.

50 Lewis, *Over the Top with the 25th*, 21.

51 Larry Worthington, *Amid the Guns Below* (Toronto: McClelland and Stewart, 1965), 44. For a discussion of who was responsible for the chaos at St. Eloi, see Tim Cook, "The Blind Leading the Blind: The Battle of the St. Eloi Craters," *Canadian Military History* 5, no. 2 (1996): 24–36.

52 *Morning Chronicle*, undated, reprinted in *Liverpool Advance*, May 3, 1916.

53 See "Surrendered as Stowaway," *The Regimental Rogue*, accessed November 11, 2016, www.regimentalrogue.com. We don't know precisely how old Laing was. His parents were married in 1897, but the family does not show up in the 1911 census or in the Nova Scotia vital statistics records except for the marriage and his father's death in 1925.

54 Joseph H. McKenzie, letter to his father, June 14, 1916, quoted in *Diocese of Antigonish*, 219.

55 Dr. Neiley, undated letter, published in *Eastern Chronicle*, June 9, 1916.

56 Winthrop "Winnie" McClare, letter to his mother, undated [circa July 20, 1915], published in P. Winthrop McClare, *The Letters of a Young Canadian Soldier during World War 1*. Edited by Dale McClare (Kentville: Brook House Press, 2000), 1. The unnamed officer visited McNab's Island on July 16. *Morning Chronicle*, July 17, 1915.

57 *Truro Daily News*, August 5, 1915 and August 9, 1915.

58 Edgar and Harold did not survive.

59 *Halifax Mail*, reprinted in *Truro Daily News*, August 7, 1915.

60 George Machum, *The Story of the 64th Battalion, CEF 1915–1916* (Montreal: privately published 1956), 20. Machum was a teacher from New Brunswick who served in the 64th Battalion.

61 Ibid., 27, 58.

62 Joseph Hayes, "Nova Scotia Medical Services in the Great War," in Hunt, *Nova Scotia's Part in the Great War*, 190.

63 Hunt, *Nova Scotia's Part in the Great War*, 202.

64 James D. Cameron, *For the People: A History of St. Francis Xavier University* (Montreal/Kingston: McGill-Queen's University Press, 1996), 161. See also Oswin Macdonald, "St. Francis Xavier Hospital Unit," in *Diocese of Antigonish*, 55.

65 Cameron, *For the People*, 161.

66 Curiously, Carruthers is listed on No. 9 Stationary Hospital's nominal roll but he is not listed in the Soldiers of the First World War database and there is no reference to him in Hunt after his appointment as adjutant. He may not have gone overseas.

67 Cameron, *For the People*, 161.

68 The third man was not a Nova Scotian.

69 The 25th Battalion was part of the 5th Brigade. See Mark G. McGowan, "Harvesting the 'Red Vineyard': Catholic Religious Culture in the Canadian Expeditionary Force, 1914–1919," *Canadian Catholic Historical Association Historical Studies* 64 (1998): 63, 64. See also David B. Hogan, "History of the No. 9 Stationary Hospital (St. Francis Xavier University), 1916–1919" (unpublished manuscript, Antigonish, n.d.), 31, cited in Matheson, "In the Dust You Will Prevail," 43.

70 Dr. Roderick MacLeod, Dr. Walter MacLean, Dr. Kenneth MacCuish, and Dr. Fielding McIsaac.

71 For a complete list of Canadian nurses who served in the war, see the *Canadian Great War Project Nursing Sisters* website, http://www.canadiangreatwarproject.com/Regimental/NursingSisters.asp.

72 They were Frieda Christie of River Hebert, Eva Clements of Liverpool, Marguerite Condon of Halifax, Bertha Cray and Lillian Edgecombe, both of Dartmouth, Marion Ellis of Upper Stewiacke, Ethel Etherington of Shelburne, Marguerite Gray of New Glasgow, Hazel King of Annapolis Royal, and Marion MacLeod of Fox Brook.

73 Harriet Graham (No. 2 Casualty Clearing Station) and Elizabeth Ross (No 10. Canadian General Hospital), both of New Glasgow, Laura Hubley (No. 7 Canadian Stationary Hospital) of St. Margaret's Bay, Katherine MacLatchy (No. 3 Canadian General Hospital) of Grand Pré, Sara MacIsaac (No. 9 Canadian Stationary Hospital) of Joggins, and Annie Strong (No. 2 Canadian Stationary Hospital) of Canning. As well, Elizabeth Doyle of Dartmouth was matron of the Cogswell Military Hospital in Halifax for four years until she signed up to go overseas in September 1918.

74 Pearl Fraser of New Glasgow and Minnie Follette of Cumberland County were victims of the sinking of the *Llandovery Castle* in June 1918. Addie Tupper of Bridgewater died of illness and exhaustion while serving in a hospital in England in December 1916. Rebecca MacIntosh of Pleasant Bay died while serving with No. 9 Canadian General Hospital at the Kinmel Park

army camp in Wales in March 1919. About 2,000 Canadian women, although not nurses, joined Voluntary Aid Detachments (VADs) in order to serve as nursing assistants in hospitals both overseas and at home. It is not known how many of them were Nova Scotians. Because she could speak French, Katharine McLennan of Sydney joined the French *Société française de secours aux blessés militaires* (SBM) and served in French hospitals. On her experiences, see A. J. B. Johnston, "Into the Great War: Katharine McLennan Goes Overseas, 1915–1919," in Kenneth B. Donovan, ed., *The Island: New Perspectives on Cape Breton History, 1713–1990* (Fredericton/Sydney: Acadiensis Press/UCCB Press, 1990), 129–44.

75 Harry Hiltz, letter to Fred Hiltz, September 20, 1916, published in *Kentville Advertiser*, October 6, 1916. Actually, there were 1,000 artillery guns in action.

76 Chute, *The Real Front*, 41–42.

77 Lewis, *Over the Top with the 25th*, 27.

78 Frank Byron Ferguson, *Gunner Ferguson's Diary: The Diary of Gunner Frank Byron Ferguson 1st Canadian Siege Battery Canadian Expeditionary Force 1915–1918*, ed. Peter G. Rogers (Hantsport: Lancelot Press, 1985), 50.

79 Lewis, *Over the Top with the 25th*, 30.

80 Harry Hiltz, letter to Fred Hiltz, September 20, 1916.

81 Hilliam, letter to GOC, 5th Brigade, quoted in McElhenny, "The 25th Battalion," 78.

82 Hilliam, undated telegram to Murray, published in *Truro Daily News*, September 25, 1916.

83 Desmond Morton and J. L. Granatstein, *Marching to Armageddon* (Toronto: Lester and Orpen Dennys, 1989), 120.

84 Howard Johnstone, letter to his mother, September 25, 1916, Nova Scotia Archives, MG 1/1500D/3.

85 Clements felt only contempt for people like Stuart Hunt who, writing in 1920, declared proudly that the men of the 25th had "made the old nickname of 'Herring-choker' one to be respected as long as memory lives and histories are written." See Hunt, *Nova Scotia's Part in the Great War*, 79, and Clements, *Merry Hell*, 153.

86 O. D. Skelton, *The Canadian Dominion* (New Haven: Yale University Press, 1921), 261.

87 Percy Willmot, letter to Dorothy Willmot, September 30, 1916, quoted in Tennyson, *Percy Willmot*, 136.

88 Clements, *Merry Hell*, 152.

89 Twenty-five Canadian soldiers were executed during the war, twenty-two for desertion, one for cowardice, and two for murder. On December 11, 2001, the government announced an official pardon for all but the two men convicted of murder, and promised that their names would be inscribed in the Book of Remembrance. The British government followed suit in August 2006

regarding the 306 men convicted of desertion or cowardice while serving in the British armed forces.

Chapter 5

1 *Amherst Daily News*, August 21, 1916.

2 *Halifax Herald*, November 6, 1915, reprinted in the *Bridgewater Bulletin*, November 9, 1915.

3 Ibid.

4 Admittedly a distinguished Nova Scotian, Fraser was also an old friend of Robert Borden who had recommended his knighthood in 1915. Perhaps more relevant was his well-established reputation as "an indefatigable lobbyist." See Janet Guildford, "Fraser, Sir Charles Frederick," *Dictionary of Canadian Biography*, vol. 15 (Toronto/Quebec: University of Toronto/Université Laval, 2003–), accessed March 24, 2016, http://www.biographi.ca/en/bio/fraser_charles_frederick_15E.html.

5 George Campbell, letter to his father, undated, published in *Kentville Advertiser*, August 1, 1916. Lieutenant George Campbell is commemorated by a brass plaque in St. Matthew's United Church in Halifax.

6 Ritchie came from a prominent Halifax legal family and had been Borden's law partner. He had moved to Vancouver in 1911 when given a plum appointment by the new government, and it is not clear why he returned to Halifax at this time. He didn't stay long, returning to Vancouver to campaign for the Conservatives in the 1917 election. For a biographical sketch, see Philip Girard, "Ritchie, William Bruce Almon," *Dictionary of Canadian Biography*, vol. 14 (Toronto/Quebec: University of Toronto/Université Laval, 2003–), accessed March 24, 2016, http://www.biographi.ca/en/bio/ritchie_william_bruce_almon_14E.html.

7 Hunt, *Nova Scotia's Part in the Great War*, 302.

8 Angus, "Living in the 'World of the Tiger,'" 98–99.

9 W. H. Muirhead, *A Short History and Photographic Record of the 219th Overseas Highland Battalion*, CEF (Ottawa, 1916), 2.

10 Quoted in *Kentville Advertiser*, January 18, 1916, and other newspapers.

11 George Cutten, quoted in *Kentville Advertiser*, November 7, 1916.

12 *Kentville Advertiser*, December 12, 1916. Her son, Norman McLeod Rogers, served overseas in the war and was later successively minister of labour and minister of national defence in the federal government.

13 This astonishing letter, dated February 14, 1916, is reproduced in full in W. James MacDonald, *Honour Roll of the Nova Scotia Overseas Highland Brigade* (Sydney: Cape Breton University Press, 2007), 7–10.

14 Hunt, *Nova Scotia's Part in the Great War*, 302.

15 Angus, "Living in the 'World of the Tiger,'" 100.

16 The two battalions that didn't come close to meeting their quota were the 246th Battalion and No. 2 Construction Battalion.

17 Sidney Oland not only served in the war but he also appeared in the most famous film made about it. He and his wife lived in Hollywood for a time after the war, and he reportedly had a small part in *All Quiet on the Western Front* before returning to Halifax to take his place in the family brewing business. Patrick Oland, "A Tale of Three Brothers," *Moosehead Beer Academy* (blog) posted November 28, 2014, accessed August 23, 2016, http://www.mooseheadbeeracademy.com/tale-three-brothers/.

18 Quoted in Matthew K. Barrett, "The Troublemakers," *Patriots, Crooks, and Safety-Firsters: Colonels of the Canadian Expeditionary Force* (blog), August 18, 2014, accessed May 15, 2016, https://matthewkbarrett.com/2014/08/18/the-troublemakers/. The problem was that the wounds had been self-inflicted.

19 LAC, Borden Fonds, C-4235/20388, Perley letter to Borden, December 15, 1916, private. I am indebted to Matthew Barrett for bringing this to my attention. See also Benjamin T. E. Fitch, "Doing their Duty: Politics and Recruitment in the Maritimes during World War 1" (MA thesis, University of Calgary, 2003), 23.

20 Modern references to him spell his name "Tremaine" but he spelled it "Tremain."

21 *Kentville Advertiser*, March 21, 1916. These figures are based on information provided in "Acadian 165th Battalion—'C' Company," accessed March 28, 2016, http://members.tripod.com/~acadie1755_165th/165th_batt_main.html; and Greg Kennedy, "Answering the Call to Serve: The Acadian Soldiers of the 165th Battalion of the Canadian Expeditionary Force and their Post-War Transition, 1911–1921" (Unpublished paper presented at the Nova Scotia's Part in the Great War Symposium, Windsor, Nova Scotia, June 11, 2016).

22 Harrington served overseas throughout the war but never got out of England. He briefly commanded the 17th Battalion at Bramshott in April 1917, then was seconded to the Ministry of Overseas Forces in London, rising to the rank of deputy minister. After the war, he resumed his law practice, was elected to the House of Assembly in 1925, and served as premier from 1930 to 1933.

23 Born in Shubenacadie, the son of a Methodist minister, he attended Mount Allison University, went to Oxford as a Rhodes Scholar, and after the war pursued an academic career at the University of New Brunswick and in the United States. He also wrote a novel entitled *Rockbound*, set on Ironbound Island at the mouth of the LaHave River, which remains in print and was the 2005 winner of CBC's Canada Reads competition.

24 Victoria County was a two-member constituency. The two members in 1914 were Premier George Murray and Angus Buchanan, both Liberals. When

Buchanan died, his seat was won by Philip McLeod, a Conservative. The result was contested, McLeod was unseated, and the seat remained vacant until the 1916 election, when John Gillis Morrison returned it to the Liberals.

25 Quoted in Matthew K. Barrett, "The Party Hack," *Patriots, Crooks, and Safety-Firsters: Colonels of the Canadian Expeditionary Force* (blog), February 23, 2015, accessed March 27, 2016, http://matthewkbarrett.com/2015/02/23/the-party-hack/.

26 F. B. McCurdy, *House of Commons Debates* (January 28, 1916), 398, quoted in Barrett, "The Party Hack."

27 Cameron, *Pictonians in Arms*, 96. Harry Murray's diary of the band's activities from March 1915 to January 1916 is available at *Harry's 85th Diary* (blog) accessed March 15, 2016, http://harrys85thdiary.blogspot.ca/.

28 Hunt, *Nova Scotia's Part in the Great War*, 146.

29 The 246th moved to Halifax and became the priority for provincial recruitment activities. Still seriously under strength in the spring of 1917, it sent two drafts overseas, both of which were absorbed into the 17th Reserve Battalion.

30 Hunt, *Nova Scotia's Part in the Great War*, 139.

31 Ibid., 140–41.

32 *Kentville Advertiser*, October 17, 1916 and October 24, 1916.

33 L. W. Totten, letter to his mother, undated, published in *Truro Daily News*, November 1, 1917.

34 *New York Times*, March 30, 1916.

35 Mackinnon, *Reminiscences*, 201.

36 Prominent men who lobbied Borden included Finlay MacDonald, president of the Nova Scotia Liberal-Conservative Association, Sydney mayor W. A. Richardson, and F. A. Crowell and J. F. Miles, executive members of the Sydney Recruiting Committee. LAC, Borden Fonds, C-4235/20386, 20387, Richardson et al., telegram to Borden, December 11, 1916. MacDonald, letter to Borden, December 14, 1916. I am indebted to Matthew Barrett for bringing this letter to my attention. George Cutten also warned Borden that disbanding the brigade would seriously affect enlistments. LAC, Borden Fonds, C-4235/20373, Cutten, telegram to Borden, December 6, 1916.

37 LAC, Borden Fonds, C-4235/20377-85. Maddin, telegram to Borden, December 9, 1916. I am indebted to Matthew Barrett for bringing this letter to my attention.

38 P. Whitney Lackenbauer, *A Commemorative History of Aboriginal People in the Canadian Military* (Ottawa: Department of National Defence, 2010), 125.

39 Don Julien, "The Mi'kmaq and the First World War" (unpublished paper presented at the Nova Scotia's Part in the Great War Revisited Symposium, Windsor, Nova Scotia, June 11, 2016.)

40 On the participation of indigenous men in the war, see Timothy C. Winegard, *For King and Kanata: Canadian Indians and the First World War* (Winnipeg:

University of Manitoba Press, 2012) and Lackenbauer, *A Commemorative History of Aboriginal People.*

41 "The Clayton Convalescent Home," *CMA* [Canadian Medical Association] *Journal* 6, no. 10 (October 1916): 925. See also Lois K. Yorke, "Best, Edna May Williston (Sexton)" in *Dictionary of Canadian Biography*, vol. 15 (Toronto/Quebec: University of Toronto/Université Laval, 2003), accessed June 23, 2016, http://www.biographi.ca/en/bio/best_edna_may_williston_15E.html.

42 "With the Colored Soldiers," *Atlantic Advocate* 1, no. 7 (January 1917): 12, 16. See also the comments of Lieutenant Colonel Charles Wood-Hill, who commanded the British West Indies Regiment, on the attitude of the War Office towards black soldiers, quoted in Stephen Bourne, *Black Poppies: Britain's Black Community and the Great War* (Stroud, UK: History Press, 2014).

43 Barrett, "The Troublemakers."

44 Bruce MacDonald, "First World War Veterans of Guysborough County," accessed May 6, 2017, http://guysboroughgreatwarveterans.blogspot.ca/2014/01.

45 Gwatkin memo, April 13, 1916, quoted in Robert Winks, *The Blacks in Canada*, 2nd ed. (Montreal/Kingston: McGill-University Press, 1997), 317.

46 The most thorough examination of No. 2 is Sean Flynn Foyn, *The Underside of Glory: Africanadian Enlistment in the Canadian Expeditionary Force, 1914–1917* (MA thesis, University of Ottawa, 1999), http://www.nl.c-bnc.ca/obj/s4/f2/ftp03/MQ48151.pdf.

47 The "civil engineers and contractors could not be found among the colored men." *Kentville Advertiser*, November 21, 1916.

48 Dr. Daniel Murray was born at Meadowville, Pictou County, in 1876 and studied medicine at Dalhousie University. He practised medicine for many years in Tatamagouche and served in the pre-war militia. In February 1917 he joined No. 2 Construction Battalion as medical officer and oversaw the building of a military hospital at La Joux and organized a military hospital at Conches to serve the Canadian Forestry Corps personnel. He and his wife, Morna, had four children, one of whom was J. Carson Murray, who also became a physician and was the father of Ann Murray.

49 Even if we accept that he was a commissioned officer, he was not the only one in the British Empire at the time. There were, in fact, three commissioned black officers in the British Army, although they were of mixed heritage, each having one white parent. The British Army's *Manual of Military Law* specifically excluded soldiers who were not "of pure European descent" from becoming commissioned officers, but George Bemand, David Clemetson, and Walter Tull were all commissioned officers. Perhaps this information serves most usefully to remind us of the absurdity of racial classifications. All three men were killed in the war.

50 *Truro Daily News*, November 16, 1916.

51 James W. St. G. Walker, "Race and Recruitment in World War 1: Enlistment of Visible Minorities in the Canadian Expeditionary Force," *Canadian Historical Review 70, no. 1 (1989): 17.*

52 R. A. Butler, letter to D. C. Mulhall, October 28, 1917, published in *Liverpool Advocate*, November 28, 1917.

53 Ibid., 20.

54 Bristol memorandum, quoted in Walker, "Race and Recruitment in World War 1," 20.

55 Robin Winks, *The Blacks in Canada*, 318.

56 Jonathan F. Vance, *Maple Leaf Empire: Canada, Britain, and Two World Wars (Don Mills: Oxford University Press, 2012), 103.*

57 Alexander O'Brien, undated letter to his father, J. S. O'Brien, published in *Casket*, June 14, 1917. Alex had enlisted in the 106th Battalion but served in the 75th and was killed near Arras on August 7; James Johnson, quoted in Reid, *Poor Bloody Murder*, 147.

58 McElhenny, "The 25th Battalion," 80.

59 Alexander O'Brien, letter to his father, undated.

60 Johnson quoted in Reid, *Poor Bloody Murder*, 148. Wallace Frail of Scotch Village could attest to this. After he was wounded, a wounded German "held onto me and helped me along" as he made his way back to seek medical treatment. Wallace Frail, letter to his mother, April 20, 1917, published in *Kentville Advertiser*, May 15, 1917.

61 Interview with Steven Toney, *Morning Chronicle*, October 12, 1918.

62 Philip Gibbs, "All of Vimy Ridge Cleared of Germans," *New York Times*, April 11, 1917.

63 Philip Gibbs, "British Fight Every Step," *New York Times*, April 16, 1917.

64 Robin Neillands, *The Great War Generals on the Western Front 1914–1918* (London: Robinson, 1998), 350.

65 John Keegan, *The First World War* (London: Hutchinson, 1998), 325, 326.

66 Tim Cook, *Shock Troops: Canadians Fighting the Great War, 1917–1918* (Toronto: Viking, 2008), 148.

67 Ibid., 146.

68 Percy Willmot, letter to Dorothy Willmot, April 16, 1916, quoted in Tennyson, *Percy Willmot*, 161.

69 Winnie McClare, letter to his mother, April 16, 1917, published in McClare, *The Letters of a Young Canadian Soldier*, 107. McClare was killed in an artillery barrage near Méricourt on May 3. He had been at the front for less than a month.

70 *Truro Daily News*, April 11, 1917.

71 *Victoria News*, May 2, 1917.

72 Cook, *Shock Troops*, 143–44.

73 My calculations suggest that more than 300 Nova Scotians, including men serving in non-Nova Scotian battalions, were killed at Vimy Ridge. The

Morning Chronicle listed fifty-nine men from the 85th, but that list is not complete. *Morning Chronicle*, April 9 and 12, 1919.

74 Lewis, *Over the Top with the 25th*, 59. Vimy Ridge was and still is popularly regarded as the Canadian Corps's greatest achievement in the war. Arthur Currie, however, considered the capture of Hill 70 four months later to be the greater achievement because the Germans put up a much stronger defence and the victory was of greater significance to the outcome of the war. It was also the first major battle in which the corps was commanded by a Canadian general. For two recent examinations of the battle and its significance, see Douglas E. Delaney and Serge Marc Durflinger, eds., *Capturing Hill 70: Canada's Forgotten Battle of the First World War* (Vancouver: UBC Press, 2016), and Holger Herwig, "'The Battle-Fortune of Marshal Hindenburg is not Bound up with the Possession of a Hill': The Germans and Vimy Ridge, April 1917," *Canadian Military History* 25, no. 2 (2016): Article 16, http://scholars.wlu.ca/cmh/vol25/iss2/16/.

Chapter 6

1 Borden diary, September 25, 1917, quoted in Tim Cook, *Warlords: Borden, Mackenzie King, and Canada's World Wars* (Toronto: Penguin, 2013), 119.

2 Walker, "Race and Recruitment in World War 1," 18. See also Chris Sharpe, "Enlistment in the Canadian Expeditionary Force 1914–1918: A Re-Evaluation," *Canadian Military History* 24, no. 1 (Spring 2015): 39–40.

3 "Men Wanted for the Navy," *Richmond County Recorder*, March 24, 1917.

4 See a sample ad in *Morning Chronicle*, April 9, 1917.

5 *Casket*, July 12, 1917. See also "Will Women Volunteer?," *Eastern Chronicle*, July 20, 1917.

6 G. S. Campbell, "National Service: An Appeal to the Coal Miners of Nova Scotia," April 7, 1917, published in *Eastern Chronicle*, April 24, 1917.

7 Borden, quoted in Morton and Granatstein, *Marching to Armageddon*, 145.

8 George Murray joined the 40th Battalion as a captain in September 1915 and Wilfrid Murray enlisted in No. 10 Siege Battery in June 1917.

9 There were two Nova Scotian vacancies in the House of Commons in 1917. Arthur DeWitt Foster (Conservative, Kings) had resigned and Bowman Law (Liberal, Yarmouth) had died in the fire that severely damaged the Parliament building in February 1916.

10 On the attitude of farmers to conscription, see W. R. Young, "Conscription, Rural Depopulation and the Farmers of Ontario, 1917–19," *Canadian Historical Review* 53, no. 3 (1972): 239–319. The attitude of Nova Scotian farmers was similar.

11 Quoted in Martin Robin, "Registration, Conscription, and Independent Labour Politics, 1916–1917," *Canadian Historical Review* 47, no. 2 (June 1966): 109.

12 Andrew Theobald, *The Bitter Harvest of War: New Brunswick and the Conscription Crisis of 1917 (Fredericton: Goose Lane, 2008), 67, 65.*

13 P. J. Veniot was elected to the New Brunswick Legislative Assembly in 1917 and became New Brunswick's first Acadian premier in 1923.

14 Lackenbauer, *A Commemorative History of Aboriginal People*, 128.

15 Calkin, letter to Borden, November 25, 1917, quoted in Roger Graham, *Arthur Meighen* (Toronto: Clarke Irwin, 1963), 2: 29.

16 J. H. Tuck, "Nova Scotia and the Conscription Election of 1917" (MA thesis, Dalhousie University, 1968), 50, 51, 53.

17 *Acadian Recorder*, May 22, 1917, quoted in Tuck, "Nova Scotia and the Conscription Election of 1917," 17.

18 Tuck, "Nova Scotia and the Conscription Election of 1917," 19.

19 Borden diary, September 25, 1917, quoted in Cook, *Warlords*, 119.

20 *Casket*, June 14, 1917.

21 *Sydney Daily Post*, August 20, 1917.

22 *Bridgewater Bulletin*, September 18, 1917.

23 *Lunenburg Progress Enterprise*, July 25, 1917; and *Richmond County Record*, June 23, 1917.

24 *Presbyterian Witness*, April 21, 1917, quoted in Angus, "Living in the 'World of the Tiger,'" 136.

25 *Bridgewater Bulletin*, July 3, 1917.

26 Reverend Charles Brewer, *The Diocese of Antigonish and World War 1* (MA thesis, University of New Brunswick, 1975), 55, quoted in Matheson, "In the Dust You Will Prevail," 79.

27 *Sydney Daily Post*, December 17, 1917.

28 Quoted in Ibid.

29 *Truro Daily News*, November 19, 1917.

30 *Sydney Daily Post*, November 29, 1917. Norman McLeod Rogers put the number at "over three hundred." Rogers, undated letter to the editor, published in *Amherst Daily News*, December 13, 1917.

31 Rogers, letter to the editor, December 13, 1917.

32 *Truro Daily News*, December 7, 1917.

33 *Amherst Daily News*, December 13, 1917.

34 Léger, undated letter [November 1917], published in *Truro Daily News*, December 3, 1917.

35 "A Message from Overseas to the People of Victoria," *Victoria News*, December 12, 1917. The lead signatory was Guy Matheson, a major in the 25th Battalion, who probably organized the appeal.

36 Keith Rogers, letter to the editor, November 24, 1914, published in *Yarmouth Herald*, December 22, 1914.

37 Manley Rafuse, July 14, 1915, published in *Yarmouth Telegram*, August 13, 1915.

38 Harold Aulenback, letter to the editor, August 29, 1915, published in *Bridgewater Bulletin*, October 19, 1915.

39 G. E. Cragg, letter to his father, November 5, 1915, published in *Bridgewater Bulletin*, December 7, 1915.

40 Patrick Whyte undated letter, published in *Sydney Daily Post*, September 7, 1917. Whyte had enlisted in the 36th Battery in January 1916.

41 Winnie McClare, letter to his father, December 29, 1917, published in McClare, ed., *The Letters of a Young Canadian Soldier*, 78.

42 Wilburn Wallace, letter to his mother, September 13, 1917, published in *Truro Daily News*, October 15, 1917.

43 Ira Moore, letter to his mother, November 5, 1917, published in *Truro Daily News*, December 1, 1917.

44 Clarence B. Smith, letter to his parents, November 14, 1917, published in *Bridgewater Bulletin*, December 11, 1917.

45 Frank McGregor, undated letter to his father, published in *Sydney Daily Post*, December 14, 1917.

46 Donald Calderwood Reid, letter to his sister, Jessie Reid, December 5, 1917, published on the Canadian Letters and Images Project website, accessed May 7, 2016; http://www.canadianletters.ca/content/document-6439?position=53&list=_MKunQF7sR-G-jU9rS8ZPavJEwmr3FNsE0ZDiPZ4ElU. Reid was killed in action on September 25, 1918.

47 Donald Calderwood Reid, letter to his father, December 7, 1917; published on the Canadian Letters and Images Project website, accessed May 7, 2016, http://www.canadianletters.ca/content/document-4210?position=54&list=_MKunQF7sR-G-jU9rS8ZPavJEwmr3FNsE0ZDiPZ4ElU.

48 MacKinlay was using the word "want" in the traditional English sense, meaning "need."

49 George R. MacKinlay, letter to his father, December 3, 1917, published in *Berwick Register*, February 9, 1918.

50 Ludlow Weeks, letter to his sister, December 6, 1917, published on the Canadian Letters and Images Project website, accessed May 7, 2016, http://canadianletters.ca/content/document-13679?position=25&list=B-F-l_trxyh0EsKFAaabvLJ3uuNTpBvDoVR9DkgWJUs. Weeks survived the war and went on to become a prominent geologist.

51 Quoted in Groom, *A Storm in Flanders*, 220–21.

52 Quoted in H. L. Livingstone et al., "Cape Bretoners in World War One," 161.

53 John William MacVicar, undated letter to his son, David MacVicar, quoted in John J. Johnson, *"The Right Spirit": A History of Birch Grove and its People 1840–1940* (North Sydney, NS: privately published, 2009), 101.

54 Elkanah Clements, letter to his father, January 14, 1918, published in Thurston, *A Monument Speaks*, 96.

55 Denis Winter, *Haig's Command: A Reassessment* (London: Penguin, 2001), 131, 141.

56 Ibid., 45–46.

57 William Ross, quoted in "The 85th fix Nova Scotia Highlanders World War 1 Monument at Passchendaele—Zonnebeke, Beglium," accessed May 27, 2016, http://www.capebretonhighlandersassociation.ca/Momuments/Passchendale%20Momument.html. Ross was from Margaree but was a miner at Sydney Mines when he enlisted in the 106th Battalion. He served overseas in the 85th Battalion.

58 Clements, *Merry Hell,* 189.

59 Quoted in Groom, *A Storm in Flanders,* 224.

60 Quoted in John Terraine, *The Road to Passchendaele* (London: Leo Cooper, 1977), xix–xx.

61 Quoted in Groom, *A Storm in Flanders,* 225.

62 Morton and Granatstein, *Marching to Armageddon,* 174.

63 *Lunenburg Progress Enterprise,* March 27, 1918.

64 Annapolis and Digby were combined, Antigonish and Guysborough were combined, Cape Breton North and Victoria were combined, and Cape Breton South and Richmond were combined.

65 Stanfield was rewarded in 1921 with a seat in the Senate.

66 Sir Wilfrid Laurier, letter to E. M. Macdonald, December 26, 1917, quoted in E. M. Macdonald, *Recollections Political and Personal* (Toronto: Ryerson, 1938), 347.

67 Mackinnon, *Reminiscences,* 209.

68 Joseph Hayes, letter to F. B. McCurdy, December 18, 1917, quoted in Desmond Morton, *A Peculiar Kind of Politics: Canada's Overseas Ministry in the First World War* (Toronto: University of Toronto Press, 1982), 143.

69 Morton, *A Peculiar Kind of Politics,* 146.

70 Edgar Rhodes, letter to D.H. McDougall, December 18, 1917, quoted in in Tuck, "Nova Scotia and the Conscription Election of 1917," 114. McDougall was the general manager of the Dominion Steel Company.

71 Rhodes, telegram to Daly, December 11, 1917, quoted in Tuck, "Nova Scotia and the Conscription Election of 1917," 136. Daly was a Manitoba lawyer and close associate of Sam Hughes. He survived the sinking of the *Lusitania* in May 1915.

72 W. T. R. Preston, *My Generation of Politics and Politicians* (Toronto: D. A. Rose, 1927), 368.

73 Hayes, letter to Rhodes, February 7, 1918, quoted in Tuck, "Nova Scotia and the Conscription Election of 1917," 135–36.

74 Morton, *A Peculiar Kind of Politics,* 147.

75 Figures are from Tuck, "Nova Scotia and the Conscription Election of 1917," 149–50.

76 Tuck, "Nova Scotia and the Conscription Election of 1917," 141.
77 See *Morning Chronicle*, October 19, 1917; and *Kentville Advertiser*, November 6, 1917.
78 *Sydney Daily Post*, October 22, 1917. This issue is incorrectly dated the twenty-first.
79 G. S. Campbell, "An Appeal to the Coal Miners of Nova Scotia," *Sydney Daily Post*, April 23, 1917. Campbell was now the director of National Service for Nova Scotia.
80 *Sydney Daily Post*, October 31, 1917
81 Ibid., November 15, 1917.
82 *Casket*, December 6, 1917.
83 Figures from J. Castell Hopkins, *Canada at War 1914–1918: A Record of Heroism and Achievement* (New York: George H. Doran, 1919), 295.
84 Agnes McGuire, letter to the editor, June 18, 1917, published in *Morning Chronicle*, June 19, 1918.
85 Ibid. None of the three men mentioned—Austin Knickle Allan Weaver, and Greville Knickle—was conscripted.
86 William Stewart, "Frustrated Belligerence: The Unhappy History of the 5th Canadian Division in the First World War," *Canadian Military History* 22, no. 2 (Spring 2013): 31.

Chapter 7

1 Edith Archibald, quoted in *Morning Chronicle*, August 11, 1914. The daughter of Sir Edward Archibald, Edith Jessie Archibald (1854–1936) was a Canadian suffragist and writer who led the Maritime Women's Christian Temperance Union (WCTU), the National Council of Women of Canada, and the Local Council of Women of Halifax. She married her second cousin, Charles Archibald, who became vice-president of the Bank of Nova Scotia.
2 *Eastern Chronicle*, August 14, 1914.
3 *Morning Chronicle*, August 6, 1914.
4 Ibid., August 22, 1914.
5 Ibid., September 19, 1914.
6 *Sydney Daily Post*, August 7, 1914.
7 LeVatte letter to Carpenter, August 20, 1914; Carpenter, letter to LeVatte, August 26, 1914, both published in *Yarmouth Herald*, September 22, 1914.
8 Canada, *House of Commons Debates*, April 15, 1915. See also E. M. Macdonald, *Recollections Political and Personal*, 291–92.
9 *Report of the Commissioner on Purchase of Horses in Nova Scotia for First Canadian Contingent* (Ottawa: King's Printer, 1917), 34. For detailed accounts of this scandal, including testimony given by some of those who sold horses,

see *Morning Chronicle*, August 12 and 14, 1915; and Cameron, *Pictonians in Arms*, 87.

10 *Eastern Chronicle*, April 9, 1915.

11 Murray letter to Harvey MacLeod, November 28, 1914, published in *Amherst Daily News*, December 19, 1914.

12 *New York Times*, June 16, 1915.

13 *Journal of Commerce*, reprinted in the *Eastern Chronicle*, May 7, 1915; and *Eastern Chronicle*, April 9, 1915 and December 10, 1915.

14 After the United States entered the war it leased the closed Ross rifle factory to manufacture pistols for its army and paid the Canadian government, which had expropriated the property, $300,000 in rent. *Morning Chronicle*, August 1, 1918.

15 *Maritime Merchant*, October 4, 1906.

16 *Eastern Chronicle*, December 17, 1915.

17 Ibid., August 28, 1917.

18 *Yarmouth Herald*, November 17, 1914.

19 *Amherst Daily News*, August 12, 1914 and December 11, 1914.

20 David Carnegie, *The History of Munitions Supply in Canada 1914–1918* (London: Longmans, Green, 1925), 20.

21 *Amherst Daily News*, March 22, 1915.

22 James M. Cameron, *Industrial History of the New Glasgow District*. (New Glasgow: Hector Publishing, 1960), 4:21; *Eastern Chronicle*, February 11, 1915.

23 Quoted in *Eastern Chronicle*, April 7, 1916.

24 *Eastern Chronicle*, May 7, 1915.

25 *Atlantic Advocate* 1, no. 1 (April 1915): 16.

26 Cameron, *Pictonians in Arms*, 99.

27 Michael Bliss, *A Canadian Millionaire: The Life and Business Times of Sir Joseph Flavelle, Bart. 1858–1939* (Toronto: Macmillan, 1978), 252. See also the views of Ian McKay, not normally a defender of industrialists, in "The 1910s: The Stillborn Triumph of Progressive Reform," in *The Atlantic Provinces in Confederation*, ed. E. R. Forbes and D. A. Muise (Toronto/Fredericton: University of Toronto Press/Acadiensis Press, 1993), 205.

28 *Eastern Chronicle*, June 23, 1916; Hopkins, *Canada at War 1914–1918*, 201, 203; and Tennyson and Sarty, *Guardian of the Gulf*, 152–53.

29 *Eastern Chronicle*, June 22, 1917.

30 Ibid., August 28, 1917; *Sydney Daily Post*, August 28, 1917 and March 1, 1918.

31 Bliss, *A Canadian Millionaire*, 287.

32 *New York Times*, March 14, 1915. The Edison family had moved from New Jersey to Nova Scotia as Loyalists and lived there until 1811.

33 This account is based on Carnegie, *The History of Munitions Supply*, 70–75.

34 *Montreal Star*, undated, reprinted in *Amherst Daily News*, April 14, 1917.

35 Carnegie, *The History of Munitions Supply*, 213.

36 *Victoria News*, May 30, 1917.

37 The ships were the 1,421-ton *War Wasp*, the 1,621-ton *War Bee*, and the *Watuka*. Some sources claim that the *Watuka* was the *War Bee*, renamed, but Tim Coulter, who has compiled a definitive shipping archive based on company records, says they were not the same ship. Tim Coulter, letter to the author, June 16, 2016.

38 *Lunenburg Progress Enterprise*, March 28, 1917.

39 *Eastern Chronicle*, April 10, 1917.

40 Victor L. Settle, "Halifax Shipyards, 1887–1978: The Economic Impact" (MA thesis, Saint Mary's University, 1999), 24.

41 Quoted in *Halifax Herald*, July 16, 1920.

42 *Morning Chronicle*, October 12, 1918; and Wolvin, quoted in *Halifax Herald*, July 16, 1920.

43 Settle, "Halifax Shipyards, 1887–1978," 29.

44 Ibid., 34.

45 Quoted in *Eastern Chronicle*, April 7, 1916.

46 *Kentville Advertiser*, November 7, 1916.

47 *Morning Chronicle*, August 24, 1918.

48 *Kentville Advertiser*, August 8, 1916; and *Eastern Chronicle*, August 4, 1916.

49 *Casket*, June 24, 1917.

50 *Eastern Chronicle*, June 12, 1917.

51 Ibid., May 2, 1916.

52 David MacKenzie, "Eastern Approaches: Maritime Canada and Newfoundland," in *Canada and the First World War: Essays in Honour of Robert Craig Brown*, ed. David MacKenzie (Toronto: University of Toronto Press, 2005), 354.

53 *Eastern Chronicle*, December 11, 1914.

54 *Kentville Advertiser*, July 27, 1917. See Lachlan Mackinnon, "Labour Landmarks in New Waterford: Collective Memory in a Cape Breton Coal Town," *Acadiensis* 42, no. 2 (Summer/Autumn 2013): 3–26.

55 *New Glasgow Evening News*, reprinted in *Truro Daily News*, December 22, 1917.

56 McKay, "The Stillborn Triumph," 207.

57 Sharpe, "Enlistment in the Canadian Expeditionary Force 1914–1918," 29–30.

58 MacLennan, *Barometer Rising*, 5, 6.

59 *Halifax, Canada's Atlantic Port: Always Open to All Shipping* (Halifax, 1930), quoted in James D. Frost, *Canada's Atlantic Gateway: An Illustrated History of the Port of Halifax* (Halifax: Nimbus, 2008), 82; John Griffith Armstrong, *The Halifax Explosion and the Royal Canadian Navy: Inquiry and Intrigue* (Vancouver: UBC Press, 2002), 23.

60 MacLennan, *Barometer Rising*, 199.

61 *Amherst Daily News*, March 15, 1915.

62 *Morning Chronicle*, August 1, 1918.

63 See the report of their grievances in the *New York Times*, August 24, 1915. Most accounts say that only one detainee was killed. The records show that Alois Clement was killed on June 1 and Fritz Claus died of gunshot wounds on June 15. Lawrna Myers, *Project 107 Report* (Vernon, BC: June 22, 2016), accessed May 25, 2016, http://www.internmentcanada.ca/PDF/CFWWIRF%20Project%20107%20Burial%20Report%20June%2022%20 2016%20Myers.pdf.

64 When twelve prisoners escaped in January 1916 by tunnelling under the walls of the building and the barbed wire fence, many people in the community, and indeed throughout the province, became alarmed, naturally assuming that they were at least potentially dangerous. Actually, their only goal was to get across the border into the United States, which was still a neutral country. Since six were recaptured, it seems likely that the others succeeded and were allowed to stay there. *New York Times*, January 20, 1916. A few months later another internee attempting to escape was killed by the guards.

65 Leon Trotsky, *My Life* (New York: Charles Scribner's Sons, 1930), 218.

66 Quoted in Silver Donald Cameron, "Trotsky in Amherst," *Canadian Geographic* (1988), accessed 5 July 2016, http://www.silverdonaldcameron.ca/trotsky-amherst.

67 Garnet White, undated letter, *Amherst Daily News*, reprinted in *Kentville Advertiser*, June 16, 1916.

68 *Kentville Advertiser*, May 23, 1916.

69 John McDougall, letter to his mother, undated [May 1916], published on the Canadian Letters and Images Project website, accessed May 7, 2016, http://canadianletters.ca/content/document-6694?position=4&list=CnSubJWF31tn CiAiWnQa1xXk2KuUyGM1f6VljEkAbVE.

70 *Kentville Advertiser*, February 15, 1916.

71 Ibid., August 22, 16.

72 Ibid., July 25, 1916.

73 More than 5,000 of them were members of the Jewish Legion. Sarah Beanlands, *Formation of the Jewish Legion at Ford Edward* (Halifax: Boreas Heritage Consulting, 2014), 6. See also Nancy Gentile Ford, *Americans All!: Foreign-born Soldiers in World War 1* (College Station, TX: A&M Press, 2001), 44.

74 Elias Gilner, *War and Hope: A History of the Jewish Legion* (New York: Herzl Press, 1969), quoted in Beanlands, *Formation of the Jewish Legion*, 16. Gilner served in the Jewish Legion.

75 Beanlands, *Formation of the Jewish Legion*, 17.

76 Ibid., 21. The event was reported in the *Hants Journal* on September 18, 1918.

77 Thomas Johnson, letter to Mr. Aitkin, October 10, 1916, published on the Canadian Letters and Images Project website, accessed May 7, 2016, http://

www.canadianletters.ca/content/document-11796?position=4&list=Zrf9AxeK1NR88Fuaq_WkgDUeeg6cuuXC_mCkaDTwzAY.

78 Among them were Caleb Goodwin, a carpenter and fisherman from Pubnico, James Redden, a farmer who gave his home address as Montreal, and Kenneth Crowell of Sandy Cove.

79 Cameron, *Pictonians in Arms*, 98.

80 *Amherst Daily News*, February 27, 1917.

81 Halifax and Richmond Counties had resisted prohibition but it was extended to the city of Halifax in July 1916. In late 1917 the federal government limited the interprovincial sale of alcohol and in March 1918 totally banned its production and sale.

82 Paul McLeod, "Loose Security at Sydney Cable Station Outraged Censor," *Halifax Chronicle Herald*, undated [2016], accessed September 15, 2016, https://thechronicleherald.ca/thegreatwar/1249597-loose-security-at-sydney-cable-station-outraged-censor#.WJjFZLYrJ0t.

83 John McCarthy, *The Story of the Establishment and Development of the Catholic Church in Amherst Nova Scotia* (Amherst: St. Charles Parish, 1962), accessed January 22, 2015, http://www.lchr.org/a/33/27/history.html.

84 *Halifax Recorder*, undated, reprinted in *Eastern Chronicle*, October 22, 1915.

85 *Morning Chronicle*, May 27, 1918.

86 *Sydney Daily Post*, September 21, 1918.

87 Ibid., November 10, 1917. There were, however, more serious incidents from time to time. See *Sydney Daily Post*, October 3, 1917, October 4, 1917 and May 31, 1918.

88 Ibid., September 3, 1918.

89 Mossman, *Going Over*, 50.

90 *Morning Chronicle*, June 19, 1918.

91 Ibid., September 24, 1914.

92 The people of Woods Harbour even declared that "many there are who would gladly give a home" to the Belgians if they could be brought to Canada. *Yarmouth Herald*, October 27, 1914.

93 Hopkins, *Canada at War 1914–1918*, 253.

94 Yorke, "Best, Edna May Williston (Sexton)," accessed October 25, 2016.

95 Charles Smith, letter, December 30, 1916, published in *Yarmouth Herald*, January 23, 1917. Cf H. W. Hiltz, letter to the secretary, Kingsport Red Cross Society, January 4, 1916, published in *Kentville Advertiser*, February 11, 1916. Harry Wentworth Hiltz of Kingsport enlisted in the 25th Battalion in November 1914 and rose to the rank of lieutenant. For other letters, see for example, Harriet Graham to New Glasgow Red Cross Society, February 22, 1915, published in *Eastern Chronicle*, March 19, 1915, and Addie Tupper, letter to the editor, May 28, 1915, published in *Bridgewater Bulletin*, June 22, 1915.

96 *Eastern Chronicle*, November 9, 1915.

97 Hopkins, *Canada at War 1914–1918*, 263.

98 W. Drummond Matheson, letter to W. G. Matheson, undated [September 1916], published in *Eastern Chronicle*, October 10, 1916.

99 Hopkins, *Canada at War 1914–1918*, 248. See also *Liverpool Advance*, April 24, 1918.

100 *Amherst Daily News*, March 7, 1916; *Bridgewater Bulletin*, April 3, 1917.

101 *Eastern Chronicle*, October 19, 1917.

102 Ibid., September 19, 1916.

103 *Bridgewater Bulletin*, March 23, 1915.

104 *Eastern Chronicle*, June 15, 1917.

105 *Morning Chronicle*, June 16, 1917, reprinted in *Liverpool Advance*, June 20, 1917. The *Deliverance* remains where it sank and is a popular site for divers.

106 Marshall, *Georges Island*, 159–60.

107 Quoted in Laura MacDonald, *Curse of the Narrows: The Halifax Explosion, 1917* (Toronto: Harper Collins Canada, 2005), 134.

108 Raddall, *In My Time*, 36.

109 Harry Chapman, *In the Wake of the* Alderney*: Dartmouth, Nova Scotia, 1750–2000* (Halifax: Nimbus, 2001), 198.

110 Ibid., 201.

111 This account of the explosion's impact on Dartmouth is based on Chapman, *In the Wake of the* Alderney, 194–204. For a good contemporary account of the explosion's impact on Dartmouth, see the account published by the Reverend J. A. McGlashen, minister of Stairs' Memorial Church, in *Lunenburg Progress Enterprise*, February 13, 1918.

112 Borden, *Robert Laird Borden: His Memoirs*, 2:764.

113 McCall telegram to Mayor Peter Martin, quoted in MacDonald, *Curse of the Narrows*, 105.

114 *Sydney Record*, undated, reprinted in *Truro Daily News*, December 24, 1917. See also *CMA Journal* 8, no. 2 (February 1918): 169. For a report on the role of physicians in the crisis, see "The Halifax Disaster," *CMA Journal* 8, no. 1 (January 1918): 59–62.

Chapter 8

1 Rudyard Kipling, quoted in *Halifax Morning Chronicle*, August 8, 1914.

2 *Sydney Daily Post*, August 3, 1914. Three days late the *Daily Post* reported that HMS *Essex* had captured a "coal laden" German ship "not far from the Cape Breton coast and bound south, evidently conveying to German cruisers off the New England coast fuel, of which they were reported short when leaving Mexican waters." *Sydney Daily Post*, August 6, 1914.

3 Quoted in Tennyson and Sarty, *Guardian of the Gulf*, 115.

4 *Sydney Daily Post*, August 6, 1914.

5 *Yarmouth Herald*, September 1, 1914.

6 John Malcolm Brinnin, *The Sway of the Grand Saloon: A Social History of the North Atlantic* (New York: Delacorte Press, 1971), 403, 404.

7 It all came to an end when Polack arranged for the vessel to be towed to Boston, "guided" by American destroyers. There it was interned and the crew was again "swept up into the cultural climate of the Hub of the Universe." But when the United States entered the war the ship was seized and became the troop transport *Mount Vernon*. Brinnin, *The Sway of the Grand Saloon*, 405.

8 *Morning Chronicle*, August 14, 1914 and August 15, 1914.

9 Ibid., August 11, 1914.

10 *Sydney Daily Post*, August 12, 1914.

11 W. H. Hayes, "On to Bermuda," *Regimental Rogue*, accessed July 8, 1915, www.regimentalrogue.com. Hayes was a member of the Royal Canadian Regiment.

12 *Toronto News*, reprinted in the *Sydney Daily Post*, August 11, 1914.

13 *Sydney Daily Post*, September 4, 1914.

14 Ibid., August 13, 1914.

15 Ibid., September 16, 1914.

16 Marc Milner, *Canada's Navy: The First Century* (Toronto: University of Toronto Press, 1999), 28–30.

17 Macdonald was born in Victoria, one of the sons of William Macdonald, who had been appointed to the Senate when British Columbia entered Confederation in 1871. He had joined the Royal Navy as an ensign and had a successful career until the accident with the *Niobe*.

18 Gilbert Norman Tucker, *The Naval Service of Canada: Its Official History (Ottawa: Department of National Defence, 1962), 241.*

19 Elson, *Canada's Bastions*, 156.

20 Hayes, "On to Bermuda."

21 Quoted in Johnston et al., *The Seabound Coast*, 266.

22 Tucker, *The Naval Service of Canada*, 245.

23 Aglionby, quoted in Johnston et al., *The Seabound Coast*, 268.

24 Marc Milner, "*Niobe*'s Brief Operational Career, Part 5," *Legion Magazine*, September 1, 2004, accessed April 22, 2016, https://legionmagazine.com/en/2004/09/niobes-brief-operational-career/.

25 *Acadian*, October 30, 1914; Purdy, letter to the editor, October 20, 1914, published in the *Yarmouth Herald*, November 24, 1914. The *Karlsruhe* exploded and sank on November 4, 1914.

26 *Yarmouth Herald*, October 27, 1914.

27 *Eastern Chronicle*, January 13, 1915.

28 "Captain Charles Owen Allen" in *Prominent People of the Maritime Provinces* (Saint John: Canadian Publicity Co, 1922), 9. This was bad luck because U-40 was torpedoed by a British submarine in the same area on June 23. Both British and German records indicate that it sank no vessels before being destroyed.

29 *Eastern Chronicle*, November 12, 1915, reprinted in *New York Times*, November 15, 1915. *U-35* was the most successful German submarine in the war, sinking 224 ships for a total of 539,741 tons. Figures are from "SM *U-35* (Germany) Explained," *Everything Explained Today*, accessed 28 April 2016, http://everything.explained.today/SM_*U-35*_(Germany).

30 *New York Times*, November 9, 1915. The three ships were the *Minnehaha* in July, the *Rio Lages* and the *Rochambeau*, both in November. A fourth ship, the Greek *Athinai*, a liner with 450 passengers, had to be abandoned before it could reach Halifax.

31 A gruff man with high standards, Pasco also knew the importance of common sense. Naval historian Marc Milner describes an occasion when Pasco found his men struggling to bring ashore a barrel marked "sugar" that rather oddly clinked as they moved it. Instead of investigating, he simply reminded the men to "send some of that sugar to my cabin, too." Milner, *Canada's Navy*, 48.

32 Quoted in Michael L. Hadley and Roger Sarty, *Tin-Pots and Pirate Ships: Canadian Naval Forces and German Sea Raiders 1880–1918* (Montreal/Kingston: McGill-Queen's University Press, 1991), 155–56.

33 *New York Times*, August 23, 1916.

34 Cecil Boyd, "Canso in 1916," *Truro Daily News*, January 5, 1917.

35 *Boston Globe*, reprinted in *Kentville Advertiser*, November 21, 1916.

36 *Kentville Advertiser*, December 12, 1916.

37 Ibid., December 19, 1916.

38 Mackinnon, *Reminiscences*, 194.

39 Michael L. Hadley, Rob Huebert, and Fred W. Crickard, *A Nation's Navy: In Quest of Canadian Naval Identity* (Montreal/Kingston: McGill-Queen's University Press, 1996), 127.

40 Tennyson and Sarty, *Guardian of the Gulf*, 155, 158

41 His name was actually James Gibson Laurier Fraser but he was commonly known as Laurier.

42 *Yarmouth Telegram*, July 5, 1918. Captain Helmut Brümmer-Patzig and two of his lieutenants were later charged with war crimes in what became known as the Leipzig Trials, but he fled to South America before the trial. The two lieutenants were convicted and sentenced to four years in prison but served only about four months before managing to escape.

43 *Eastern Chronicle*, July 9, 1918.

44 *Bridgewater Bulletin*, August 13, 1918.

45 *Morning Chronicle*, June 29, 1918.

46 *Kentville Advertiser*, August 9, 1918.

47 Other Nova Scotian vessels sunk that summer were the *Annie M. Perry* (Captain James Goodman), the *Elsie Porter* (Captain Irvin Isnor), the *Potentate*, and the *Agnes G. Holland*. The *Walrus* (Clayton Morrissey) had a near escape when, instead of surrendering his vessel Morrissey tried to ram the U-boat,

which quickly submerged; the *Walrus* returned safely to port. *Yarmouth Herald*, August 20, 1918. Vessels registered in other countries that were sunk at this time also showed up in Nova Scotian ports. When the captain of *U-155* discovered that the freighter he had just sunk off Sable Island was Portuguese, he reportedly exclaimed, "Ach du lieber Gott, I have wasted a torpedo!" *Morning Chronicle*, September 18, 1918.

48 Captain Eldridge Nickerson, captain of the *Muriel*, reported that he and his crew were taken aboard the submarine and given "a meal of bully beef and rice and were assured by their captors that the U-boats meant them no personal harm." Quoted in *Gloucester Herald*, August 5, 1918. See also the *Bridgewater Bulletin*, August 13, 1918, and US Navy Department, Historical Section, *German Submarine Activities on the Atlantic Coast of the United States and Canada* (Washington: Government Printing Office, 1920), 58. The crew of the *Dornfontein* was told the same thing when it spent five hours on *U-156* and was given a meal. *Morning Chronicle*, August 5, 1918.

49 *Morning Chronicle*, June 5, 1918.

50 William Johnston, "The Royal Canadian Navy and the First World War," in *The Naval Service of Canada 1910–2010: The Centennial Story*, ed. Richard H. Gimblett (Toronto: Dundurn, 2009), 37.

51 That vessel, the *Mackay-Bennett*, was the first to arrive on the scene to recover bodies after the sinking of the *Titanic* in April 1912. It retrieved 306 of the 328 bodies found from the 1,517 who died. Popular Canadian author Thomas Raddall based some of his short stories on his experiences as a wireless operator on the *Mackay-Bennett*.

52 Milner, *Canada's Navy*, 54.

53 *Sydney Daily Post*, August 28, 1918.

54 Tennyson and Sarty, *Guardian of the Gulf*, 160.

55 S. F. Wise, *Canadian Airmen and the First World War: The Official History of the Royal Canadian Air Force* (Toronto: University of Toronto Press, 1980), 1:604.

56 *Sydney Daily Post*, September 30, 1918.

57 *Morning Chronicle*, July 29, 1918.

58 Ibid., July 31, 1918.

59 Ibid., August 14, 1918.

60 Ibid., August 19, 1918.

61 *Halifax Herald*, undated, reprinted in *Bridgewater Bulletin*, August 20, 1918.

62 Ibid.

63 *Bridgewater Bulletin*, September 3, 1918.

64 Quoted in the *Morning Chronicle*, 23 August 1918.

65 *Morning Chronicle*, 5 June 1918.

66 *Bridgewater Bulletin*, August 13, 1918.

67 William Bell Clark, *When the U-Boats Came to America* (Boston: Little Brown, 1929), 169.

68 US Navy Department, *German Submarine Activities*, 58. This source identifies the man as the Second Officer.

69 *Lunenburg Progress Enterprise*, September 11, 1918. The *Eastern Chronicle* embellished the story when it reported that the captain of a fishing vessel recently sunk by a submarine had said the U-boat captain was "a Lunenburg fishing captain well known to all the shore people of Lunenburg. He told the captain of the schooner who has a brother master of a large fishing schooner that he would get the brother's schooner too, in a day or so." *Eastern Chronicle*, undated, reprinted in *Yarmouth Herald*, September 10, 1918.

70 Quoted in J. D. F. Kealy and E. C. Russell, *A History of Canadian Naval Aviation 1918–1962* (Ottawa: Naval Historical Section, Canadian Forces Headquarters, Department of National Defence, 1965), 4.

71 *Morning Chronicle*, August 31, 1918.

72 Ibid., November 4, 1918.

73 Ibid.

74 Quoted in Tom Sheppard, *Historic Bridgewater* (Halifax: Nimbus, 2008), 185.

75 *Morning Chronicle*, November 4, 1918.

76 Kealy and Russell, *A History of Canadian Naval Aviation*, 4.

77 *Bridgewater Bulletin*, November 5, 1918. The *Industrial* had been built by J. N. Rafuse & Sons and was owned by the LaHave Outfitting Company.

78 US Navy Department, *German Submarine Activities*, 141.

79 Roger Sarty, "Hard-Luck Flotilla: the RNC's Atlantic Coast Patrol, 1914–18," in *The RCN in Transition 1910–1985*, ed. W. A. B. Douglas (Vancouver: University of British Columbia Press, 1988), 125.

80 Milner, *Canada's Navy*, 39.

Chapter 9

1 Herbert Cunningham, letter to unknown, November 21, 1917, published in *Yarmouth Herald-Telegram*, January 15, 1918. Herbert Cunningham was an engineer in Yarmouth when he enlisted in the 40th Battalion in April 1915. He served in the 60th Battalion, was wounded in early 1917, and spent nearly a year in hospitals in England before returning home. He was the lighthouse keeper at Cape Forchu from 1922 to 1952.

2 For thorough examinations of this sordid affair, see Joel Zemel, *Scapegoat: The Extraordinary Legal Proceedings following the 1917 Halifax Explosion* (Halifax: SVP Productions, 2012) and Janet Maybee, *Aftershock: The Halifax Explosion and the Persecution of Francis Mackey* (Halifax: Nimbus, 2015).

3 Born in 1864, Rogers was named after William Tecumseh Sherman, the American Civil War general. He was a prominent lawyer in Amherst before moving to Halifax and ran unsuccessfully as a Conservative candidate in the

1904 federal election. Wallace subsequently served the royal commission appointed in 1926 to investigate Maritime claims. Fowke was a prominent businessman in Oshawa and had served as mayor from 1898 to 1907. He was also a Liberal Member of Parliament from 1908 to 1911, but in 1917 he supported Union government. Ralph Pickard Bell was a prominent Halifax businessman who, among other things, founded the company that became National Sea Products. One almost gets the impression that Cutten was not anxious to return to Acadia. He left in 1922 to become president of Colgate University in Hamilton, New York.

4 Suzanne Morton, "The Halifax Relief Commission and Labour Relations during the Reconstruction of Halifax, 1917–1919," *Acadiensis* 18, no. 2 (Spring 1989): 73–92.

5 *Morning Chronicle*, August 14, 1918.

6 "Six Nurses Win Military Medal," *Toronto World*, September 25, 1918, published on The Great War Project website, accessed July 25, 2016, http://www.canadiangreatwarproject.com/transcripts/transcriptDisplay.asp?Type=N&Id=714. .

7 J. L. Granatstein, *Hell's Corner: An Illustrated History of Canada's Great War* (Vancouver: Douglas & McIntyre, 2004), 177. The Canadian Corps's success in the Hundred Days partly reflected the fact that Canadian divisions were significantly larger than British divisions, which had been reduced in size because of the shortage of men. Currie had refused to do this and instead the 5th Division was broken up to reinforce the four divisions in the field. Because the Canadian divisions operated at full strength with two battalions up and two in reserve, follow-up attacks had 50% more men than British divisions, as well as more artillery, machine guns and engineers. As Chris Sharpe has pointed out, this "contributed to the tremendous success enjoyed by the corps during The Hundred Days that ended the war." Sharpe, "Enlistment in the Canadian Expeditionary Force 1914–1918," 42.

8 Granatstein, *Hell's Corner*, 180.

9 Sharpe, "Enlistment in the Canadian Expeditionary Force 1914–1918," 47.

10 E. F. Miller, letter to unknown, August 13, 1918, published in *Morning Chronicle*, September 26, 1918.

11 L. R. Peebles, undated letter to the editor, published in *Morning Chronicle*, September 25, 1918.

12 John Ronald McLellan, letter to his cousin, undated [August 1918], published in *Catholics of the Diocese of Antigonish*, 231. McLellan died at Cambrai on September 29.

13 Miller, letter, August 13, 1918. Peebles said the same thing. See Peebles, letter, September 25, 1918.

14 Sergeant William Adams, letter to his mother, August 30, 1918, published in *Kentville Advertiser*, October 11, 1918.

15 Arthur Johns, undated letter to his wife Amy, published in *Kentville Advertiser*, September 24, 1918.

16 Ibid.

17 *The Times* (London), quoted in Hopkins, *Canada at War 1914–1918*, 170; Byng, quoted in Jonathan F. Vance, *Maple Leaf Empire: Canada, Britain, and Two World Wars* (Don Mills: Oxford University Press, 2012), 108; and Denis Winter, *Haig's Command: A Reassessment* (London: Penguin, 1991), 271.

18 Clements, *Merry Hell*, 213.

19 The Reverend A. J. MacDonald, letter to the editor, September 9, 1918, published in *Presbyterian Witness*, October 12, 1918. According to Lieutenant Reginald Herman, the men in the 25th respected MacDonald because "he went over the top with us and did wonderful work amongst the wounded." See Herman, letter to his mother, September 1, 1918, published in *Lunenburg Progress Enterprise*, October 2, 1918.

20 Quoted in Berton, *Marching as to War*, 209.

21 Granatstein, *Hell's Corner*, 169.

22 Ibid., 171.

23 Quoted on *The Fort Garry Horse* website, accessed August 18, 2016, http://fortgarryhorse.ca/wp/1914-1919.

24 He is referring to Dan Mooney, the director of the Stellarton Brass Band, which became the 78th regimental band, then became the 85th Battalion band. Charles Murray, letters to the editor, *Eastern Chronicle*, October 21 and 24, 1918; and *Eastern Chronicle*, November 12, 1918.

25 Jack McCorry, quoted in John Hawkins, *The Life and Times of Angus L.* (Windsor: Lancelot, 1969), 52. McCorry had enlisted in the 106th Battalion but was transferred into the 25th. Hawkins says he was from Queens County but he gave his address as Wolfville. Angus L. Macdonald was born in Dunvegan but grew up in Port Hood. He was attending St. Francis Xavier University when the war broke out. He joined the 185th Battalion in February 1916 with the rank of lieutenant and went to France in May 1918 with the 25th Battalion. He went on to serve as premier of Nova Scotia 1933-40, minister of national defence for naval services 1940-45, and premier again 1945-54. Cf Stephen Henderson, *Angus L. Macdonald: A Provincial Liberal* (Toronto: University of Toronto Press, 2007).

26 George Chapman, letter to Mary Chapman, November 9, 1918, quoted in Hebb, ed., *Letters Home*, 135.

27 Virtually all references to Price say he was a native of Canning, Nova Scotia. In fact, he was born at Falmouth but grew up in Church Street, a small community situated between Port Williams and Canning.

28 There is a tendency to focus on the "last" man or the last few men who died on the last day of the war because of the obvious poignancy and sense of tragedy. To put the deaths of these unfortunate men in context, however, about 10,900 soldiers, both Allied and enemy, were killed that day. David Laskin, *The Long*

Way Home: An American Journey from Ellis Island to the Great War (New York: HarperCollins, 2010), 311.

29 Some sources state that he was born in 1898 but the 1901 and 1911 Canadian census records give his birth date as 1894. Some sources give his birthplace as McLennan's Mountain but this is also incorrect.

30 George Chapman, letter to Mary Chapman, November 9, 1918, quoted in Hebb, ed., *Letters Home*, 135. He was actually referring to the false announcement of peace on the ninth.

31 Clements, *Merry Hell*, 221, 222.

32 Elva E. Jackson, *Windows on the Past: North Sydney, Nova Scotia* (Windsor: Lancelot, 1974), 133–34.

33 *Sydney Daily Post*, November 8, 1918.

34 *Truro Daily News*, November 5, 1918.

35 *Morning Chronicle*, November 12, 1918.

36 Ibid., 28 October 1918.

37 Ibid., November 12, 1918.

38 *Sydney Daily Post*, November 11 and 12, 1918.

39 Ibid., November 13, 1918.

40 Ibid., November 14, 1918.

41 Ibid., November 13, 1918.

42 Ibid., November 16, 1918.

43 Ibid., November 18, 1918.

44 Ibid., November 14, 1918.

45 Ibid.

46 In North Sydney, for example, there were "several clashes between returned soldiers and American sailors" on Commercial Street, apparently the only serious incidents of violence. "Several arrests were made of disturbers on both sides of the argument, and the climax was reached about eleven o'clock when some person set fire to a mattress in the jail, which necessitated the calling out of the firemen." *Sydney Daily Post*, November 14, 1918.

47 *Digby Courier*, undated [November 12, 1918?], quoted in Irma Walker with Gerald Handspiker, *A Culloden Chronicle: A West Nova Scotia Farming and Fishing Village 1783–2013* (Yarmouth: privately published, 2014), 102.

48 *Morning Chronicle*, November 12, 1918.

49 *Bridgewater Bulletin*, November 12, 1918.

50 *Casket*, November 14, 1918.

51 *Truro Daily News*, November 11, 1918.

52 Ibid, November 12 and 15, 1918.

53 Clements, *Merry Hell*, 222.

54 The most thorough account of this episode is Julian Putskowski, "The Kinmel Park Camp Riots, 1919," *Flintshire Historical Society Journal* 32 (1989): 55–107, http://welshjournals.llgc.org.uk/browse/viewobject/llgc-id:1219213/article/000069512.

55 Debbie Marshall, "The Death of a Nurse amidst the Tumult at the End of the War," *Finding the Forty-Seven: Canadian Nurses of the First World War* blog, June 5, 2012, accessed July 19, 2016, http://rememberingfirstworldwarnurses.blogspot.ca/2012/06/death-of-nurse-amidst-tumult-at-end-of.html.

56 Johnson, *"The Right Spirit,"* 247.

57 Gillan's family was never given an explanation for his death. See Roberta Avery, "The Calamity of Death at War's End," *Toronto Star*, November 11, 2007.

58 The body of John Hickman of Dorchester, New Brunswick, was brought home.

59 On the origins of the epidemic in Canada, see Mark Osborne Humphries, "The Horror at Home: The Canadian Military and the 'Great' Influenza Pandemic of 1918," *Journal of the Canadian Historical Association* 16, no. 1 (2005): 235–60.

60 *Sydney Daily Post*, October 4, 1918. Tefft spoke "in the highest terms" of the treatment that the American men received at Sydney, adding he thought it "a big thing that we should have allowed these sick men to land in Sydney and be cared for in the hospitals at much inconvenience and some danger to the people." Asked if the men had any complaints about their treatment, Tefft said they did not but admitted that they didn't really appreciate the frequent cups of tea offered to them!

61 Beanlands, *Formation of the Jewish Legion*, 19.

62 *Truro Daily News*, November 12, 1918.

63 Robert Hirtle, "Life, Death and the Ironies of War," *Lunenburg County Progress Bulletin*, February 26, 2014.

64 *Morning Chronicle*, October 14, 1918.

65 Ibid., October 28, 1918.

66 Ibid., October 29, 1918 and November 2, 1918.

67 Ibid., October 16, 1918.

68 Mackinnon, *Reminiscences*, 217.

69 Will R. Bird, *Ghosts Have Warm Hands* (Toronto: Clarke Irwin, 1968), 171.

70 Bertram Hayes, *Hull Down: Reminiscences of Wind-jammers, Troops and Travellers* (New York: Macmillan, 1925), 241.

71 Innes McCartney, *Lost Patrols: Submarine Wrecks of the English Channel* (Penzance: Periscope Publishing, 2003), 36. Hayes's recollection of the event, which took place on May 12, 1918, was rather hazy. He thought the *Olympic* was en route from Southampton to New York, and picked up seventeen survivors.

72 James Johnson was frankly astonished that "inside of an hour I had my money and my discharge." Quoted in Reid, *Poor Bloody Murder*, 249.

73 Hunt, *Nova Scotia's Part in the Great War*, 172.

74 Fetherstonhaugh, *The Royal Canadian Regiment*, 382.

75 *Morning Chronicle*, April 7, 1919.

76 Mullins, *Some Liverpool Chronicles*, 129.

77 Ibid.

78 See "The Race Riots of 1919: The Lives of the Old North End," *The Old North End* blog, accessed August 26, 2016, https://oldnorthend.wordpress.com/2014/03/11/the-race-riots-of-1919; and Constance Barkhouse, "'I Was Unable to Identify with Topsy:' Carrie M. Best's Struggle Against Racial Segregation in Nova Scotia, 1942," *Atlantis* 22, no. 2 (1998): 17.

79 *Morning Chronicle*, April 22, 1919.

80 Ibid., April 24, 1919.

81 Lynn Moar, "Comrades in Arms," *Valley Harvester*, November 5, 2015.

82 *Morning Chronicle*, May 17, 1919.

83 Ibid., May 17, 1919. Matheson enlisted in November 1914 and rose to the rank of major and second-in-command of the battalion. He was awarded the Military Medal, the Military Cross, and the Distinguished Service Order. He returned to his farm at Baddeck with Robert the Bruce.

84 *Morning Chronicle*, May 17, 1919.

85 Hayes, *The Eighty-Fifth*, 242.

86 *Yarmouth Herald*, 10 June 1919.

87 Hayes, *The Eighty-Fifth*, 242.

88 Ibid.

89 *Yarmouth Herald*, May 20, 1919.

90 *Morning Chronicle*, April 12, 1919.

91 Ibid., April 21, 1919.

92 *Yarmouth Times*, May 30, 1919. Sara Corning was a remarkable Nova Scotian, although largely unknown in her own province. Born in Chegoggin, Yarmouth County, she trained as a nurse and joined the US Red Cross when the United States entered the war. She then joined Near East Relief, a charitable organization established to assist the displaced populations of the Balkans and the Middle East. She worked for years with the Armenians, who were being persecuted by the Ottoman government, and helped to rescue 5,000 Greek children from Smyrna. Indeed, she spent most of her life in Turkey, working in an orphanage and residential training school, returning to Chegoggin in her retirement. In 2012 the Sara Corning Centre for Genocide Education was established in Toronto to carry out research and education in the fields of human rights and genocide.

93 *Yarmouth Herald*, June 17, 1919.

Afterword

1 Robert Borden, *The War and the Future* (London: Hodder and Stoughton, 1917), 47.

2 Newfoundland was similarly affected, of course, but it was not then part of Canada.

3 Stuart Hunt claims that the Militia Department thought the province could contribute 53,500 men but this is not correct. Hunt, *Nova Scotia's Part in the Great War*, 300.

4 Sharpe, "Enlistment in the Canadian Expeditionary Force 1914–1918," 39. Officially, the army only accepted British citizens between the ages of eighteen and forty-five. It was calculated that about 20% of such men were medically unfit and another 15% were fit enough to serve but unfit for combat. See J. L. Granatstein, "To Win at Any Cost: Politics and Manpower," in *Capturing Hill 70: Canada's Forgotten Battle of the First World War*, ed. Douglas E. Delaney and Serge Marc Durflinger (Vancouver: UBC Press, 2016), 207.

5 Halifax's Book of Remembrance lists 1,360 men who it claims were from Halifax County but it is very inaccurate because it includes men and women who attested there but came from other parts of the province. To cite just three examples, Steven Bird, brother of Will Bird, is included even though he was from Amherst, Gabriel Bishara was from Yarmouth, and Nursing Sister Minnie Follette was from Port Greville. Similarly, monuments in the larger towns can be misleading because they often list men and women who actually came from surrounding communities. We do have figures for some counties. Pictou County lost 406 men, Cumberland 336, Colchester 176, Yarmouth 173, Guysborough at least 136, and Shelburne 93. For more data, see the *"We Will Remember" War Monuments in Canada* website, accessed on August 15, 2016, https://www.cdli.ca/monuments/ns.htm; and *Nova Scotia Monuments: War Memorials, Historic Monuments and Plaques —Nova Scotia's Electric Scrapbook*, accessed on August 15, 2016, http://ns1763.ca/remem/plaques.html.

6 *Lunenburg Progress Enterprise*, November 6, 1918.

7 Angus, "Living in the 'World of the Tiger,'" 2.

8 Ibid., 2–3.

9 Ibid., 109.

10 *Yarmouth Herald*, April 1, 1919.

11 *Morning Chronicle*, April 22, 1919. On the experience of veterans after the war, see Desmond Morton and Glenn Wright, *Winning the Second Battle: Canadian Veterans and the Return to Civilian Life 1915–1930* (Toronto: University of Toronto Press, 1987).

12 For more on this, see T. W. Acheson, "The National Policy and the Industrialization of the Maritimes, 1880–1910," *Acadiensis* 1, no.2 (Spring 1972): 3–28; and E. R. Forbes, "Misguided Symmetry: The Destruction of Regional Transportation Policy for the Maritimes," in Ernest R. Forbes, *Challenging the Regional Stereotype: Essays on the 20th Century Maritimes* (Fredericton: Acadiensis Press, 1989), 114–35.

13 *Truro Daily News*, November 7, 1918; and *New York Times*, January 28, 1919.

14 David Frank, "The 1920s: Class and Region, Resistance and Accommodation," in *The Atlantic Provinces in Confederation*, ed. E. R. Forbes

and D. A. Muise (Toronto/Fredericton: University of Toronto Press/ Acadiensis Press, 1993), 254.

15 Stephen Leacock, *The Unsolved Riddle of Social Justice* (New York: John Lane, 1920), 127–28.

16 Frank, "The 1920s," 245.

17 The reference here is to the song "Rise Again," written by Leon Dubinsky in 1984 for the stage musical *The Rise and Follies of Cape Breton.* Dubinsky has explained that the song is about "the cycles of immigration, the economic insecurity of living in Cape Breton, the power of the ocean, the meaning of children, and the strength of home given to us by our families, our friends and our music." It seems applicable to the economic and social crisis endured by Nova Scotia generally, at least until the 1960s. "Rise Again: (The Rankin Family Song)," *Wikipedia*, accessed on May 14, 2017, https://en.wikipedia.org/wiki/Rise_Again_(The_Rankin_Family_song)#cite_ref-2.

BIBLIOGRAPHY

Newspapers

Amherst Daily News, 1914–18
Antigonish Casket, 1914–18
Arichat Richmond Recorder, 1914–18
Atlantic Advocate (Halifax), 1915–17
Baddeck Victoria News 1914–18
Bridgewater Bulletin 1914–19
Digby Weekly Courier 1914–19
Halifax Morning Chronicle, 1914–19
Kentville Advertiser, 1916–19
Liverpool Advance, 1914–18
Lunenburg Progress Bulletin, 1914–19
New Glasgow Eastern Chronicle, 1914–18
New York Times, 1914–19
Sydney Daily Post, 1914–19
Truro Daily News, 1914–18
Wolfville Acadian, 1914
Yarmouth Herald, 1914–18

Publications and Theses

Allen, Ralph. *Ordeal by Fire: Canada 1910–1945.* Toronto: Doubleday, 1961.

Anderson, Eleanor L. *Broughton: Cape Breton's Ghost Town.* [Sydney]: privately published, n.d., [2004].

Angus, Murray E. "Living in the 'World of the Tiger': The Methodist and Presbyterian Churches in Nova Scotia and the Great War, 1914–1918." MA thesis, Dalhousie University, 1993.

Anonymous. *A History of Beaver Brook, 1760 to 1959.* Beaver Brook Branch of the Women's Institutes of Nova Scotia, 1959. Accessed April 9, 2016. http://www.canadagenweb.org/archives/ns/bbrook.txt.

———. *Catholics of the Diocese of Antigonish, Nova Scotia, and the War 1914–1919, with Nominal Enlistment Rolls by Parishes.* Antigonish: St. Francis University Press, n.d.

———."The Clayton Convalescent Home." *CMA* [Canadian Medical Association] *Journal* 6, no. 10 (October 1916): 925.

———. "With the Colored Soldiers." *Atlantic Advocate* 1, no. 7 (January 1917): 12, 16.

Armstrong, John Griffith. *The Halifax Explosion and the Royal Canadian Navy: Inquiry and Intrigue.* Vancouver: UBC Press, 2002.

Ashton, John. "Pictou County 'Aces' of First World War." *New Glasgow News.* September 7, 2014. Accessed April 16, 2016. http://www.ngnews.ca/Community/2014-09-07/article-3861145/Pictou-County-%26lsquo%3Baces%26rsquo%3B-of-First-World-War/1.

Avery, Roberta. "The Calamity of Death at War's End." *Toronto Daily Star,* November 11, 2007.

Barkhouse, Constance. "'I Was Unable to Identify with Topsy': Carrie M. Best's Struggle against Racial Segregation in Nova Scotia, 1942." *Atlantis* 22, no. 2 (Spring 1998): 16–26.

Beanlands, Sarah. *Formation of the Jewish Legion at Ford Edward.* Halifax: Boreas Heritage Consulting, 2014.

Berton, Pierre. *Marching as to War: Canada's Turbulent Years 1899–1953.* Toronto: Anchor Canada, 2002.

Beswick, Aaron. "Leon Trotsky Forged Notable Month at Amherst Foundry Turned Internment Camp." *Halifax Chronicle-Herald,* January 2, 2015.

Bird, Will R. *And We Go On: A Memoir of the Great War.* Toronto: Hunter-Rose, 1930.

———. *Ghosts Have Warm Hands.* Toronto: Clarke Irwin, 1968.

Bliss, Michael. *A Canadian Millionaire: The Life and Business Times of Sir Joseph Flavelle, Bart.* Toronto: Macmillan, 1978.

Boileau, John. *Halifax and the Royal Canadian Navy.* Halifax: Nimbus, 2010.

Borden, Robert Laird. *Robert Laird Borden: His Memoirs.* Vol. 2, edited by Henry Borden. Toronto: Macmillan, 1938.

Brinnin, John Malcolm. *The Sway of the Grand Saloon: A Social History of the North Atlantic.* New York: Delacorte Press, 1971.

Brown, Robert Craig and Donald Loveridge. "Unrequited Faith: Recruiting the CEF 1914-1918." *Canadian Military History* 24, no. 1 (Spring 2015): 61–88.

Byers, Daniel. "J. L. Ralston and the First World War: The Origins of a Life of Service." *Canadian Military History* 22, no. 1 (Winter 2013): 3–16.

Cameron, James D. *For the People: A History of St. Francis Xavier University.* Montreal/Kingston: McGill-Queen's University Press, 1996.

Cameron, James M. *Industrial History of the New Glasgow District.* New Glasgow: Hector Publishing Co., 1960.

———. *Pictonians in Arms: A Military History of Pictou County, Nova Scotia.* New Glasgow: privately published, 1969.

Cameron, Silver Donald. "Trotsky in Amherst." *Canadian Geographic* (1988). Accessed July 5, 2016. http://www.silverdonaldcameron.ca/trotsky-amherst.

Caplan, Ronald, ed. *Cape Bretoners in the First World War in Their Own Words.* [Sydney]: Breton Books, 2014.

Carnegie, David. *The History of Munitions Supply in Canada 1914–1918.* London: Longmans, Green and Co., 1925.

Chambers, Sheila, Joan Dawson, and Edith Wolter. *Historic LaHave River Valley.* Halifax: Nimbus, 2004.

Chapman, Harry. *In the Wake of the* Alderney*: Dartmouth, Nova Scotia, 1750–2000.* Halifax: Nimbus, 2001.

Christie, Michael. *The Barrington Passage Wireless Station.* Yarmouth: privately published, 2002.

Chute, Arthur Hunt. *The Real Front.* New York: Harper & Brothers, 1918.

Clark, William Bell. *When the U-Boats Came to America.* Boston: Little, Brown, 1929.

Clements, Robert N. *Merry Hell: The Story of the 25th Battalion (Nova Scotia Regiment).* Edited by Brian Douglas Tennyson. Toronto: University of Toronto Press, 2013.

Comeau, Louis V. *Historic Kentville.* Halifax: Nimbus, 2003.

Cook, Tim. *At the Sharp End: Canadians Fighting the Great War, 1914–1916.* Toronto: Viking, 2007.

———. *Shock Troops: Canadians Fighting the Great War, 1917–1918.* Toronto: Viking, 2008.

———. "'The Blind Leading the Blind: The Battle of the St. Eloi Craters." *Canadian Military History* 5, no. 2 (1996): 24–36.

Cowley, Deborah, ed. *Georges Vanier: Soldier: The Wartime Letters and Diaries, 1915–1919.* Toronto: Dundurn, 2000.

Crerar, Duff W. "Bellicose Priests: The Wars of the Canadian Catholic Chaplains 1914–1919." *Canadian Catholic Historical Association Historical Studies* 58 (1991): 21–39.

———. "In the Day of Battle: Canadian Catholic Chaplains in the Field, 1885–1945." *Canadian Catholic Historical Association Historical Studies* 61 (1995): 53–77.

Davison, James Doyle. *Mud Creek: The Story of the Town of Wolfville, Nova Scotia.* Wolfville: Wolfville Historical Society, 1985.

Donovan, Ken, ed. *Cape Breton at 200: Historical Essays in Honour of the Island's Bicentennial, 1785–1985.* Sydney: UCCB Press, 1985.

———. *The Island: New Perspectives on Cape Breton History, 1713–1990.* Fredericton/Sydney: Acadiensis Press/UCCB Press, 1990.

Doucette, Keith. "First World War Touched Everyday Lives in Halifax, Atlantic Canada." CBC News Nova Scotia, August 2, 2015. Accessed October 25, 2016. http://www.cbc.ca/news/canada/nova-scotia/first-world-war-touched-everyday-lives-in-halifax-atlantic-canada-1.3177160.

Edwards, Reverend William X. "The MacPherson-Tompkins Era of St. Francis Xavier University." *Canadian Catholic Historical Association Report* 20 (1953): 49–65.

Elson, Bryan. *Canada's Bastions of Empire: Halifax, Victoria and the Royal Navy 1749–1918.* Halifax: Formac, 2014.

———. *First to Die: The First Canadian Naval Casualties in the First World War.* Halifax: Formac, 2011.

Erickson, Paul A. *Historic North End Halifax.* Halifax: Nimbus, 2004.

Everett, Frances D. "Barrington Passage Wireless Station." *The Canadian Amateur* (1987). Accessed 12 February 2016. http://radioalumni.ca/z_1987_barrington_passage_wireless_stat.htm.

Ferguson, Frank Byron. *Gunner Ferguson's Diary: The Diary of Gunner Frank Byron Ferguson 1st Canadian Siege Battery Canadian Expeditionary Force 1915–1918.* Edited by Peter G. Rogers. Hantsport: Lancelot Press, 1985.

Fetherstonhaugh, R. C. *The Royal Canadian Regiment 1883–1933.* Ottawa: Department of National Defence, 1936.

Fitch, Benjamin T. E. "Doing Their Duty: Politics and Recruitment in the Maritimes during World War 1." MA thesis, University of Calgary, 2003.

Forbes, E. R. "Prohibition and the Social Gospel in Nova Scotia." *Acadiensis* 1, no. 1 (Autumn 1971): 11–36.

———. *The Maritime Rights Movement, 1919–1927: A Study in Canadian Regionalism.* Montreal: McGill-Queen's University Press, 1979.

Ford, Nancy Gentile. *Americans All! Foreign-born Soldiers in World War 1.* College Station, TX: Texas A&M Press, 2001.

Fox, Brent. *Camp Aldershot: Serving Since 1904.* Kentville: Kings Historical Society, 1983.

Foyn, Sean Flynn. "The Underside of Glory: Africanadian Enlistment in the Canadian Expeditionary Force, 1914–1917." MA thesis, University of Ottawa, 1999.

Frank, David. *J.B. McLachlan: A Biography.* Toronto: James Lorimer, 1999.

———."The Cape Breton Coal Industry and the Rise and Fall of the British Empire Steel Corporation." *Acadiensis* 7, no. 1 (Autumn 1977): 3–34.

———. "The 1920s: Class and Region, Resistance and Accommodation." In *The Atlantic Provinces in Confederation,* edited by E. R. Forbes and D. A. Muise,

233–71. Toronto/Fredericton: University of Toronto Press/Acadiensis Press, 1993.

Frost, James D. *Canada's Atlantic Gateway: An Illustrated History of the Port of Halifax*. Halifax: Nimbus, 2008.

———. *Merchant Princes: Halifax's First Family of Finance, Ships and Steel*. Toronto: James Lorimer, 2003.

Gagnon, Jean-Pierre. "Canadian Soldiers in Bermuda during World War One." *Histoire sociale/Social History* 23, no. 5 (May 1990): 9–36.

Gass, Clare. *The War Diary of Clare Gass, 1915–1918*. Edited by Susan Mann. Montreal/Kingston: McGill-Queen's University Press, 2000.

Gibson, Charles Dana. "Victim or Participant? Allied Fishing Fleets and U-Boat Attacks in World Wars I and II." *The Northern Mariner* 1, no. 4 (October 1991): 1–18.

Gillis, Rannie. *Historic Sydney*. Halifax: Nimbus, 2003.

———. "North Sydney Cable Office Busy Place in 1910," *Cape Breton Post*, 6 April 2014.

Graham, Roger. *Arthur Meighen: And Fortune Fled*. Toronto: Clarke Irwin, 1963.

Granatstein, J. L. "Conscription in the Great War." In *Canada and the First World War: Essays in Honour of Robert Craig Brown*, edited by David MacKenzie, 62–75. Toronto: University of Toronto Press, 2005.

———. *Hell's Corner: An Illustrated History of Canada's Great War*. Vancouver: Douglas & McIntyre, 2004.

———. "To Win at Any Cost: Politics and Manpower." In *Capturing Hill 70: Canada's Forgotten Battle of the First World War*, edited by Douglas E. Delaney and Serge Marc Durflinger, 205–25. Vancouver: UBC Press, 2016.

Grescoe, Audrey and Paul Grescoe, eds. *The Book of War Letters: 100 Years of Private Canadian Correspondence*. Toronto: McClelland & Stewart, 2003.

Groom, Winston. *A Storm in Flanders: The Ypres Salient, 1914–1919*. New York: Atlantic Monthly Press, 2002.

Gwyn, Sandra. *Tapestry of War: A Private View of Canadians in the Great War*. Toronto: HarperCollins, 1992.

Hadley, Michael L., Rob Huebert, and Fred W. Crickard. *A Nation's Navy: In Quest of Canadian Naval Identity*. Montreal/Kingston: McGill-Queen's University Press, 1996.

Hadley, Michael L. and Roger Sarty, *Tin-Pots and Pirate Ships: Canadian Naval Forces and German Sea Raiders 1880–1918*. Montreal/Kingston: McGill-Queen's University Press, 1991.

Haliburton, Gordon M. *Horton Point: A History of Avonport*. Wolfville: Gaspereau Press, 1998.

Hayes, Bertram. *Hull Down: Reminiscences of Wind-jammers, Troops and Travellers*. New York: Macmillan, 1925.

Hawkins, John. *The Life and Times of Angus L*. Windsor: Lancelot, 1969.

Hayes, Joseph. "Nova Scotia Medical Services in the Great War." In M. Stuart Hunt, *Nova Scotia's Part in the Great War*, 177–225. Halifax: Nova Scotia Veterans Publishing, 1920.

———. *The Eighty-Fifth in France and Flanders.* Halifax: Royal Print & Litho, 1920.

Hayes, W. H. "On to Bermuda." Accessed July 8, 2015. *The Regimental Rogue*, www.regimentalrogue.com.

Hearn, Wilfred. "17th Battery (6th Battery, CFA)." In M. Stuart Hunt, *Nova Scotia's Part in the Great War*, 31–40. Halifax: Nova Scotia Veteran Publishing, 1920.

Hebb, Ross, ed. *Letters Home: Maritimers and the Great War, 1914–1918.* Halifax: Nimbus, 2014.

Hirtle, Robert. "'Dear Jo': Wartime Letters Home Uncovered in Attic." *Lunenburg County Progress Bulletin*, November 6, 2013.

———. "Life, Death, and the Ironies of War." *Lunenburg County Progress Bulletin*, February 26, 2014.

Hogan, David. "History of the No. 9 Stationary Hospital (St. Francis Xavier University), 1916–1919." Antigonish: St. Francis Xavier University, unpublished paper, n.d.

Hopkins, J. Castell. *Canada at War 1914–1918: A Record of Heroism and Achievement.* New York: George H. Doran, 1919.

Howe, Glenford D. "A White Man's War? World War One and the West Indies." *BBC History.* Accessed April 25, 2015. http://www.bbc.co.uk/history/worldwars/wwone/west_indies_01.shtml.

Howell, Colin. "The 1900s: Industry, Urbanization, and Reform." In *The Atlantic Provinces in Confederation*, edited by E. R. Forbes and D. A. Muise, 155–91. Toronto/Fredericton: University of Toronto Press/Acadiensis Press, 1993.

Humphries, Mark Osborne. "The Horror at Home: The Canadian Military and the 'Great' Influenza Pandemic of 1918." *Canadian Historical Association Journal* 16, no. 1 (2005): 235–60.

Hunt, M. Stuart. *Nova Scotia's Part in the Great War.* Halifax: The Nova Scotia Veteran Publishing, 1920.

Jackson, Elva E. *Windows on the Past: North Sydney, Nova Scotia.* Windsor: Lancelot, 1974.

Johnson, John J. *"The Right Spirit": A History of Birch Grove and its People 1840–1940.* North Sydney: privately published, 2009.

Johnston, A. J. B. "Into the Great War: Katharine McLennan Goes Overseas, 1915–1919." In *The Island: New Perspectives on Cape Breton History, 1713–1990*, edited by Kenneth B. Donovan, 129–44. Fredericton/Sydney: Acadiensis Press/UCCB Press, 1990.

Johnston, William. "The Royal Canadian Navy and the First World War." In *The Naval Service of Canada 1910–2010: The Centennial Story*, edited by Richard H. Gimblett, 23–40. Toronto: Dundurn, 2009.

———, G. P. Rawling, Richard H. Gimblett, and John MacFarlane. *The Seabound Coast: The Official History of the Royal Canadian Navy, 1867–1939.* Vol 1. Ottawa: Department of National Defence, 2010.

Julien, Don. "The Mi'kmaq and the First World War." Unpublished paper presented at the *Nova Scotia's Part in the Great War Revisited* Symposium, Windsor, Nova Scotia, June 11, 2016.

Kealy, J. D. F. and E. C. Russell. *A History of Canadian Naval Aviation 1918—1962.* Ottawa: Naval Historical Section, Canadian Forces Headquarters, Department of National Defence, 1965.

Kennedy, Greg. "Answering the Call to Serve: The Acadian Soldiers of the 165th Battalion of the Canadian Expeditionary Force and their Post-War Transition, 1911–1921." Unpublished paper presented at the *Nova Scotia's Part in the Great War Revisited* Symposium Windsor, Nova Scotia, June 11, 2016.

Lackenbauer, P. Whitney. *A Commemorative History of Aboriginal People in the Canadian Military.* Ottawa: Department of National Defence, 2010. Accessed November 15, 2015. http://publications.gc.ca/collections/collection_2010/forces/D2-250-2-2009-eng.pdf.

———. "Soldiers Behaving Badly: CEF Soldier 'Rioting' in Canada during the First World War." In *The Apathetic and the Defiant: Case Studies of Canadian Mutiny and Disobedience, 1812 to 1919,* edited by Craig Leslie Mantle, 195–260. Toronto: Dundurn, 2007.

Leddin, Des. *The Headmaster's War: George Sylvester and the Great War for Civilization.* Halifax, 2009.

———. *The No. 7 Stationary Hospital (Dalhousie University) in World War One.* Skibbereen: Redbarn, 2015.

Lester, Nancy Joan Mason. "Nova Scotian Attitudes toward the Conscription Crisis of 1917." BA Honours thesis, Acadia University, 1976.

Lew, Byron and Marvin McInnis. "Guns and Butter: World War 1 and the Canadian Economy." Trent University Department of Economics Working Paper, 2007. Accessed October 28, 2015. https://www.trentu.ca/economics/WorkingPapers/LewMcInnis_Toronto_05.pdf.

Lewis, Ralph. *Over the Top with the 25th Battalion: Chronicle of Events at Vimy Ridge and Courcellette* [sic]. Halifax: Marshall, 1918.

Livingstone, H. L., Howard Reid, Dan E. MacQuarrie, John Angus MacNeil, Ken MacLeod, Bill Daye, Leo Sears, Thomas Gillard, Thomas R. Langley and Kristopher Mayich "Cape Bretoners in World War One." *Cape Breton's Magazine* 33 (June 1983): 1–9, 11–15, 17–27.

Longley, Ronald Stewart. *Acadia University, 1838–1938.* Wolfville: Kentville Publishing Company, 1939.

Macdonald, Bruce. "First World War Veterans of Guysborough County," accessed May 6, 2017; http://guysboroughgreatwarveterans.blogspot.ca/2014/01.

———. "Jack Tate: First Nova Scotia Soldier Killed on the Western Front." *Chronicle Herald*. Accessed October 15, 2016. http://thechronicleherald.ca/thegreatwar/1271932-jack-tate-first-nova-scotia-soldier-killed-on-the-western-front#.WER3GuErJ0s.

Macdonald, E. M. *Recollections Political and Personal.* Toronto: Ryerson, 1938.

MacDonald, F. B. and John J. Gardiner, *The Twenty-Fifth Battalion Canadian Expeditionary Force: Nova Scotia's Famous Regiment in World War One.* Sydney: J.A. Chadwick, 1983.

MacDonald, Hilda and Helen Kendall. "World War One Continues: Nursing Sisters in England and France." *Cape Breton's Magazine* 34 (August 1983): 1–7.

MacDonald, Laura M. *Curse of the Narrows.* New York: Walker & Company, 2005.

Macdonald, Oswin. "St. Francis Xavier Hospital Unit." In *Catholics of the Diocese of Antigonish, Nova Scotia, and the War 1914–1919, with Nominal Enlistment Rolls by Parishes* (Antigonish: St. Francis University Press, n.d.).

Macdonald, Stuart. "Myth Meets Reality: Canadian Presbyterians and the Great War," *Canadian Society of Church History Historical Papers* (2012): 103–120.

MacDonald, W. James. *Honour Roll of the Nova Scotia Overseas Highland Brigade.* Sydney: Cape Breton University Press, 2007.

———. *Nova Scotia's [sic] Born Casualties of World War One (1914–1918) Canadian Overseas Expeditionary Force.* Baddeck: Elder Brook Books, 2014.

MacDonnell, Angus J. "Angus J. MacDonnell's War Memories." *Inverness Oran*, November 6, 1996. Accessed April 7, 2016. http://archiver.rootsweb.ancestry.com/th/read/NS-CAPE-BRETON/2002-11/1037046637.

MacGregor, Francis. *Days That I Remember.* Windsor: Lancelot Press, 1976.

Machum, George. *The Story of the 64th Battalion, CEF 1915–1916.* Montreal: privately published, 1956.

MacKenzie, David. "Eastern Approaches: Maritime Canada and Newfoundland." In *Canada and the First World War: Essays in Honour of Robert Craig Brown*, edited by David MacKenzie, 350–76. Toronto: University of Toronto Press, 2005.

Mackinnon, Clarence. *Reminiscences.* Toronto: Ryerson, 1938.

MacKinnon, D. A. "The 36th Battery, CFA." In M. Stuart Hunt, *Nova Scotia's Part in the Great War*, 43–55. Halifax: Nova Scotia Veteran Publishing, 1920.

MacKinnon, Robert. "The Historical Geography of Agriculture in Nova Scotia, 1851–1951." PhD thesis, University of British Columbia, 1991. Accessed July 15, 2016. https://open.library.ubc.ca/cIRcle/collections/ubctheses/831/items/1.0100608.

MacLennan, Hugh. *Barometer Rising.* Toronto: McClelland & Stewart, 2007.

MacLeod, Alistair. "Afterword." In Hugh MacLennan, *Barometer Rising*, 305-21. Toronto: McClelland & Stewart, 2007.

MacLeod, Ken and Leslie Reid. "World War 1 Continues: The Halifax Explosion and Going to Siberia." *Cape Breton's Magazine* 34 (August 1983): 7–12.

MacPhail, Andrew. *Official History of the Canadian Forces during the Great War 1914–19: The Medical Services.* Ottawa: Department of National Defence, 1925.

Mann, Susan. *Margaret Macdonald: Imperial Daughter.* Montreal/Kingston: McGill-Queen's University Press, 2005.

March, William. *Red Line: The Chronicle-Herald and The Mail-Star 1875–1954.* Halifax: Chebucto Agencies, 1986.

Marshall, David B. "Methodism Embattled: A Reconsideration of the Methodist Church and World War 1." *Canadian Historical Review* 66, no. 1 (March 1985): 48–64.

Marshall, Dianne. *Georges Island: The Keep of Halifax Harbour.* Halifax: Nimbus, 2014.

Matheson, Scott. "In the Dust You Will Prevail: The Mobilization of Acadia, Dalhousie, Mount Allison, and St Francis Xavier Universities, 1914–1918." MA thesis, St. Mary's University, 2010.

Maybee, Janet, *Aftershock: The Halifax Explosion and the Persecution of Pilot Francis Mackey.* Halifax: Nimbus, 2015.

———. "The Persecution of Pilot Mackey." *The Northern Mariner* 20, no. 2 (April 2010): 149–73.

McCann, Larry. "The 1890s: Fragmentation and the New Social Order." In *The Atlantic Provinces in Confederation*, edited by E. R. Forbes and D. A. Muise, 119–54. Toronto/Fredericton: University of Toronto Press/Acadiensis Press, 1993.

McCarthy, John. *The Story of the Establishment and Development of the Catholic Church in Amherst Nova Scotia.* Amherst: St. Charles Parish, 1962. Accessed January 22, 2015. http://www.lchr.org/a/33/27/history.html.

McCartney, Innes. *Lost Patrols: Submarine Wrecks of the English Channel.* Penzance: Periscope Publishing, 2003.

McClare, P. Winthrop. *The Letters of a Young Canadian Soldier during World War 1.* Edited by Dale McClare. Kentville: Brook House Press, 2000.

McElhenny, G. C. "The 25th Battation." In M. Stuart Hunt, *Nova Scotia's Part in the Great War*, 70–91. Halifax: Nova Scotia Veteran Publishing, 1920.

McGowan, Mark G. "Harvesting the 'Red Vineyard': Catholic Religious Culture in the Canadian Expeditionary Force, 1914–1919." *Canadian Catholic Historical Association Historical Studies* 64 (1998): 47–70.

McKay, Ian, "Drummond, Robert," *Dictionary of Canadian Biography.* Vol. 15, Toronto/Quebec: University of Toronto/Université Laval, 2005. Accessed August 20, 2016. http://www.biographi.ca/en/bio/drummond_robert_1840_1925_15E.html.

———. "The 1910s: The Stillborn Triumph of Progressive Reform." In *The Atlantic Provinces in Confederation*, edited by E. R. Forbes and D. A. Muise, 192–229. Toronto/Fredericton: University of Toronto Press/Acadiensis Press, 1993.

McLeod, Paul. "Loose Security at Sydney Cable Station Outraged Censor," *Halifax Chronicle-Herald*, undated [2016]. Accessed September 15, 2016. https://thechronicleherald.ca/thegreatwar/1249597-loose-security-at-sydney-cable-station-outraged-censor#.WJjFZLYrJ0t.

Miller, Carman. *A Knight in Politics: A Biography of Sir Frederick Borden.* Montreal/Kingston: McGill-Queens University Press, 2010.

Milner, Marc. *Canada's Navy: The First Century.* Toronto: University of Toronto Press, 1999.

———. "*Niobe*'s Brief Operational Career, Part 5." *Legion Magazine* (September 1, 2004). Accessed April 22, 2016. https://legionmagazine.com/en/2004/09/niobes-brief-operational-career/.

Moar, Lynn. "Comrades in Arms." *Valley Harvester.* November 5, 2015.

Moody, Barry. "Acadia and the Great War." In *Youth, University and Canadian Society,* edited by Paul Axelrod and John G. Reid, 143–60. Montreal/Kingston: McGill-Queen's University Press, 1989.

Moogk, Peter. "From Fortress Louisbourg to Fortress Sydney: Artillery and Gunners on Cape Breton, 1743–1980." In *Cape Breton at 200: Historical Essays in Honour of the Island's Bicentennial 1785–1985,* edited by Kenneth Donovan, 127–82. Sydney: UCCB Press, 1985.

Morgan, Robert J. *Rise Again: The Story of Cape Breton Island: From 1900 to Today.* Sydney: Breton Books, 2009.

Morton, Desmond. *A Peculiar Kind of Politics: Canada's Overseas Ministry in the First World War.* Toronto: University of Toronto Press, 1982.

——— and J. L. Granatstein. *Marching to Armageddon.* Toronto: Lester & Orpen Dennys, 1989.

Morton, Suzanne. "The Halifax Relief Commission and Labour Relations during the Reconstruction of Halifax, 1917–1919." *Acadiensis* 18, no. 2 (Spring 1989): 73–93.

Mossman, David. *Going Over: A Nova Scotian Soldier in World War I.* Lawrencetown Beach: Pottersfield Press, 2014.

Muirhead, W. H. *A Short History & Photographic Record of the 219th Overseas Highland Battalion, C.E.F., Lt. Col. W. H. Muirhead, Commanding Officer.* Ottawa: privately published, n.d. [1916].

Mullins, Janet E. *Some Liverpool Chronicles.* Liverpool: Liverpool Advance 1941.

Murray, David. "Garrisoning the Caribbean: A Chapter in Canadian Military History." *Revista/Review Interamericana* 7, no. 1 (Spring 1977): 73–86.

Myers, Lawrna. *Project 107 Report.* Vernon, BC, June 22, 2016. Accessed July 10, 2016. http://www.internmentcanada.ca/PDF/CFWWIRF%20Project%20107%20Burial%20Report%20June%2022%202016%20Myers.pdf.

Nelson, Gary. "Remembering a Hero: Ernest John Brooks." *Canadian Association for Baptist Freedoms Bulletin* (Spring 2015): 10–13.

Nichols, Mabel G. *The Devil's Half Acre.* Kentville: Kentville Centennial Committee, 1986.

Oland, Patrick. "A Tale of Three Brothers." *Moosehead Beer Academy,* November 28, 2014. Accessed August 23, 2016. http://www.mooseheadbeeracademy.com/tale-three-brothers/.

O'Reilly, George. "Londonderry: Nova Scotia's Giant from the Past May Still Have a Future." *Nova Scotia Minerals Update Newsletter* 7, no. 3 (Winter 1996): 3. Accessed August 20, 2015. https://www.novascotia.ca/natr/meb/data/pubs/ftmif/mif07.pdf.

Pachai, Bridglal. *Beneath the Clouds of the Promised Land: The Survival of Nova Scotia's Blacks 1800–1989.* Halifax: The Black Educators Association, 1990.

Piers, Harry. *The Evolution of the Halifax Fortress 1749–1928.* Halifax: Public Archives of Nova Scotia, 1947.

Preston, W. T. R. *My Generation of Politics and Politicians.* Toronto: D. A. Rose, 1927.

Putskowski, Julian. "The Kinmel Park Camp Riots, 1919." *Flintshire Historical Society Journal* 32 (1989): 55–107. Accessed July 20, 2016. http://welshjournals.llgc.org.uk/browse/viewobject/llgc-id:1219213/article/000069512.

Raddall, Thomas H. *Halifax: Warden of the North.* Toronto: McClelland and Stewart, 1971.

———. *In My Time: A Memoir.* Toronto: McClelland and Stewart, 1976.

———. "Sam Glode: Travels of a Micmac." *Cape Breton's Magazine* 35 (December 1983): 21–29.

Radley, Kenneth. *Get Tough Stay Tough: Shaping the Canadian Corps 1914–1918.* Solihull: Heleon, 2014.

Reid, Gordon, ed. *Poor Bloody Murder: Personal Memoirs of the First World War.* Oakville: Mosaic Press, 1980.

Reid, Mark Collin, ed. *Canada's Great War Album: Our Memories of the First World War.* Toronto: HarperCollins, 2014.

Reilly, Nolan. "The General Strike in Amherst, Nova Scotia, 1919." *Acadiensis* 9, no. 2 (Spring 1980): 56–77.

Roberts, Michael D. *Dictionary of American Naval Aviation Squadrons.* Vol. 2. Washington: Naval Historical Center, 2000.

Robin, Martin. "Registration, Conscription, and Independent Labour Politics, 1916–1917." *Canadian Historical Review* 47, no. 2 (June 1966): 101–18.

Rudolf, R. D. "Boulogne in War Time." *CMA Journal* 5, no. 3 (March 1915): 255–59.

Sarty, Roger. "Hard-Luck Flotilla: the RCN's Atlantic Coast Patrol, 1914–18." In *The RCN in Transition 1910–1985,* edited by W. A. B. Douglas, 101–25. Vancouver/London: University of British Columbia Press, 1988.

——— and Bruce Ellis. "Connaught Battery and the Defence of the Atlantic Coast, 1906–1941." *Canadian Military History* 18, no. 2 (2009): 57–66.

Settle, Victor L. "Halifax Shipyards, 1887–1978: The Economic Impact." MA thesis, Saint Mary's University, 1999. Accessed October 25, 2015. http://library2.smu.ca/xmlui/bitstream/handle/01/22312/settle_victor_l_masters_1994.%20PDF?sequence=1.

Sharpe, Chris. "Enlistment in the Canadian Expeditionary Force 1914–1918: A Re-Evaluation." *Canadian Military History* 24, no. 1 (Spring 2015): 17–60.

Sheppard, Tom. *Acadia University*. Halifax: Nimbus, 2013.
———. *Historic Bridgewater*. Halifax: Nimbus, 2008.
———. *Historic Wolfville*. Halifax: Nimbus, 2003.
Skelton, Oscar D. *The Canadian Dominion*. New Haven: Yale University Press, 1921.
Snowie, J. Allan. *Collishaw & Company: Canadians in the Royal Naval Air Service 1914–1918*. Bellingham, WA: Nieuport Publishing, 2010.
Stewart, William. "Frustrated Belligerence: The Unhappy History of the 5th Canadian Division in the First World War." *Canadian Military History* 22, no. 2 (Spring 2013): 31–47.
Tennent, A. J. *British Merchant Ships Sunk by U-Boats in World War One*. Penzance: Periscope Publishing, 2006.
Tennyson, Brian Douglas. "A Cape Bretoner at War: Letters from the Front." *Canadian Military History* 11, no. 1 (Winter 2002): 37–48
———. "Canada and the Commonwealth Caribbean: The Historical Relationship." In *Canadian-Caribbean Relations: Aspects of a Relationship*, edited by Brian Douglas Tennyson, 1–57. Sydney: University College of Cape Breton Centre for International Studies, 1990.
———. *Percy Willmot: A Cape Bretoner at War*. Sydney: Cape Breton University Press, 2007.
———. "Preparing for War: The 25th Battalion in Halifax, 1914–15." *Canadian Military History* 20, no. 1 (Winter 2011): 61–74.
———. "Sydney, Nova Scotia, and the U-boat War, 1918." *Canadian Military History 7, no. 1 (Winter 1998): 29–41*.
———. *The Canadian Experience of the Great War: A Guide to Memoirs*. Lanham: Scarecrow Press, 2013.
———. "'Wild Bill' Livingstone Goes to War: A Diary and Letters 1916–19." *Royal Nova Scotia Historical Society Journal* 12 (2009): 119–44.
——— and Roger Sarty. *Guardian of the Gulf: Sydney, Cape Breton, and the Atlantic Wars*. Toronto: University of Toronto Press, 2000.
Terraine, John. *The Road to Passchendaele*. London: Leo Cooper, 1977.
Theobald, Andrew. *The Bitter Harvest of War: New Brunswick and the Conscription Crisis of 1917*. Fredericton: Goose Lane, 2008.
Thurston, Harry. *A Monument Speaks...and Tells the Story of its Dead*. Yarmouth: privately published, 1989.
Trotsky, Leon. *My Life*. New York: Charles Scribner's Sons, 1930.
Tuck, J. H. "Nova Scotia and the Conscription Election of 1917." MA thesis, Dalhousie University, 1968.
Tucker, Gilbert Norman. *The Naval Service of Canada: Its Official History. Vol. 1.* Ottawa: Department of National Defence, 1962.
United States Navy Department, Historical Section, *German Submarine Activities on the Atlantic Coast of the United States and Canada*. Washington: Government Printing Office, 1920.

Vance, Jonathan F. *Maple Leaf Empire: Canada, Britain, and Two World Wars.* Don Mills: Oxford University Press, 2012.

———. "Provincial Patterns of Enlistment in the Canadian Expeditionary Force." *Canadian Military History* 17, no. 2 (2012): 75–78.

Waite, P. B. *The Lives of Dalhousie University.* 2 vols. Montreal/Kingston: McGill-Queen's University Press, 1994, 1998.

Walker, Irma with Gerald Handspiker. *A Culloden Chronicle: A West Nova Scotia Farming and Fishing Village 1783–2013.* Yarmouth: privately published, 2014.

Walker, James W. St. G. "Race and Recruitment in World War I: Enlistment of Visible Minorities in the Canadian Expeditionary Force." *Canadian Historical Review 70, no. 1 (1989): 1–26.*

Willson, J. Beckles. *Nova Scotia: The Province that Time Has Passed By.* London: Constable, 1912.

Windsor, Lee and Roger Sarty. "New Brunswick's Artillery Goes to War, 1914–1915." *Canadian Military History* 24, no. 1 (2015): 103–39.

Winks, Robin. "Negro School Segregation in Ontario and Nova Scotia." *Canadian Historical Review* 50, no. 2 (June 1969): 164–91.

———. *The Blacks in Canada: A History.* 2nd ed. Montreal/Kingston: McGill University Press, 1997.

Winter, Denis. *Haig's Command: A Reassessment.* London: Penguin, 1991.

Wise, S. F. *Canadian Airmen and the First World War: The Official History of the Royal Canadian Air Force.* Vol. 1. Toronto: University of Toronto Press, 1980.

Worthington, Larry. *Amid the Guns Below.* Toronto: McClelland and Stewart, 1965.

Yorke, Lois K. "Best, Edna May Williston (Sexton)." In *Dictionary of Canadian Biography.* Vol. 15. Toronto/Quebec: University of Toronto/Université Laval, 2005. Accessed October 25, 2016. http://www.biographi.ca/en/bio/best_edna_may_williston_15E.html.

Zemel, Joel. *Scapegoat: The Extraordinary Legal Proceedings Following the 1917 Halifax Explosion.* Halifax: SVP Productions, 2012.

Websites

Nominal Rolls*

17th Battalion http://data2.archives.ca/e/e444/e011089509.pdf
25th Battalion http://data2.archives.ca/e/e444/e011089517.pdf
40th Battalion http://data2.archives.ca/e/e444/e011089532.pdf
64th Battalion http://data2.archives.ca/e/e444/e011092656.pdf
85th Battalion http://data2.archives.ca/e/e444/e011092677.pdf
106th Battalion http://data2.archives.ca/e/e444/e011092698.pdf
112th Battalion http://data2.archives.ca/e/e444/e011092704.pdf
165th Battalion http://data2.archives.ca/e/e444/e011087803.pdf

185th Battalion http://data2.archives.ca/e/e444/e011087823.pdf
193rd Battalion http://data2.archives.ca/e/e444/e011087831.pdf
219th Battalion http://data2.archives.ca/e/e444/e011087789.pdf
246th Battalion http://data2.archives.ca/e/e444/e011087928.pdf
No. 2 Construction Battalion http://data2.archives.ca./e/e444/e011087797.pdf
6th Canadian Mounted Rifles Battalion http://data2.archives.ca/e/e444/e011092734.pdf
No. 14 Brigade, Canadian Field Artillery http://data2.archives.ca/e/e444/e011087952.pdf
No. 23 Battery, Canadian Field Artillery http://www.canadiangreatwarproject.com/Regimental/23rd-Battery-CFA.asp
No. 1 Tunnelling Company http://data2.archives.ca/e/e444/e011087907.pdf
No. 1 Canadian Clearing Hospital http://data2.archives.ca/e/e444/e011087858.pdf
No. 7 Canadian Stationary Hospital http://data2.archives.ca/e/e444/e011087862.pdf
No. 9 Canadian Stationary Hospital http://data2.archives.ca/e/e444/e011087863.pdf

* *Nominal rolls list the officers and men who were in the unit at the time it went overseas. They do not include officers and men who became members after that date.*

General

Antigonish and Pictou Counties during the Great War http://www.parl.ns.ca/greatwar/
Canadian Great War Project http://www.canadiangreatwarproject.com/index.asp
Canadian Letters and Images Project http://www.canadianletters.ca/
Canadian Soldiers of the First World War http://www.bac-lac.gc.ca/eng/discover/military-heritage/first-world-war/personnel-records/Pages/search.aspx
Canadian Virtual War Memorial http://www.veterans.gc.ca/eng/remembrance/memorials/canadian-virtual-war-memorial
Guysborough First World War Veterans http://guysboroughgreatwarveterans.blogspot.ca/2015/05/lieutenant-catherine-nichols-gunn.html
Yarmouth Those Who Served
http://wartimeheritage.com/whawwi/whawwi_those_who_served_yarmouth.htm

IMAGE CREDITS

Acadia University Archives 5.1, 5.4
Beaton Institute, Cape Breton University 2.2, 3.1, 8.3, 9.5
Bruce MacDonald 5.2, 5.3
Canadian War Museum 4.5, 6.2, 6.4, 8.1, 8.2, 9.1, 9.2
DesBrisay Museum 8.4
Nova Scotia Archives 1.1, 1.2, 1.4, 2.1, 4.1, 4.3, 6.1, 6.3, 7.1, 7.3, 9.4
Nova Scotia Museum of Industry 7.2
Parks Canada and Mr. George Barkhouse and Family 9.3
Queens County Museum 3.2
St. Francis Xavier University Archives 4.4
Yarmouth County Museum and Archives 1.3, 3.3, 4.2

INDEX